Tales of the Congaree

CONGAREE SKETCHES

BY E. C. L. ADAMS

WITH AN INTRODUCTION BY PAUL GREEN

The University of North Carolina Press

Chapel Hill, N. C.

The original dust jacket for *Congaree Sketches*

TALES OF THE

Congaree

EDWARD C. L. ADAMS

EDITED WITH AN INTRODUCTION

BY ROBERT G. O'MEALLY

THE UNIVERSITY OF NORTH CAROLINA PRESS

CHAPEL HILL AND LONDON

Manufactured in the United States of America

Library of Congress Cataloging-in-Publication Data
Adams, Edward C. L. (Edward Clarkson Leverett),
1876–1946.
Tales of the Congaree.
Includes Congaree sketches (1927) and Nigger to nigger (1928).
Bibliography: p.
Includes index.
1. Afro-Americans—South Carolina—Literary collections. 2. Congaree Swamp (S.C.)—Literary collections. 3. Afro-Americans—Folklore—Literary collections. 4. South Carolina—History—Literary collections. 5. Slavery—South Carolina—Literary collections. I. O'Meally, Robert G., 1948– II. Adams, Edward C. L. (Edward Clarkson Leverett), 1876–1946. Nigger to nigger. 1987. III. Title.
PS3501.D21755A6 1987 813'.52 86-30912
ISBN 0-8078-1709-0
ISBN 0-8078-4188-9 (pbk.)
92 91 90 89 88 87 5 4 3 2 1

For Jacqui, Douglass, & Gabriel

Contents

Acknowledgments

During the three years it has taken to complete this edition, I received a great deal of assistance, for which I am extremely grateful. Wesleyan University has helped immeasurably with research grants and a sabbatical leave. I am especially indebted to colleagues and friends Joseph Reed, Richard Slotkin, Clarence Walker, Daniel Aaron, William J. Harris, Robert Hemenway, Robert Stepto, and Ernest J. Wilson III, who read parts of the manuscript and offered encouragement as well as comments and suggestions for research and analytical approaches.

I am indebted to more librarians and libraries than I can name. For their extraordinary professionalism and kindness, I am pleased to thank Steven Lebergott at Wesleyan's Olin Library, Ernest Kaiser at the Schomburg Library of New York, and the research librarians at the Moorland-Spingarn Research Center of Howard University and the Beinecke Library of Yale University. I am especially grateful to the tireless and dedicated Henry Fulmer, Thomas Johnson, and Alan Stokes at the South Caroliniana Library in Columbia, South Carolina.

For permission to use documents in the Langston Hughes Papers at Yale, I am grateful to Arnold Rampersad. For information on New World Africanisms in Adams's work, I am grateful to Robert Farris Thompson. For suggesting approaches to problems concerning the history of southern racial etiquette, I am indebted to Joel Williamson. For leading me, through his own writings, to Adams's books in the first place, and for offering wise counsel and warm encouragement, I am grateful (again) to Sterling A. Brown.

E. C. L. Adams's family took me in; made pictures, manuscripts, and memorabilia available to me; fed me; corresponded with me; and shared with me their memories of their illustrious family member. Thanks especially to Stephen and Pam Adams, Mr. Stephen B. Adams, and Mrs. George C. S. Adams. I also wish to thank these others who made me feel at home in Columbia and led me to information about Dr. Adams: Rev. J. P. Neal, Sr., Rev. J. P. Neal, Jr., and Mrs. Mamie Blakeley.

I am very pleased to thank the highly skilled typists who prepared the manuscript—Mrs. Gloria Cone, Mrs. Carol Foell, and Mrs. Georgianne Leone.

And thanks to my wife Jacqueline Malone for listening to it all, and for her patience and insight.

Introduction
Masks of Edward C. L. Adams

One of the first epithets that many European immigrants learned when they got off the boat was the term "nigger"—it made them feel instantly American. But this is tricky magic. Despite his racial difference and social status, something indisputably American about Negroes not only raised doubts about the white man's value system but aroused the troubling suspicion that whatever else the true American is, he is also somehow black.

—Ralph Ellison, in *Time*, 1970

I wanted to restore the language that black people spoke to its original power.

—Toni Morrison, in *New Republic*, 1981

Scip: Well, things is gettin' wusser.

—E. C. L. Adams, "Murder vs. Liquor"

Most standard guides and histories of American writing omit all notice of Dr. Edward Clarkson Leverett Adams, author of *Congaree Sketches* (1927) and *Nigger to Nigger* (1928). If mentioned at all, generally his books are consigned to a footnote or parentheses, in which he often is listed with other South Carolina writers of the 1920s: DuBose Heyward, Julia Peterkin, and Ambrose Gonzales. Sometimes it is noted that all these writers were white and that all of their principal works centered around the lives of unlettered blacks. Heyward's *Porgy* (1925) and Peterkin's *Scarlet Sister Mary* (1927) are usually the works selected by literary historians as the touchstones for this period and place. Both won Pulitzer Prizes (Heyward for *Porgy* in its dramatic form), and the opera based on *Porgy* has become a sainted perennial. Gonzales's anecdotes about life among the Gullah and Adams's sketches of life on the black Congaree are selected out and are little known, if at all.

Yet Adams's books have lasting power, perhaps more than those of the writers with whom he is usually bracketed. No others rendered scenes from black life with his control of dramatic tension; none presented scenes so true to the blacks' own sense of reality and poetic idiom. Adams took pains to distinguish the talk of his black characters not only according to where they came from—his occasional Gullah or "Geechee" speakers sounding quite unlike his Congaree speakers—but also according to more subtle peculiarities of individual style: his characters yarn in eloquent flourishes as well as in ironic asides full of turns and silences. For Adams's true literary counterparts one looks not to his fellow white South Carolinians but to Zora Neale Hurston, Langston Hughes, and Sterling A. Brown—black writers associated with the New Negro Renaissance.

Like the New Negro writers, Adams knew that black American language was much more than "Tom Show" or carnival stage patter, that it could express the full range of the experience of the people using it.[1] His ballads and elegies show this sensitivity. (One elegy, "Elizabeth Coleman," was the favorite of all of the works Adams would test on his black employees.) He believed that black preachers' sermons, alive with language from the Old Testament and the spirituals and charged with calls and countercalls between preacher and congregation, constituted "the best poetry in America." Some Adams pieces capture this sermonic poetry, not as the facile comedy of popular fiction and theater but as tragic funeral rhetoric or as the poetry of exultation. Most of his sketches are set up as secular exchanges among blacks themselves—hence the second book's albeit offensive title—not as performances to reassure white bosses that all was fine on the old plantation. No whites appear in this work, except as rare background figures and topics of conversation by Tad, Scip, and other black storytellers who have their say as if no whites were in earshot. As Tad says at one point: "We talkin' to we."

In these books, "we" tell timeless stories of gossipers and hypocrites, rabbits and "hants," tales that could have turned up (minus Joel Chandler Harris's crippling frames) in an Uncle

Remus collection. But in addition to such relatively mild Harrislike twice-told tales—often, true to the folkloric tradition, sounding their own partially concealed notes of protest and agony—Adams also collects sterner stuff about here and now: real-sounding conversations about blacks who were falsely set up as crooks and rapists, jailed, Jim Crowed in court, chainganged, beaten, lynched; tales about desperate, bitter, and angry blacks in encounters with racist whites and the vicious systems they controlled. As one journalist wrote of Adams in the early 1930s: "Chaingang reform is one of his most rabid interests. Any story of injustice or cruelty to the black people sets him afire."[2] Adams's tales are "realer," more direct in their willingness to point up the jagged grain in southern black experience, than those in any other black lore collection of the period. Even Zora Neale Hurston (the only New Negro writer who collected and published folklore per se) failed to gather tales so encompassing of the ambiguous facts of black life, the bleak and the tragic as well as the farcical and comic. Perhaps because of her white patrons and editors, and because of her own race pride and romanticism, Hurston tended not to publish tales about the deadliest of hard times along the southern color line.[3]

That Adams was told such tales at all is certainly part of the mystery here. It was in the plantation tradition for black slaves and even freedmen to be brought forward to give "Old Master" and his guests an after-dinner song, dance, or other entertainment, thus to confirm in ritual form the white man's different way of life, his paternal beneficence, and his power over the blacks.[4] In the South Adams knew, where in spite of segregation white and black cultures infused each other intimately and thoroughly, perhaps he like other whites depended heavily upon these rituals to preserve his sense of who he felt he was—as a white man. Adams's home was well known as a place where whites could enjoy such ritualized "Negro entertainment"—not by professionals but by local blacks who knew how to put on an unprettified Congaree show. Adams must have gathered much of his material from just such parties. In the plantation tradition, too, he hosted all-black affairs (except for Adams himself) to celebrate holidays or special events like the end of the harvest. At these more private

EDWARD C. L. ADAMS
(courtesy of Stephen B. Adams)

THADDEUS "TAD" GOODSON

(courtesy of Stephen B. Adams)

sessions, "Dr. Ned" (as blacks called him) stood within the circle of tale-tellers around the big fireplace in his country lodge and heard certain tales, songs, and pieces the blacks thought too risqué or otherwise inappropriate for the white general public. These would have certainly been unavailable to most whites in his time.

In 1931, Adams attended Langston Hughes's poetry reading in Columbia, South Carolina, and invited the black poet to his farm lodge outside of town. Hughes had read some of Adams's tales and heard that his farm was run by "the doctor's relatives on the colored side," and he eagerly accepted the chance to survey the scene for himself. Hughes's account of the visit makes clear that Adams was not only operating within the typical plantation tradition but extending its boundaries. He greeted Hughes at the front door.

> There was nothing inhibiting or self-consciously Southern about Dr. Adams [writes Hughes]. . . . He invited me to have a seat in the living room, sat down himself, conversed most cordially, and made me feel quite at home. Presently he sent to the fields for the plantation hands whose dialogues he featured in his stories. They came and they, too, seemed perfectly at home, joking and telling tales. One of them brought a guitar and hit a few tunes. We had a very good time that afternoon. . . . A buxom colored woman in a neat headrag and spotless apron brought in food and drinks, and served the white doctor and myself as the taletelling and music went on. I was having a wonderful time.

Hughes did not fail to point out that his host on the trip to Adams's place was Dr. Green, a black physician from Columbia, who got out of his car to greet Adams. He did not venture inside Adams's house, however, but waited in the car. En route back to town, Hughes asked Green why he had not come in. "Well, in the South," said Green, "there are some things colored people just can't do." He went on: "Dr. Adams is a fine man. To him my coming would mean nothing. But had I gone through the front door as a guest, and word of it got around among the white people of Columbia, it could ruin my hospital. The white drugstores might refuse to honor my prescriptions, and no more white businessmen would contribute to our building fund for the new hospital Negroes hope to erect."[5] Adams's free behavior toward blacks, especially toward the radical Hughes, his breaches of southern etiquette that so challenged the extant social order that Green scrupled to hold back, marked Adams as a maverick, one to whom certain "tales blacks tell on themselves"—and even "on the white man"—might be risked.

But what about works like "Thirteen Years," a harsh lynching tale (based on a real case) that was hardly an entertainment set piece? Why was Adams permitted to hear such frank black talk on such a taboo theme? Here it is crucial to consider that if Adams's black informants knew him as a maverick, they also knew him as an upper-class white man, a widely respected authority figure. (As an upper-class white man he could get away with being a maverick.) In addition, he was a medical doctor who occasionally treated black patients and thus could hear some inside talk.

To blacks "Dr. Ned" was nothing if not "quality white folks," one who played the part of the gentle patriarch and who, within the limits of a rigidly divided system, sought to be benevolent and protective of all who lived on and near his property.[6] It was Adams, for example, who answered an appeal from local blacks by donating an acre of land for them to build the A.M.E. Rock Hill Church. By telling Adams the relatively unexpurgated truth about their lives, perhaps some of his tale-tellers believed they were exercising a vague political power. They could not vote, of course, or express controversial political views in public; perhaps somehow Dr. Ned would state their case where it would matter. No doubt blacks also found it a cathartic experience to speak the bitter words of "Thirteen Years" directly to the face of a prestigious white man of the South.[7]

As Scip and Tad knew well, like many upper-class whites, Adams felt more sympathy for "his" blacks than for the poor whites, or "crackers." Like the blacks, Adams saw crackers as a dangerously lawless class whose increasing political power threatened to deal out both blacks and white aristocrats. In one tale Adams defines crackers as "mostly cruel . . . they hate alike the successful white men and the more unfortunate Negro, whom they intend to keep in his place." Sensing this alliance with a white aristocrat, Scip and Tad would be encouraged to tell Adams a story at a cracker's expense, even a wry and bitter version of a lynching tale with a Jim Crow court scene. Nor did Adams seem to have felt much fraternity with the striving white middle classes: the businessmen, lawyers, politicians, and doctors of these pieces are little better than the crackers when it comes to fair play for the darker brother. For Adams the color-based alliance between the cracker and Judge Foolbird (Judge Lynch) is deadly—not just for blacks but for the Congaree as a whole and for American democracy. If ever a white man might be trusted by blacks with their complaints (against all but white aristocrats) about life along the killing color line, it was Adams. They had enemies in common.

That he was privy to certain insiders' lore also proves, I believe, that Adams must have become something of what the rare white man who could play good jazz had to become: an initiate within the world of predominantly black experts. As his books show, he knew how to shape and trade a story. He had a good tale-teller's voice, and he loved to act out a story, playing all the parts. Beyond that, he must have known when to keep his mouth shut and virtually disappear so that veteran storytellers in the tradition, like Scip and Tad, could hold forth. "I've got one mind for the white folks to see, and another mind for myself, which is *me*," is a black saying that surely applied to Tad's and Scip's relationship to Adams. But what they let him see seems close to what they might have said "is me." Very often in these tales one seems to overhear blacks conversing not just as if no white men were present but as if everyone, including the silent Adams, were of the same turn of mind. To a significant degree, these storytellers let Adams hear their tales because they not only respected and trusted him, they liked him and accepted him into their circle of "big picture talkers . . . using the side of the world for a canvas."[8] So confident was Hughes of Adams's consanguinity that when he got home he sent the doctor a note he had prepared soliciting funds for the defense of the Scottsboro boys.[9]

True as they were to black life, Adams's sketches inevitably told his own story, too. Like Hurston's *Mules and Men*, Adams's books are subtle collaborations between the subject/tale-teller, the author, and the various (immediate and imagined) audiences. Adams could not have been what he sometimes told his friends he was: an objective tape recorder of folklore. The face behind the storyteller's mask in *Mules and Men* tells of Hurston's journey home and her attempts to comprehend life there. It is Hurston's own. The face behind the mask (or masks) in *Tales of the Congaree* is Adams's. How, beyond what I have said about class and caste, did white Adams happen to frame his own story as one told "nigger to nigger"?

Ralph Ellison comes closest to solving this puzzle when he writes about the American impulse to speak one's piece from behind a mask: "Here the 'darky' act makes brothers of us all. America is a land of masking jokers. We wear the mask for purposes of aggression as well as for defense; when we are projecting the future and preserving the past. In short, the motives hidden behind the mask are as numerous as the ambiguities the mask conceals." "Welcome to the United States of Jokeocracy," says an Ellison character who hears the high whine of hysteria in the laughter among whites after a white man tells a "Negro joke."[10] Somehow, through the black mask white Americans have been able to confront feelings and ideas that are virtually unspeakable through any other medium. Obviously, this was the case in the minstrel shows wherein whites in blackface wisecracked about sex, politics, and other taboo subjects.[11] Ironically, Adams also "blacked up" to speak taboo truths—in his case through the medium of black characters represented as speaking privately of white/black tensions and violence. Wearing his black mask, he could project attitudes and values that the unmasked Adams, and certainly most whites of his place and time, would have disavowed as their own. To complicate matters, over his black mask Adams put on a *white* mask, that is, he gave winks and nods to his genteel white southern readers, racial supremacists who felt fondly toward "niggers" so long as they were held "in their place." Crouching securely behind both masks—feeling a double distance between himself and his readers—Adams described a full scene as he himself saw it: snarled in complexity and steeped in trouble.

In sum, as unusual as it is to reprint accounts of black life in South Carolina written by a white man in 1927 and 1928, there are compelling reasons to do so. Adams's tales provide scholars and general readers alike with well-wrought and authentic versions of black folklore and of life along the southern color line. Adams's own life history is a significant reason for reprinting these tales: he was a white man torn between his heritage of paternalism and his personal sense of humanity. For Adams, masking was more than a literary device; it was also his way of confronting the world. And as such it reflects the masking psychology of liberal white southerners of his era and tells us much about the deepest recesses of the mind of the South. Published at the time of the New Negro Renaissance, when black writers were strongly asserting the imperatives of black culture, Adams's work forms an important part of that movement's periphery. It joined—and usually surpassed, both in accuracy and in artistic quality—the stream of books by white fellow travelers of the New Negro movement: Peterkin, Heyward, and Green.

Adams's Heritage

Edward Clarkson Leverett Adams was born on January 5, 1876. His own names bespeak his aristocratic lineage. He was also a Hopkins. His birthplace, Weston, South Carolina, is a hamlet named for a branch of his family. His was a gold and silver line of South Carolina's first families, many of whom were active in politics and planting throughout the state's history. Both of his parents were descendants of colonists. On his father's side, he is descended from Stephen Bull, who sailed from England on the ship *Carolina* and who was captain of the fort at Charles Towne in 1670, the first permanent settlement in South Carolina. Adams's mother traced her family line back to Thomas Leverett, a Pilgrim father, and to John Leverett, a governor of colonial Massachusetts knighted by an English king. His great-great-grandfather was a revolutionary war general. Other forebears include a Harvard president and a president, successively, of Brown, Union College, and the

University of South Carolina. Though Adams downplayed his family's prestige—and requested his publishers after 1928 to list him not as Dr. E. C. L. Adams but merely as Ned Adams—still the suppressed letters and their histories stood for a vital part of his story. On an American scale, E. C. L. Adams spelled royalty.[12]

Adams's eccentricity no doubt was possible because of the security of his upper-class position. He could let Langston Hughes in the front door without caring who disliked it. His relative willingness to eschew strict Jim Crow codes also reflected the variety of his personal experience—always a challenge to the notion that a system is immutable. He had grown up with books at home and reread certain favorites throughout his life: Edgar Allan Poe's poems, Rudyard Kipling, *Uncle Remus*, *Gulliver's Travels*, *The Memoirs of Casanova*. He attended elementary and secondary schools in and around Columbia before going off to Clemson College in the state's northwest corner. After Clemson, he served in the Spanish-American War, being stationed at Jacksonville, Florida, and Chickamauga, Georgia. He returned to South Carolina to attend Charleston Medical College, earning his M.D. there (with a year out as a transfer student at Maryland Medical College in Baltimore). He pursued medical study further at the University of Pennsylvania in Philadelphia, and at Rotunda Hospital in Dublin, Ireland.

It was during his 1908–9 stint in Dublin that Adams first met Padriac Colum, who became a lifelong friend. When Adams met him, Colum—along with William Butler Yeats, John Millington Synge, and other Irish writers—was hotly engaged in a literary struggle to counteract English stereotypes of the "stage Irishman" with portraits drawn from Irish history, folklore, and sympathetic firsthand experience. These Irish writers' ideas about the vibrancy of realistic portraiture were inspiring to Adams,[13] who had long felt that Americans had rarely seen or heard the Negro as Adams knew him in central South Carolina. Two decades after Adams left Dublin, just before *Congaree Sketches* was published, six of the book's sketches appeared in the *Dublin Magazine*. In the pages of that magazine, whose policy was "to look at life primarily and profoundly from an Irish point of view,"[14] Adams could speak his mind not just "in blackface" but from the perspective of the Irish, another group with whom Adams strongly identified and another group called at times by other Americans an "alien race."

In 1910, when Adams married Amanda M. Smith from Wilkes-Barre, Pennsylvania, his immediate family's fortunes had dwindled almost to nothing. By 1911, however, with money from his wife's family, he bought a large tract of land a few miles below Columbia. That it was land formerly owned by members of his family made the purchase a special pleasure. It was on this former slave plantation that he first met most of the tale-tellers of his books. Adams opened a general medical practice in town and managed a farm and grain mill business outside of town. As the humdrum life of a small town doctor began to bore him, he spent less and less time at his practice in Columbia and more at "the place" (he hated the term "plantation") outside of town.

In aristocratic southern fashion, Adams was an amateur naturalist. He was "the place's" chief birdwatcher, fisherman, and hunter, and he became the first president of South Carolina's Audubon Society. He attempted, with some success, to domesticate several species of wild ducks in the area, and he perfected a breed of wild game chickens. He even imported some pigs from Europe and used them, too, in trying to create a new native strain; a few of the hybrids survived to roam for years through the vastness of the Congaree swamp. Somehow he once brought home a herd of zebu, the sacred hump cattle of India, which grazed and occasionally stampeded through Richland County until government officials captured and removed them.[15]

According to one of Adams's sons, Stephen, when the local zoo closed its doors, Adams took in all the animals—snakes, monkeys, strange mammals, unlikely looking fowl—everything but the elephants. "For years we had monkeys in our woods," said Stephen in 1983. "And even now you're never quite sure what you're likely to run into deep in the swamp." Occasionally, Adams also donated some Congaree animals to the Bronx Zoo in New York City, sometimes transporting them himself. Family members recall one spirited episode when Adams and Thaddeus Goodson drove from Columbia with a forty-pound turtle strapped to each running board. Adams told those gathered to see the car off that time would tell whether the southern specialty would be received by a New York zoo or a New York restaurant. E. C. L. Adams enjoyed experimenting with his crops—cotton, fruits, and vegetables—and inspecting the garden, and just for pleasure he would ride his horses through the avenues of oak and bamboo that lined his property. He was an expert horseman, a trick rider who at a party sometimes entertained guests by reaching down at full gallop to lift a row of handkerchiefs from the ground.[16]

From 1915 through the 1920s, three to four hundred people, most of them black, lived and worked on the land. Adams would ride through the property in a car driven by his right-hand man, Thaddeus Goodson, to whom *Nigger to Nigger* was dedicated: "To the Sportsman, Humorist, Fatalist, Philosopher Thaddeus Goodson, The Tad of These Sketches." Goodson had been born seven years before Adams and had always lived on the land that Adams eventually bought. He was Adams's chauffeur, overseer, night watchman, handyman, confidante, and friend. "He was not just a worker," recalled Stephen Adams; "he was Dad's alter ego." They shared bootleg corn liquor, philosophized about politics and the world, and swapped tall tales. Often when Adams would take off for Atlanta or New Orleans, Tad Goodson was his driver and sharer of his adventures. When Adams gave parties at his lodge on the place, Goodson played key parts. A veteran cook, known for his venison, goat, "coota" (turtle), and catfish and for his barbecue, he was also the main entertainer: "Make it over to Doctor Ned's place," blacks would say. "It'll be enough to eat and Uncle Taddy will be rattling them bones."[17] Goodson played "bones" as well as knife-and-fork and guitar. Other blacks would play accordion, harmonica, and even mandolin. "Come on down and stay at my place for a while," Adams frequently wrote to friends, fellow-artists, and business associates up north. "I believe that I can make it both interesting and amusing." The interesting and amusing time—enjoyed over the years by such notables as Sally Rand, Harry Hopkins, Joseph Hergesheimer, and Edgar Lee Masters—would feature Tad's songs and dances as well as local yarns, his specialty.[18]

Typical of the southern gentleman of his time, Adams took his turn as a candidate for public office. Twice he ran for lieutenant governor: in 1916 (when he was the first ever to challenge an incumbent for that office) and in 1922. One might have expected the man who would write *Congaree Sketches* to speak out against lynching, Jim Crow politics, and legal outrages against blacks. One journalist writing in about 1931 said that reports of cruelty or injustice that was "too heinous" would make Adams "seize a soap box and rush to the nearest crossroads."[19] But in both formal political contests he studiously avoided even a hint of radical or "racial" issues. Instead, his stands were unvaryingly bland and vague: he was for good roads and against cutting taxes at the expense of schools. The main issues raised by all candidates involved lawlessness: crimes of "blind tigers" (smugglers and bootleggers), murderers, and robbers. But there was no mention of the newly vitalized night riders. Adams stated in speech after dull speech that he wanted "to be placed on record as the foe of crime and the friend of law and order."[20]

Some of the feelings his flat rhetoric concealed bristled out in his attacks, including physical ones, upon his opponents. During the 1916 campaign, Adams heckled his right-wing opponent, Andrew J. Bethea, as a "coattail swinger" of his associates Henry Ford and William Jennings Bryan. On another occasion he persisted in interrupting a speech by Bethea until the police forced him to be quiet. Three weeks later, Adams socked and bloodied the face of John DesChamps, an archconservative candidate for governor. (Adams did not directly call down DesChamps for trying to organize a far right-wing "White Party.") Later, Adams branded as false the rumor that he had struck a man from behind with "a pair of knucks." Late in the 1916 campaign, he gave a speech characterizing Bethea as "a Christian at one end of the line and a crook at the other." In response, one of Bethea's supporters met Adams leaving the podium and "landed a heavy blow on Adams's chin." The two "struggled and writhed until they were dragged apart." On that day, the *State*, Adams's hometown paper, carried the headline: "Another Scrap Marks Campaign, Dr. Adams Again Engaged in Actual War."[21]

In 1916, the electorate chose Bethea over Adams by a nearly two-to-one margin. That Adams carried his home county of Richland was his only consolation.

The same story was repeated in 1922. Again, the campaign's small portion of excitement was stirred not by the political positions publicly taken by the candidates. All spoke of "law and order." But there was not a word about racial issues: it was as if such issues were too painful and enormous to broach, at least directly. Adams tried to heat things up by accusing his main opponent, this time E. B. Jackson, of being overly indebted to certain supporters. (He did not mention that Jackson was warmly endorsed by the Ku Klux Klan.) Now it was Jackson's turn to beat Adams, again by nearly two to one. In 1928, Adams again considered running for lieutenant governor. He never entered the race, though, complaining to friends that his chances for winning had been ruined by Paul Green's introduction to *Congaree Sketches*, which implied that Adams was a radical. In his own ways—at points in roughneck ways that challenged his identity as an upright aristocrat—Adams fought the political machinery around him. When Paul Green revealed "the black mask of humanity" (behind the white mask) in his work, however, Adams retreated and never entered politics again.

At age forty-one, between political contests, Adams left his wife and two sons at home to volunteer for World War I. Typical of him, he was a frontline serviceman, who, as captain of the Eighty-first ("Wildcat") Division, participated in the battles of Château Thierry and Argonne Forest. Nor is it unlike him that although he received no medals for bravery, he did get himself officially reprimanded for reckless endangerment of himself and his men. The following year Adams resumed his medical practice at home. But with his own health impaired by overseas service, and in any case with less enthusiasm than ever for his work as a doctor, gradually he saw fewer and fewer patients. Around 1920 he announced his retirement. When blacks on the place were sick and sent word to his house that help was needed, his routine response was to dispatch his car to transport the patient to another doctor. He had given up his ambitions to be a political officeholder, and now he gave up medicine, too. He told friends he was a full-time planter, just a country farmer.

From 1925 through 1930, however, Adams was no more "just a farmer" than William Faulkner was. He had begun another southern gentlemanly occupation, that of a man of letters. He now filled his days writing down tales by blacks—along with their sermons, prayers, and songs—"not merely for his own diversion," he later told a reporter, "but at the insistence of his friends who delighted to hear his anecdotes and wished to have them 'hot from the griddle.' "[22] Once he began to collect the material, he started serving it up in local journals. In 1925 two tales were published together as "Congaree Sketches" in the *Reviewer*, a North Carolina journal edited by the playwright Paul Green.[23] These pieces, "Tournament in Heaven" (later called "The Hopkins Nigger") and "Jonas," show that as soon as he began to publish his "Negro works," forty-nine-year-old Adams's method was formed. Rich with black talk and dealing wryly with social issues from a black viewpoint, these first "Congaree Sketches" paved the way for the book of the same name. He had found the vehicle for channeling his enormous energies and for expressing his huge dissatisfactions with the world he knew.

Publishers and Critics

In 1927, *Congaree Sketches* was published by the University of North Carolina Press and was a very important landmark. The young new assistant editor, William T. Couch, had immediately found the book attractive and believed that it would bring to life some of the press's scholarly analyses of black folklore. That the tales might prove objectionable to conservative southern readers had, of course, occurred to Couch. But outside evaluators pronounced the manuscript acceptable on that score. Paul Green, whose North Carolina magazine had first brought the Adams sketches into print, was one of these evaluators. He liked the book and, at Adams's request, agreed to write an introduction.

Green's introduction turned out to be the part of the book

that caused problems. In it, Green hailed "the Negro's artistic genius recognized the world over—in that great creation the Spiritual. In folklore, in song, in dance, in drama, fiction, in every art . . . the Negro [is] coming to his own hearthstone." Of the New Negro movement, whose architects believed black cultural advancement to be the key to black political and economic gains, Green wrote: "This recent exuberant outburst of the Negro in art and literature . . . is as sound as a people's life." White artists such as Adams and others drawing upon black sources thereby did a service for their darker brethren as well as themselves. In this sense they were, Green implies, partners with the New Negro writers. Perhaps most disturbing to racial separatists was Green's assertion that "the United States is awakening to the fact that the destiny of the Negro is its destiny, that black and white are inextricably mingled in blood and bone and interaction, and that as the white man fails he fails and as the Negro rises the white man rises." Thus it was as senseless, in Green's formulation, for whites to try to segregate themselves from blacks as it was for blacks to speak of retreating with Marcus Garvey "back" to Africa.[24]

Couch felt Green had stated his case in a way that was "perfectly clear and . . . as inoffensive as possible";[25] the essay "fits exactly in with the spirit of the sketches and expresses their fundamental tone," he said.[26]

Adams's divided mind shows up in this controversy over the introduction. He had specifically requested that Green be asked to write it and had personally paid him fifty dollars to do so. He could not have been uninformed about Green's liberal politics (Green's own books were clear on that score). And yet he told Couch in advance that he did not need to see Green's essay: anything he wrote would have his approval. When the essay was more explicitly liberal than even Couch had anticipated, the editor dispatched an assistant to Columbia to show Adams the essay. But Adams would not look at it; he said to go ahead and put it in the book. Later, he could disavow the essay, complaining that the introduction had no connection with his work and that it had foiled his political ambitions.[27]

How, in the first place, did Couch get the introduction past the press's cautious Board of Governors? The young editor quietly worked around them. He described his predicament and strategy in a letter to a friend:

> You will remember when I saw you recently that I said something about the possibility of our starting some fireworks sometime soon. My opinion is that the next month or so is going to be a rather hot time for us. Under separate cover I am sending you a copy of CONGAREE SKETCHES by E. C. L. Adams with an introduction by Paul Green. After reading Paul's introduction, if I did not tell you you would certainly wonder how it happened to be in a book with the University imprint on it. For the seeming negligence of our watchdogs I must plead guilty. We had printed prefaces before without submitting them to the inspection of members of our Board of Governors and this time we merely followed our usual procedure. Needless to say, I have received explicit instructions how to proceed in future cases, and unless something remarkable happens, it must not seem that we will commit such an error again at any time soon.[28]

The University of North Carolina Press "watchdogs" first saw Green's introduction when they received finished copies of *Congaree Sketches* from the bindery. They called an emergency meeting with Couch and decided unanimously that there was nothing to do but to "destroy all existing copies of the book forthwith and to reprint it without the introduction." Green's essay bore no relation to the sketches, they argued; worse, it was a work of "propaganda" that would release a bullet storm of criticism from southern readers. "Having just weathered a pitched battle between the university and North Carolina Fundamentalists over the teaching of evolution," the historian Daniel Singal reports, the board was in "no mood for taking chances." But the cagey Couch had a trump card for the board. Singal recounts:

> In as matter-a-fact a tone as he could muster, Couch explained certain facts the board did not know: on his special instructions, more than a hundred advance copies of *Congaree Sketches* had already been distributed to reviewers,

> leading literary figures, and major bookstores throughout the country. The *New York Times* had a copy, as did the *New York Herald-Tribune*, along with Walter Lippmann and Oswald Garrison Villard, editor of the *Nation*. If the press stopped publication of the book now, Couch asked, would not some of these people suspect foul play and start inspecting the book closely to see what was wrong? Perhaps it was best to do nothing, he suggested. Again a vote was taken, this time with each member agreeing in turn to follow Couch's advice.[29]

When book and introduction turned out to cause no crash of outraged reaction from reviewers, politicians, or general southern readers—the press received not a single letter of protest—Couch was vindicated. More than that, although he did not officially become the press's director until 1932, after the 1927 publication of *Congaree Sketches*, Couch was indisputably the prime mover of the press. For twenty years he directed it toward scholarship that was more analytical and critical than had been this southern publisher's fare in its brief earlier history.

At first Adams had been entirely satisfied with the first edition of *Congaree Sketches*, Green's essay and all. "Tremendously pleased with book from cover to cover," he wired Couch after receiving an advance copy. "Believe Green's introduction will have tremendous influence on its sales."[30] (By now, presumably, Adams had read that introduction.) But when sales turned out to be sluggish, he grew irritated about the introduction and wanted a second edition issued without it. He came to agree with those who, like the reviewer for the *State* (his conservative hometown paper), raved about the sketches but strongly disliked Green's introduction, which that reviewer said "clogs the little batch of fine sketches like a bundle of wet blankets." Adams was especially incensed that the introduction mentioned his own work only in a perfunctory final paragraph. "If I could," he wrote a friend, "I would withdraw from sale every volume and make a bonfire of them. The entire pleasure of the book has been destroyed for me by this introduction."[31] Adams also felt little joy about favorable notices by reviewers who gave little more than a polite nod in the general direction of his "Uncle Remus stories" as if they were mere footnotes authenticating Green's hot essay.

James Weldon Johnson (then executive secretary of the National Association for the Advancement of Colored People [NAACP]) called the introduction "one of the finest approaches by the written word to interracial understanding and good will ever made."[32] Mary White Ovington (chair of the NAACP's Board of Directors) liked the sketches well enough but found the introduction "generous," "beautiful," and "the best thing in the book."[33] Adams felt uneasy about being thus upstaged. Then, too, he grew annoyed and, in the end, very angry about the imputation, encouraged by Green, that his sketches had too definite, and radical, a political motive: "It strikes me," wrote Adams privately, "that he has used my book as a vehicle for ideas that I personally do not stand for."[34] Adams also may have disliked the note of optimism sounded in Green's essay: what would cynical Scip or Hatchet say to Green's coolly confident pronouncements?

In fact, Green's essay is directly on target when it suggests that these tales cry out for social change. And it is helpful that Green considers *Congaree Sketches* in the context of works by black and white writers whose subject is the folk Negro. Still the essay is weak insofar as it makes only the scantiest mention of the particular work it purports to introduce.[35] With a word or two changed it could serve as the polemical introduction to many works: it is an all-purpose "folk Negro" book introduction, perhaps originally written for some other publication. In this sense, Adams's objections were legitimate. But Adams also was unhappy to have Green point up the political implications present in *Congaree Sketches*. He preferred to turn his white mask toward his (white) readers and claim that he was simply recording local knee-slappers and songs of black pathos.

Interestingly, even commentators who focused solely on the tales were divided over their meaning. White reviewers, North and South, tended to praise Adams for keeping out of the picture and letting the "African types" sing their "idyllic" swan songs without white interruption.[36] Here, according to the *Saturday Review*, one could "rejoice in the fertility and ingenuity of the untutored negro mind"; here are "snippets of dialogue" along with "metrical versions of darkey legend."[37] A Boston reviewer found that the sketches gave true representations of "the illiterate, shiftless, easy-going men and women living in what was once the slave states. . . . These little tales . . . are full of casual humor, as easy-going as the slow nervous systems of our colored brothers."[38] Commenting on Adams's comedy in *Nigger to Nigger*, a South Carolina reviewer noted: "It is here . . . that we see and know the negro for the child that he really is—a shrewd, observing, keen, watchful, wary child, but essentially a child after all."[39] Another reviewer in South Carolina evidently interviewed Adams for his article and perhaps presented the case as Adams would have. He admitted the tales to be "bitter, cruel and grim," but still he assured his readers that the works intended no incentive to social change: "They are not written with any intention of presenting race problems or to consciously alleviate existing conditions."[40]

Black commentators saw Adams's work quite differently. In an unpublished piece entitled "You Don't Know Us Negroes," Zora Neale Hurston mocked and excoriated most white writers dealing with black themes and characters. (Roark Bradford, she said, wrote a "Negro book" with "just about as much Negro folklore in it as Cal Coolidge had in him.") But she included "the author of 'Congaree Sketches' " among those who "looked further than the too-obvious outside." Like T. S. Stribling, she said, Adams sought meanings of black life "beyond the laugh." Sterling A. Brown called *Congaree Sketches* "one of the most faithful representations of Negro folk life." He continued: "The author, E. C. L. Adams . . . kept out of the scene, and allowed his Negro characters to speak for themselves. The result was neither sentimentality or clowning." Of *Nigger to Nigger*, which he considered even more realistic, Brown wrote: "Some of the sketches deal with slavery in a manner far removed from the plantation tradition. The unusual chorus of Tad and Scip and their fellows reveals that though they may be unlettered, they are cynical realists, and certainly they are not being fooled."[41] Both white and black reviewers called Adams's work "real"; but, obviously, for the blacks what was "real" went beyond childish watchfulness and humorous "darkey" banter.

Less than a year after the appearance of *Congaree Sketches*, Adams was contacted by Maxwell Perkins of Scribner's in New York. Perkins had heard that Adams had written a new series of Negro sketches and told him that Scribner's might wish to publish it—a sampling first in *Scribner's Magazine*, then a collection in book form. If Adams wished, Scribner's would also take over *Congaree Sketches* and issue it in a new edition without the troublesome introduction.[42] Adams jumped at the New York offer, much to the dismay of editor Couch, who had put so much effort into the University of North Carolina Press volume. The Scribner's edition of *Congaree Sketches* was delayed and delayed and finally dropped. As planned, however, excerpts from *Nigger to Nigger* appeared in *Scribner's Magazine*, and that book was published in 1928, one year after *Congaree Sketches*.

The title of *Nigger to Nigger* was an issue. Adams had wanted it to be *Just a Damn Nigger*, the title of one of his new sketches dealing with the law. Perkins advised against this title, fearing that some readers might be put off by the use of the word "damn." He recommended *Nigger to Nigger*, which would set it off from the "Uncle Remus" type of collection and emphasize the work's "absolutely negro quality."[43] Adams agreed. In later years he regretted the title, though, and let family and friends know that it was never his idea. But in 1928 neither Perkins nor Adams realized that the title *Nigger to Nigger* would offend many potential readers and probably help drive this excellent book into obscurity. Neither man seems to have considered the possibility of a black readership that would be offended by seeing this hated epithet printed twice on a book's cover.

After the Books

After *Nigger to Nigger*, Adams published a series of sketches about Sand Hill whites, tales told, as it were, "cracker to cracker." Then he wrote more "Negro" sketches, some framed as conversations among blacks, some as exchanges with "Dr. Adams" playing straight man to wisecracking Tad.[44] But none seemed close enough to the mark set by his two books for

Adams to submit them for publication. The cracker tales, published in *Scribner's Magazine* under the title "The Carolina Wilderness," worked as sequels or background appendixes to his Negro sketches. (They appear as such in the present volume.) They also hold up as a self-contained series, but Adams never seems to have had a book-length work in mind to contain them. In 1929, he reworked the *Congaree Sketches* piece entitled "Big Charleston" as a play, *Potee's Gal* (which also appears as an appendix here). But as a play the work was leaden: much of what had worked as a sketch was boring in extended dramatic form, even for only one act. For a time, though, Adams tried to launch the play, first in Columbia, then in New York. In Columbia, a production of *Potee's Gal* began rehearsal, using a cast of 150 blacks, but local white opposition to the all-black play stopped the show. Thus lacking momentum—and perhaps lacking Adams's own wholehearted belief in its artistic qualities—the play never reached New York. Indeed, it seems never to have played before an audience.

"Congaree Sketches" resurfaced in another form in 1929 and 1930, when a music teacher in San Antonio, Texas, Lilia A. MacKay-Cantell, set some of the poems and sketches to music. There were several performances in Texas of cantatas called "Congaree Sketches," and for a brief moment Adams was heralded as a skilled librettist in a vernacular idiom. Here again the parallel with DuBose Heyward's *Porgy* is inescapable.[45]

E. C. L. Adams died at the age of seventy on November 1, 1946. He had lived as an aristocrat who enjoyed all the privileges of rank, including the privilege of wearing his proprieties loosely. A drinker of fine as well as homemade whiskey, he was quick to anger and to fight. He loved the South, but he despised its treatment of blacks—particularly by crackers but also by their abettors from other classes. Not surprisingly, he was unable to face directly the implications of his feelings concerning blacks. He was most successful in this regard when he tried to capture the note and trick of black life in his sketches. But even here one is aware that Adams is divided, off-balance; his tales are part-white, part-black. His "tragic mulatto" sketches, in particular, bespeak what may have been his deep fear of racial mixing as well as his miserable guilt about his black truth-telling and his happy associations with black friends and "relatives on the colored side." Still, the tales, masked black and masked white, endure. And they tell a part of the 1920s southern story that no one else (certainly no other white writer) seemed willing or able to tell.

Masks

As Ralph Ellison has observed, Mark Twain and other great American writers, especially of the nineteenth century, also "wore the mask" of blackness to project some of their strongest images and ideas about the American experience. Though in many respects he is a predictable minstrel stereotype, Nigger Jim is nonetheless the character in *Huckleberry Finn* most strongly embodying humanity and value. In so doing he symbolizes the American yearning to be free. The Negro slave, the man lowest down in the social hierarchy, personified Twain's loftiest national ideals.[46]

Joel Chandler Harris, whose work Adams admired throughout his life, was another writer who wore the mask of blackness to express himself. Both Harris and Adams were white writers of the Deep South, somewhat liberal for their place and time, who skillfully recorded Negro lore. Both indeed were extraordinarily careful to set down their findings "uncooked," to use Harris's term, as if direct from their black sources. Like Adams's black narrators, Harris's Remus described the South as blacks saw it: full of trouble, self-absorption, deceit, and casual violence—particularly against those with the least power.

But of course there is a trick here. Faithful as they usually are to blacks' own view of life in the South (the part they let him see), Joel Chandler Harris's retellings of black folktales are undercut by the tales' frames, which derive uncooked from the plantation tradition. Surrounding the true-to-the-folk folktales are frame-tales about good old Uncle Remus reciting bedtime stories to a golden-haired white child; these frame-tales palliate and even counterstate the complex, stinging messages crooned, snarled, and embodied by Rabbit, Wolf, and their cautious, hungry "brers."[47] The odd result was that Harris's white supremacist readers of the late nineteenth century were given a huge dose of reality from a black perspective, but then it was so thickly coated with the white sugar of plantation novel and Tom Show conventions, including the Tom Show's seemingly indelible image of the gentle Negro "Uncle" and the white child, that no harm seemed done. This is by no means to say that Harris himself was a "closet revolutionary"; he merely reflected the divided mind of the white southerner of his time, burdened with his history and unable to fit together the puzzle pieces of the society in which he lived. White Harris wore a black mask (the language, the true-to-idiom inner tales) to describe with unusual accuracy his ravenous and racially torn society.[48] No doubt he did so also to project his own anger and bitterness over the way the world was turning. But over that black mask he wore yet another one, a white one, which he used to tickle the funnybone, to rhapsodize with familiar stereotypes, and otherwise to appeal to and appease his genteel white readers—to prepare them to stomach (but never truly to comprehend) the uncooked black tales of violence, disarray, and revenge.

Adams also wore one mask over another. Again, his black tales were as true to the black angle of vision and idiom as were Harris's, even more so. Yet as with Harris's stock Remus and little white boy, it is Adams's white mask that one sees quickly, perhaps even first, when one picks up one of his books. The white face of *Congaree Sketches* shows when, in his glossary (see the entries for "Free Issue," "purtty or pritty," and "Tad"), Adams uses the words "darky" and "mammy" as if they were equivalent to "Negro" and "black woman." Furthermore, Adams's work reflected the typical white prejudice against Negroes of mixed white and black bloodlines. One literary form this prejudice took was that of the convention, used by Harriet Beecher Stowe and many others (including, in his turn, Faulkner), of the evil mulatto.[49]

During slavery, mulattoes born to white women were legally free, but "dey was discounted by white folks and dey was scorned by niggers," Adams makes a character say. To one tale's "Free Issue," who is not only a "tragic mulatto" but a stagey "wretched freedman"[50] as well, "a real nigger were pison," so his spirit wanders even now, and when it is seen "a nigger always die." In another tale, mixed-blood Simon, who kills a white woman, is described in terms more befitting a Thomas Nelson Page or Thomas Dixon novel than a work of the New Negro Renaissance. Adams's black character Old Daniel is made to recite these unlikely words:

> Simon daddy white, Simon' mammy black, Simon ain't nothin'; He got a nigger heart an' a white man head, an' dat's a mighty poor mixtry. What Simon head say Simon heart ain't know, an' what Simon heart say Simon head tangle up. He ain't white an' he ain't black, an' he ain't nothin'. White man spiles the nigger in him an' nigger spiles the white man. He born tangle up an' he guh die tangle up, an' all I can say is God forgive he Daddy and God love he Mammy an' God have mercy on Simon. He ain't nigger, an he ain't white, an he ain't nothin'. He born tangle up.

Adams's other "yaller niggers" are also weaklings, killers of "real niggers," and mad wildmen who hate everybody. That all of Adams's "yaller niggers" fit these categories makes clear that they are inhabitants not of the Congaree but of the gallery of "mulatto" stereotypes dating back to nineteenth-, eighteenth-, and even seventeenth-century American culture. Here we meet the lily-white Dr. E. C. L. Adams—or, more accurately, the double-masked man, with his reassuring white mask of convention turned toward his white audience.

If these stereotyped characters and casually antiblack uses of such explosive terms as "darky" and "nigger" made Adams's sketches palatable even to white supremacists, so did his characters' statements concerning black ambition. In one tale Sam hears a black preacher talk about how "de nigger is guh prosper. He say dey is guh be great rulers an' big bosses, dat heben is full on 'em an' God got 'em crowded 'roun' de throne an' nigger angels is flyin' ever which a way an' dey got great 'thority. Dey settin' 'roun' de foot-stool an' roostin' all 'round on de bannisters an' sunnen dey self on de golden stairs." Sounding again like a Page or Dixon mouthpiece, Scip has the last word here: "God ain guh have a passel of niggers messen up in he business. Niggers got dey place an' dat ain't on top. Has you ever see a tumble bug roll he load? He ain't never satisfy wid it any way he got it. He always try to roll up a hill. He gits up a piece and then he roll down again, 'en that's a nigger." Likewise, Preb heard a "passel er lies" about Scip's son, who comes home talking about improving "the race."

> *Preb:* . . . He tell dem niggers ef dey jine togedder dey can rise up an' take dey own place in de worl', an' he been talkin' 'bout schoolin' an' 'bout respect dey self an' how dey will be respected. He say dey got a long road to travel, an' it's up hill all de way, dat dey's down in de valley of darkness now, but bright lights is shinin' at de top.

Tad replies that "dat ain't nothin' but nigger talk"; but Spencer adds the summary judgment that gives "White Folks is White Folks" its title and the book a white mask:

> *Spencer:* A nigger's a nigger. If he tempts t be better'n a nigger a nigger pulls him down an' a cracker pushes him down. Down is de nigger's cry. He's got two main enemies—crackers and niggers. White folks is white folks, crackers is crackers an' niggers is niggers.

These tales, "Sunning on de Golden Stairs" and "White Folks Is White Folks," show Adams with both masks in sight. Through one he appeals to the white supremacist, obviously. But through another he also tells the truth as many blacks themselves doubtless knew it. Surely mixed bloods, "brass ankles," *were* sometimes viewed with suspicion by their darker brothers. And surely Spencer's lines about blacks with ambition could have been spoken by a dubious black person almost as easily as by a white racist. Easy race-uplift rhetoric, especially when voiced by outsiders, was viewed by blacks with suspicion if not contempt.

Like *Congaree Sketches*, Adams's second book was double-masked. Ironically, the very title of this "absolutely negro" book marked it as a white man's work. So did its cover, with drawings of old "uncles" (very close to the Remus or Tom stereotypes) and their grimly defeated nephews. "The book is attractively gotten up," wrote one reviewer, "save that its jacket depicts black men with a mentality of the baboon or an animal that might have a vocabulary of fifty words, not the clever talker of the volume to whom the right word always comes."[51] White masking also appears here in the form of Adams's own "Foreword" (inevitably a revision of Paul Green's), which opens the second volume with academic clichés about "primitive peoples" of a "high type" alongside a Thomas Dixonism about the speech of his informants as "pure nigger" dialect with a phonetic system obeying "no rule." Again in this book we find stock scenes involving "yaller niggers" who are crazy, weak, and wondering what they are.

In *Nigger to Nigger*'s "Education," as in certain pieces in *Congaree Sketches*, one again sees Adams with both masks in sight. Echoing a Joel Chandler Harris tale in which he uses Uncle Remus to decry the uselessness of schooling for blacks ("Dey better be home pickin' up chips. Wat a nigger winter l'arn outen books? I kin take a bar'l stave an fling mo' sense inter a nigger in one minnit dan all de schoolhouses betwist dis en de State er Midgigin."),[52] Adams's "Education" shows Tad and Scip differing about the ends of "education" for "a nigger." Scip states the case cynically, in a way that would appeal to readers Adams might share with Harris, Dixon, or Page: "I never has seen a nigger and education fitten for nothin'. Ef you send him off to school, he sho' God forgits how to plow, an' a axe, or pick or a hoe looks like pizen to 'em." With scorn, Scip goes on to apply the "give-the-nigger-an-inch-and-he'll-take-an-ell" analysis to a black visitor who has brought black advancement ideas to Congaree. The man is no more than one of these "slick niggers wid all dey scheme. . . . First thing you know, he'll be tryin' to have you settin' at de table wid white folks." Tad agrees that that would be an unwelcome turn: "I'd feel wusser 'bout it dan dey does," he says.

Perhaps some blacks of the 1920s would have said that and meant it. But what Scip says next certainly is consistent with other accounts of black suspicion toward "outside agitators": "Dey comes here wid all dey notions an' leffs us wid de calf to hold." Adams's revision of the Harris tale becomes still more believably black when Tad says that in his view the visitor "have got some good ideas. . . . I ain' think that nigger all fool. . . . By the help er God we mought better we condition ef we trys. Maybe de white folks will help we." Tad even chides Scip for his relentless cynicism: "Scip, I 'clare to God," he says, "you oughter git over you' disheartenin' ways." Scip's rejoinder is real, too: "I been here a good while," he says. Like *Nigger to Nigger* as a whole, Adams's "Education" is white and black masked, double-masked.

William Faulkner, whose first novel appeared in the same year as *Congaree Sketches*, provides the clearest example of the white American writer of this century who tells his truth from behind a black mask. The epic of the South that emerges from his Yoknapatawpha books would not be imaginable without Dilsey Gibson and her family, Joe Christmas, Sam Father, Charles Bon, Lucas Beauchamp, or Rider Spoot. As Thadious M. Davis has observed, the presence (one might say the omnipresence) of "Faulkner's Negro" in this created world mirrors the divided (and yet much shared) black-and-white South and the possibility of wholeness.[53] Referring not just to Faulkner but to other writers of the 1920s choosing black characters, Davis writes:

> For the artist inclined to explore "life," the Negro had a special appeal. By virtue of his enslavement and separation from his African homeland, the Negro is a dramatic representation of human struggle for survival in a world (especially in a modern, industrial world) bereft of traditional customs and values. His African heritage also makes him particularly attractive as an exotic primitive offering a vicarious escape from mundane concerns. Because of his traditional position in southern life, the Negro evokes a wide range of associations and is capable of interaction with all levels of society. For instance, only the Negro has traditionally had contact with every possible caste and class in the South, from aristocrat to poor-white, from plantation owner to industrial worker. His presence alone can evoke myths of "blackness" as evil, damned, or mysterious; or it can recall theories of blacks as descendants of Ham and the progeny of Cain. The Negro can be used to suggest conceptual structures: slavery, sexuality, primitivism, fraternity, endurance, hope. He may symbolize historical contexts:

> the antebellum South, the Civil War, Reconstruction. Or he may represent change: the destruction of the cavalier and plantation myths; the failure of King Cotton; the conversion power of faith or love; the rise of the modern South. Largely because of the Negro, the southern artist found a coherent locus of meaning in the South. By observing and synthesizing the Negro's experience, the artist saw that the tragedy and the comedy of fundamental human experience could be approached directly. Or, as in the case of [Faulkner's] works such as *Soldiers' Pay* and *The Sound and the Fury*, Negro experience could place the experience of southern life in wider perspectives and less parochial contexts. However, Negro life, even when considered superficially, made accessible to the artist (no matter the degree of his talent or powers of observation) the inner realities of southern culture. In addition, Negro life laid bare complex personal emotions and responses to the vicissitudes of existence. For both artist and average southerner, "the Negro" personified life's simpler functions and its serious problems; in a pseudo-theoretical sense he represented an attitude toward being that counteracted the more destructive conditions of industrialization and the breakdown of rural patterns.
>
> Paradoxically, though the Negro became the South's metaphor for change, he remained the region's lone constant while traditions crumbled. He contributed much to the southerner's need for continuity and stability. Within a context of change and conflict, the Negro provided a central rallying point of order and meaning for the diverse ideologies about both "the Negro" and the "New South." There was much truth to an old saying about the Mississippi Delta region: "The variable factors are high water and the price of cotton; the constant is the Negro."[54]

Adams's project was far less ambitious than Faulkner's: the Negro characters of Congaree are much less richly evocative in meaning. But like Faulkner's, Adams's Negroes speak more than a narrow caste truth. Through his renditions of their conversations, which one editor called "absolutely negro," Adams offers his own critique of the culture of the South and the nation. Things, he feared, were "gittin' wusser."

The Tales Themselves

Granted that Adams's tales were "part-white," what did he tell us from behind his black mask? His first published sketches set the stage. "Tournament in Heaven," which first appeared in the *Dublin Magazine* (1925) was the first narrative piece in *Congaree Sketches.* It retraces the much-recorded tale of the Negro who went to heaven only to be put out for flying too fast.[55] Adams's technique in this story is typified by its fine, uncluttered representation of black talk. "Time dat nigger hit heben," the unnamed tale-teller says, "he hit it a throwin' them foots an' shouting. Peter walk up to him and say, 'Hole on nigger, the Lord want to see you.'" True to this folktale as blacks themselves often have told it, the Lord, Peter, "Gabel," and "de tall angel" all conspire with poor white angels ("dem buckra") to remove the quick-winged "Hopkins nigger" from heaven. The fixed tournament among the angels results in the injury of the Negro flier. "Atter while de Lord and he Son and de white angels come up and dere lay de nigger, he pearley whings broke, he silver feathers scattered on de groun', he head twist one side and he gold claw curl up." But the Lord is without mercy: He "look at him an' say, 'jest like a nigger, persisely like a nigger.'" Peter packs him off in a wheel barrow rolling down "a hill on de back side of heben to de grand trash pile, and he was mummerin' and a mutterin'. This comes from bein' like a nigger. 'Just like a nigger! Persisely like a nigger!'"

Here the black storyteller makes clear again that pride goeth before a fall. Why did the angel announce himself as "er Hopkins nigger, like dat been sumpen great?" This particle of vainglory—not just in his earthly residence but in his association and perhaps family connection with the prestigious Hopkinses (Adams's cousins)—mark him as the inevitable dupe. Still the tale-teller here performs the verbal jujitsu again true to black folk sources, the sudden twist involved in seeming to accept for the moment of the tale certain traits ascribed stereotypically to blacks: extravagantly improper behavior, gullibility, reckless waste of precious "pearley" gifts. He knows the lies whites tell on blacks and merely laughs them off. So what if they are true! Is it not *human* after all ("persisely like a nigger" or anybody) not just to mess up a good thing but to crash even after St. Peter himself warns you to "Hole on?" Is not self-mockery, too, a hard-won, therapeutic, and even nobly human talent?

On another level, the tale is a parable of the harsh 1920s southern scene in which blacks who dare to fly from "their place" are hated and scapegoated by powerful whites as well as by "dem buckra." Peter dislikes "de Hopkins nigger" on first sight, perhaps because he shows up at heaven's front door. When he turns out to be a superior flier—naturally better than the winged "buckra"—Peter and others with power fix things so the black angel is crushed. If the Hopkins flier strikes the Lord and Peter as being "persisely like a nigger," they act "persisely" like most southern whites of their time. Despite its "realistic" message of fixed social roles, this rich tale retains this turn: even if God Himself is dead set against the Negro, who is guilty of nothing more than being human, for a shining moment at least "the Hopkins nigger" is nonetheless the fastest flier in heaven. "De nigger stretch hisself and flop he whing three or four times an' create a dust, den he riz up an' he fly an' he flewed and there never been seen such flyin' since heben been heben an' de Lord look on an' was 'stonished." In the end, in spite of the white pettiness of the Lord and Peter, true transcendence belongs to "de nigger" from Hopkins.

The other sketch Adams published in Dublin in 1925, "Jonas," was set not in heaven but in the Congaree. Perhaps the real-world setting makes this piece more fatalistic in tone. Here the white bosses do not protect "dem buckra" from blacks so much as "dem buckra," who in this sketch control the court as jurymen, look out for themselves. In the conversation between cynical Scip and an unnamed "Voice"—used by Adams in many sketches as a chorus calling for the tale's main teller to clarify and amplify his tale—Scip returns from the trial of "Un' Fed boy, Jonas." In this terse account, all official charges or legal defenses are utterly beside the point:

Scip: Dey done finish.
Voice: Wha' dey do wid him.
Scip: You talk like a fool. Axe me what dey guh do wid him. Ain't I tell you dey try him? Ain't I tell you dey done finish try him? You axe me wha' dey do wid him. Ain't you know who set on de jury?
Voice: White folks.
Scip: Yes, white folks, and dat ain't all,—poor white folks, poor buckra, cracker,—ain't dat 'nuf? Dat what set on de jury.
Voice: But Jonas ain't do nuttin'.
Scip: Dat ain't make no difference. I done tell you who set on de jury.

As in the previous tale, here again the white-controlled game is rigged against the black man. Jonas is trapped beyond all help. No moments of humor or symbolic victory relieve this tale's tension. If there is hope in "Jonas," it is the tightly muffled hope that comes from the stoic acceptance of immutable facts:

Voice: Is he pa fret much?
Scip: No he ain't fret. He know dey ain't no nuse to fret. He raise he chillun right and he ain't fret. He got sense. He know wha' guh be, guh be, en he ain't fret.

Adams's most telling messages lie not just in the narrative line of his tales, but in their structure and symbolic geography. The full title of *Congaree Sketches* includes the cumbersome but summarizing subtitle *Scenes from Negro Life in the Swamps of the Congaree and Tales by Tad and Scip of Heaven and Hell with Other Miscellany*. These fifty-four scenes, tales, and "other miscellany" include explanation tales, lyrical descriptive pieces, animal stories, poems, sermons, and narratives about relations among Congaree residents, black and white, present and past. Like Harris's Remus tales, these sketches, most framed as conversations, are structured as tales-within-tales and follow a prologue-tale-epilogue pattern. But here both outer tale and inner tale generally (though, as we have seen, not always) are told from a compellingly black point of view: the Harris formula of outer tale = "white world," inner tale = "black world"[56] is not followed here. When the white mask appears, it is more subtle than Harris's "white" bracketing tales.

Generally, Adams's outer tales (prologue and epilogue) take place in a linguistic "demilitarized zone," apart from the swampland "combat zone" of the inner tales. An early version of "A Freshet on the Congaree" defines this safer area into which Leck emerges from the Congaree swamp. Adams sets the scene as if it were part of a play: "Scene: *Group of Negroes gathered about old shop, talking. Leck approaches. His clothes are yellow with mud, boots caked. Horn swung over his shoulder and old time shot gun under his arm.*"[57] These outer tales situate the tale-tellers as aloof—if only for the moments of the tales' telling—from the Congaree swamp itself and from the terror of the inner tales' action. Set in the present, the outer tales are full of ritual greetings that signal fraternity within a close group and reflections on the meanings of excursions to the troubled, past-haunted world of the inner tale. The prologue of "A Freshet on the Congaree" is repeated in structure, tale after tale:

Leck: Gentlemens!
Voice: Sorter slow. Wuh's de time, Ber Leck?
Leck: Time ain't so much.
Voice: Wey you come from?
Leck: Jes come out of de Congaree swamp.
Voice: How come time ain't so much, Ber Leck?
Leck: Jes come out de Congaree swamp and de old river sho' is ragin'.

Then comes the inner tale, Leck's prose-poetic account of the sudden and destructive flooding of the Congaree River: "I never is seen a wusser freshet. . . . Every which er way I look I see 'struction. I see sturgeon tangle up in a wire fence an' de birds quit singin' and went to hollerin', and I look down on de yaller water and I see wey buzzard cast his shadow. . . . If your heart ain't right, my brother, de big swamps will 'stroy it. Dey 'stroy your body, an' if dey ain't 'stroy it, look like dey 'stroy your soul." Following the inner tale is the epilogue, which brings the reader back into the present for an amplifying comment typically full of repeated phrases, spoken this time by the choral "Voice":

> Did you hear Ber Leck? He ain't tell no lie. I see a heap of mens come out de big swamps. If dey stay dere long enough, when dey come out dey look more like beasts or varmints dan dey does like mens. Brother, God ain't make dem swamps for mens. Dey de home of de devil, de home of 'struction; dey de home of serpents, de home of buzzards, and if you put mens in dem swamps, de only way dey can live is to be like de critters dat live dere, and take on dere ways. Yes, my brother, stay 'way from de big swamps.

Most of the inner tales are set in these frightful swamps of the Congaree. Their setting deep down in the swamps, where men take on the ways of "beasts or varmints" and where animals talk and hold court, is no Yoknapatawpha, but still it is a created world, a place tense with historical associations, symbols, and signs. In his word list, Adams gives the following gloss for the word "Congaree":

> The Congaree swamps lie on both sides of the Congaree River a few miles from Columbia, South Carolina. They vary in width from seven to twelve miles, and extend along the river about forty miles. A series of other swamps continue below them for a hundred miles or so toward the sea. Congaree is possibly the last surviving word of a lost language, the speech of the vanished Congaree Indians who once inhabited the region. There are no more Congaree Indians living, but many of the Negroes of this district plainly have Indian blood in them.[58]

The original Congarees were decimated by the British in the Yemassee War of 1715; those who were not killed or driven out were sold as slaves on the West Indian market. Although the knowledge of the precise meaning of the word "Congaree" vanished with the Congaree Indians, still it has connotations that are significant here. For not only did the name apply to a river and its swampland, along with a church, a railroad station, and other area landmarks, but Columbia, the nearby state capital, was originally known as "the Congarees."[59] Furthermore, the Congaree Swamp, covering seventy thousand acres, is "one of the last of the South's great virgin swamp forests" and boasts cypress, giant pine, and oak trees more than seven hundred years old, "the redwoods of the East."[60] And, of course, the blacks of Congaree, according to Adams, have mixed so with the Congaree Indians that many are part Congaree. Indeed, for blacks the resonance with the African word "Kongo" might have made calling oneself a "Congaree" a form of self-celebration. So, too, might all the region's residents be called Congarees. Something rotten in Congaree would suggest much more than did the "dying Indian" stories of a century before, sentimental tales of "noble savages" who "disappeared" with the clearing of the land. It would bring to mind ancient blood wars and a pattern of betrayal, slavery, and the threatened destruction of the very spark of life in the state and the nation, if not in nature itself.

And something is terribly rotten in Adams's Congaree. That fact is clear in the first tale in *Congaree Sketches*, "The Big Swamps of the Congaree," in which Tad exchanges the usual ritual greetings with the group before the inner tale begins. In this instance the inner tale consists of a kind of "song of the swamp," telling in a general way what it means to have been "down in de big swamps on the Congaree." His lyrical speech recalls his trip to the strange, deathly region:

> *Tad:* I been down in de big swamps on de Congaree. . . . I been down to de Congaree in de big swamps, where de trees is tall an' de moss long an' gray, where de Bullace grow, an' where I hear de tune of de bird in de mornin'; down wey de wild turkey gobbles, way down on de Congaree; wey God's mornin' leads to de devil's night; down on de river, where night make her sign, where owls on a dead limb talks of de dead, talks wid de dead and laughs like de dead, way down in de big swamps of de Congaree; down where de blunt-

> tailed moccasin crawls in de grass, where de air is stink wid he smell; where de water is green, where de worms is spewed out of de groun', where de groun' is mud, where de trees sweat like a man; down in de home of de varmint an' bugs, down in de slick yallow mud, de black mud an' de brown, way down in de big swamps of de Congaree; down in de land of pizen, where de yallow-fly sting, in de home of de fever an' wey death is de king. Dat wey I been, down in de big swamps. Down in de land of mosquito, way down in de big swamps, down on de Congaree.

It is a journey decidedly *down*: Tad uses that word fifteen times in the one-page sketch; four times he makes clear that the place he has traversed is "*wey* down." If Tad reports signs of health in this lower region—bird calls, tall trees, wild grapes ("Bullace")—they are overshadowed by a plague of other less hopeful images: long gray moss, death owls, snakes in grass, worms, bugs, "varmints," and "pizen." The atmosphere here is "unnat'ral": the air is stinking with snakes, the water is green, trees "sweat like a man." The mud underfoot is black, brown, and yellow—but in the swamp, "where de yallow-fly sting," yellow is the dominant hue. No wonder when, in "A Freshet on the Congaree,"[61] Leck emerges from the underworld of the swamp, "his clothes are yellow with mud, boots caked." He, Tad, and other *Congaree* narrators have traveled to the frightening "devil's night" world, to the frightening realm "way down" in the swamp of yellow death and signs.

One walker in the Congaree lowlands gives a detailed report of the swamp that goes beyond realism:

> De swamp look evil wid de yaller mud from de high water up on de trees higher 'an a man's head, and shadows from de trees and flies and things flyin' 'round. And up in de air a hawk been sailin' 'round and a buzzard way up dere in de sky; and through de yaller swamp de yaller crane and the goose eye yaller Issue was passin', in de distance mixin' wid everything else dat were yaller, an' passin' dis way comin' into sight one minute and fadin' de nex' till dey all was swallowed up and everything were like it were not in a human world.

The only truly hopeful sign in these tales is that Leck, Tad, and most (not all) of the other swamp travelers do reemerge from the swamp and from the mad world of the inner tale; somehow they return home to tell their stories, even to tell them with gusto. Leck surfaces from the killing swamp to join friends and has only the slight complaint that "time ain't so much."

Strangely enough, this night world swamp that kills and drives men and beasts mad and "unnat'ral" is as devilishly alluring as it is dangerous: it "draws people like a trap draws flies, an' people dies in de big swamps like flies dies in traps." "The spirit world of the Negro," reports Adams, "is usually one to be feared, full of goblins and ghosts."[62] It is the world of lost owls that embody the restless spirits of dead men, jaybirds that fly to and from the lower world delivering wood for hellfire, and even "spirit dogs and barking snakes" that "tangles twixt de feets of men." The dreadfully alluring spirits of the Congaree are its eternal wanderers, dead sinners dwelling in the hell of the deep swamp. The most tempting of these is the "Jack-ma-lantern," "sinful old folks" barred from heaven and hell, whose punishment is "to wander in de bad places and on de bad night, and dey business is enticing mens to follow 'em, an' dey ain't got no res', les' dey entice mens to lef' de right road." Hock followed a jack-ma-lantern down a hole and through briars and knee-deep mud. When they found him he was frozen in a cringing posture with his eyes open, "and he was stiff dead." Likewise, "Transmigration" has a moral aspect: a former slave is doomed to haunt the darkness of the swamp because "he ain' live right in dis world." What lures men to the swamp has to do with guilt, sin, and unresolved historical tensions and tragedies endemic not only to the South but to the nation.

More than any other subject, the sketches of Adams's first book concern these alluring but doomed, dead, and deadly wanderers. Most of them died during slavery; their eternal travels in Congaree punish them for their wicked lives and serve as a warning to the living. That they wandered from slavery to Adams's era suggests, too, that problems from the slave past still haunted Adams's present world. Ole Man Rouse was a slaveholder who punished his black slaves and then black freedmen by drowning them. Once when he was fishing the Big Cypress, where he did the drownings, blacks ambushed him and pushed him into the water. Now Rouse's spirit lives near the place where he was drowned; fishermen passing that spot may see Rouse in the form of a turtle as well as blacks shaped as lizards laughing at Rouse in his torment.

In another tale, we meet Ole Man Rogan, whose "great pleasure" during slavery was to break up black families by selling mothers from children, husbands from wives. At night his spirit travels the territory where he died: one knows he is near when in the swamp one hears a chain rattle, a black mother or child calling for one another, or Rogan laughing at their pain. "He laugh like he satisfied, but he ain't had no res'." Another doomed sadist moving through the swamp is a "yaller" man who rode a gray mule and whose job during slavery was to capture runaways: "Dat been he juty and dat been he pleasure, to say he ain' love nothen but he mule and he houn' and he old marster. And dey say dey ain' certain he love he old marster but he wants to be he friend wid him so he can have he pleasure." His spirit still chases the spirits of those he ran down during slavery. "Dey 'pears as a warnin' to mens."

"The past is never dead," wrote Faulkner. "It's not even past."[63] Adams's Congaree Swamp is a hellish underworld as haunted as Yoknapatawpha with ghosts from slavery days. And like Faulkner's Jefferson, the principal town in his postage stamp county, Adams's civilized town is, ironically, at least as bad as the forests and swamps surrounding it. His tale-tellers' reports of encounters with the law describe this disordered section of deathtrap Congaree. We have seen Jonas, who has done nothing, tried and doomed by "poor white folks, poor buckra, cracker jurymen." "Poor buckra" drive the black men on the chain gang, too. When Wash (whose crime is that he "done cross de path of de law") prays and cries for mercy from his gang bosses, one "poor buckra" kicks him and says, "Holler if you wants to, gee him twice as much." Then he orders salt rubbed into the black man's sores. "Poor buckra" are defined by Adams as "crackers, poor white trash, the lowest kind of white men." He adds: "In the language of the Calabar Coast *buckra* means 'demon, a powerful and superior being.'" In Adams's work, middle-class whites are usually not more fair to blacks than are "dem buckra."[64] Middle-class whites' ideas of proper racial etiquette are mocked in "Judge Foolbird" when Ole Man Hall, a white store owner, overhears black Noah say "God-dam" to another black shopper in Hall's store. Hall, "a Christian gentleman," tells Noah to leave the premises. Noah apologizes and leaves. But "atter while ole man Hall walk out an' follow him up an' he walk up to Noah an' bus' him over de head wid er axe halve an' beat him up." Both are arrested. Once Hall and Noah are in court, the judge inevitably sides with the white man despite the facts of the case, which make it ludicrously plain that Noah has committed no crime: "Jedge Foolbird axe ole man Hall what de nigger do when he follow him up and ole man Hall say 'He ain't do nuthin', but he look like he goin' say sumpen,' and Jedge Foolbird fined Noah one hunnerd dollahs." Hall is fined five dollars. Why was the white man fined at all? "Ain't he white folks?" asks one initiated listener. Yes, but "Jedge Foolbird is de law, an' he goin' do what he goin' do. He de law, and de law is de law." Such is much of the comedy in the world of E. C. L. Adams.

In "Big Charleston" the black man whose name gives the sketch its title has committed a real crime: he has killed another man. But his victim is only another black man, so the white boss sends his lawyer to Big Charleston's defense. "When he lawyer git up and tell dat jury wuh kind of hand Big Charleston been and how much work he can do, he say he [Charleston] ain't never been in no trouble wid no white folks, and he say, 'You all ain't got nothin' 'gainst Charleston, wuh he do?'" So the good workman is released. In another sketch the confused mulatto Simon commits the ultimate sin of killing a white woman. The court says he must die.

In sketch after sketch set in the 1920s civilized world beyond the swamp, liquor is the issue, with Judge Foolbird and colleagues, legal and extralegal, giving time and death. In these liquor sketches, Adams touches upon an explosive set of issues. Bootlegging was big business during Prohibition, and in the 1920s the Klan and other white vigilante groups patrolled their members' stills, often scapegoating black salesmen or deliverymen when white owners were threatened.[65] Black Reuben was sent to the penitentiary for seven years "fer a little liquor." Suspected black liquor dealers were sometimes awakened in their homes by lawmen and killed if they resisted—even if no liquor was found. "De jedge is de jedge, an' de law mus' be helt up," comments one of Adams's characters. "De jedge is a great man. He is a hones' man. He know he business an he guh broke up liquor."[66]

In "The Animal Court," Buzzard eats Rabbit and is sentenced to die. Bur Fox is selected as Buzzard's executioner. But Fox is "mighty perticular 'bout what he do an' what he put he mout' on." So he leaves the job undone. "An' nobody didn't do nuthen to Bur Buzzard, an' ain't never done nothen to Buzzard. Dat's why so much buzzard. Dey always gits off." A black man has seen this animal court in session by the light of the moon in slavery time. But its counterpart also operated in the Congaree of Adams's era. Here too the weak black "rabbits" were preyed upon by the strong white "buzzards." Once a weak one was in the court's clutches, no amount of earnest explaining, prayer, Uncle Tom acting, or appeals to mercy would soften the "buzzard's" heart. Ole Man Tooga and his son try all of these to no avail. Nor is trickery—the black strategy of first and last resort—of any help to Tooga or his son. Of Tooga's chances to outscheme "de cracker" Scip remarks, "Is you ever see a mice when de cat's got him? Schemin' helps him."

Adams's Congaree is a nether region where dead men wander, tempting the living to death. But the ghouls of the past are not the only ones rattling chains and laughing horribly. Sixty years after slavery's end the white men who run the courts, not just "poor buckra" but businessmen, politicians, and judges, all conspire together under the banner of Christ, decency, and whiteness to scapegoat and "legally lynch" the black man accused of crime.

Sterling A. Brown is certainly correct when he favorably compares *Nigger to Nigger* with *Congaree Sketches*; the former is "fuller and even more forceful."[67] *Nigger to Nigger* is a larger book, with nearly twice as many entries as Adams's first. And its range of expression is much wider. There are more descriptive gems here. For instance, Tad says, "De last time I see Mensa, he wave he hand to me an' walk off. I kin see him now walkin' like a tiger cat. He look back onct an' swing his self away like a piece er music on de air. . . . He jes connect up pleasant feelin's wid danger." The funny tales in *Nigger to Nigger* are extremely funny and true to the idiom. The unknowing Negro of "The Telephone Call" has not received the "fine sixteen dollar suit er clothes" he has ordered from Sears in Chicago, so he uses the boss's phone to check on it. He talks up $167.28 worth of inquiry. The boss is so upset when he returns that "he hover 'twix' life an' death. Dey was talk 'bout havin' dat nigger 'rested for makin a 'tempt on de white folks' life." In "A Good Looking Man," Tad noticed his boss "all dress up an' shave."

> An' Tad look at him an' say:
> "Boss, you sho' God is a good lookin' man. You de best lookin' man I ever see."
>
> An' de boss look at him an' say:
> "You think so, Tad?"
>
> An' Tad say:
> "You sho' is. I reckon the reason wuh make I think so is you moest generally look so wuss."

What is most impressive about this second series of tales is the comprehensiveness of their view of black American history. Here again, it is as though once he was double-masked Adams felt he could say precisely what was on his mind. With his black mask in place, Adams deals with the meanings of Africa for the black dweller in Congaree. Debunking any notions of a purely glorious African past is "The King Buzzard," which concerns a chief "'way back in Africa" who catches and sells thousands of his brethren to white slave traders. On their last trip to that coast, the white slavers chain the chief himself and bring him to America. His spirit is among those unfit for heaven or hell and doomed to wander forever. Tad encounters it in the form of a large buzzard, "de King Buzzard," feeding on dead beasts deep in the Congaree Swamp.

"Gullah Joe" tells of a slave born in Africa who recalls being lured to a slave trader's ship. He recounts for Tad the horror of traveling through the Middle Passage on a ship of disease and cruel death. He also tells Tad that he "has a longin' to walk in de feenda." He goes on: "I wants to see it one more time. I has a wite an' chillun here, but when I thinks er my tribe an' my friend an' my daddy an' my mammy an' de great feenda, a feelin' rises up in my throat an' my eye well up wid tear." Adams glosses "feenda" as "an African word for 'forest.'" More particularly, "feenda" is a creolized word for the classical Ki-Kongo term for "forest," "nfinda." According to Robert Farris Thompson, "nfinda" means "forest" in "a deep sense of realm of the ancestors, as boundary, threshold to the superior wisdom of the ancestors, liminality, all these things and more."[68]

Adams does not use Gullah Joe's moment of yearning to sing of an Edenic African homeland, for Gullah Joe does not want to take his wife or his children born in America "back" to live in "de feenda." Yet Adams's unwillingness to dismiss utterly this man's desire to see his birthplace results in a sketch of rare power and poignancy. Unlike most "African" pieces of the New Negro Renaissance, Adams's African sketches are not drawn from dream-visions or nightmares of primitive villages, full of drums, twilight, shadows, and superstitions. For Gullah Joe, Africa is a real place full of actual remembered experience, in all its ambiguity.

Nigger to Nigger's section "Slavery Time" includes only five pieces: two about memories of Africa, three about white violence toward black slaves. But elsewhere in the volume, slavery and slaves' techniques for enduring it are Adams's subjects. Tales about preachers and accounts of their sermons—many of them, not surprisingly in the deadly Congaree, funeral sermons—make up more than one-fifth of the book. He heard a black preacher chant the words:

> I vision God standing
> On the heights of heaven,
> Throwing the devil like
> A burning torch
> Over the gulf
> Into the valleys of hell.
> His eye the lightning's flash,
> His voice the thunder's roll.

Wid one hand He snatched
The sun from its socket,
And the other He clapped across the moon.

Adams's black dwellers in the Congaree saw God as a protector, "a rock in a weary land." But preachers were human. In these sketches, they hollar too loud—"like God can't hear ef dey whisper"—and then "eat up all de grub you kin put on you' table, set down an' go to pickin' dey teet' an' lookin' at you' baby gal." They preach faith and prayer, but these men are practical, too. Deacon Jones, when called on to tell of his spiritual travels, alludes to an attack by a bear: "My brothers an' sisters," he says, "all I kin say is: God is good. I loves God. I sho' loves Him, and I puts my faith in Him. God is good an' He'll help you in a lot er little things, but, my brothers an' sisters, good as God is, He ain' worth a damn in a bear fight." Scip "was a minister," according to Adams, "but something of a skeptic and a fatalist." In *Congaree Sketches* he remarks that when God "drap" a black man "in de han' of er cracker he done wid him, he done quit noticin' prayer, Him and he Son an' all un um. Dey got too much else to 'tend to." A man on the chain gang "mought pray to de cracker ef he wants to create a laugh an' game makin'. Luh him pray." Likewise Scip tells Tad it helps a man in deep trouble to pray sometimes. "He ain' foolin' God, but it helps him to fool his self, an' it sounds good when he gits out."

If religion tempered with skepticism provided one way for slaves and their children to face the world, so did the strategies celebrated in black trickster tales, a series of which is recorded in *Nigger to Nigger*. Through both books, in fact, Adams's characters sustain a discussion of the necessary art of lying. Lying is a defensive weapon. In *Congaree Sketches*, when Spencer pretends to scold Tad for "fixin' to make Preb lie," Tad continues the once-upon-a-time prelude to the tale by offering Preb more encouragement:

Tad: Luh him lie. It ain't hurt nobody when he lie. I an' you an' him all know he guh lie. Luh him lie. He ain' fool no nigger, an' if he keep in practice hit will help him wid de white folks.

Even Tad says that Jazy "oughter be 'shame" for telling white children that to kill an owl in a tree they need simply walk in a circle around the base of the tree until the stupid bird twists "he head right on 'round an' wring it off." But Scip defends the lie:

> *Scip:* Dat's good for em chillun. It's good to tell 'em lie an' create s'picion in dey mind, kaze dey guh listen to lie all dey life an' dey better be prepared. Dis world ain' much more 'an one big lie anyway. Luh him learn dese chillun while dey young.

As Robert Bone argues, black tale-telling is more than just a defensive game against white bosses or an initiation into a lying world. It involves "creating a fiction" by which to live, a world in which one's values and sense of life are sustained. It is more than mere escapism. "Fiction," says Bone, "is perceived as a source of survival. With this perception, we are very close to the sources of the black man's storytelling art."[69] Through his carefully wrought "lies" (or stories with a point), the teller may record a means of avoiding the worst excesses of enemies; and ironically, too, the liar also may face, in the compressed but comprehensive way that fiction allows, truths that may be, as Ernest Hemingway says, truer than the facts. Of Congaree's Napoleon, a master tale-teller often quoted by Adams's liars, Voice says: "He tell a lie so nat'ral till I ain' know if it de trute or a lie. I heared him 'scribe a thing till dey jes look like a natu'al picture somebody drawed."

Some of Adams's liars tell of black badmen so bad the world backs up when they approach. But these tales' most stalwart of survivors are the artful dodgers, the tricksters. In his "Bur Rabbit" tales, Rabbit is the master of lies and deception, whose province is the interstices of whatever place he inhabits. So he appears "in de dead er night" when "de moon was shakin' an' every star in de element was geeving light." "He a sportin' man" who likes to dance and put on "more airs dan a poor buckra wid a jug er liquor an' a new suit er clothes on," yet he lives and loves to party in the graveyard. "He ain' no Christian. An' he got more stucked up ways"; yet he calls a dead man back to life.[70] It is not surprising that "Bur Spider and Bur Rabbit use' to run together . . . both of 'em had low ways." Both live in the in-between world, the spider hanging from the ceiling, the rabbit crouching in his hole in the ground: in the interstices of the places they pester.

Adams's Rabbit is no drummer or player of the quills, like the Brer Rabbit recorded in the Remus tales. But like his ancestor he is a singer. And this Rabbit accompanies himself with his fiddle—a sort of magic wand with which he performs his tricks. Rabbit "ain' care nothin' 'bout nothin' cep playin' he fiddle an' frolicin' wid de gals. . . . Ef you was to take dat fiddle 'way from him, he would perish 'way an' die." Playing and singing along, Rabbit plays the part of the wish-fulfillment hero. With his music he calls the other animals to a graveyard party on Christmas night. When Fox approaches he gives a sign for the other animals to scatter and hide. Fox lights out after Rabbit, who takes him to where hound dogs are sleeping and touches his fiddle just enough to wake the hounds. Rabbit "got a heap er sense an' heaper scheme" and knows no hound would chase a rabbit when a fox is near. "De las' I hear on it," the taleteller says, "Bur Rabbit was settin' on a stump playin' he fiddle, an' dem hound had Bur Fox stretched like a string runnin' a race wid death." With his games and his mastery of art, Bur Rabbit turns the tables on the beast that threatens the whole animal neighborhood.

Adams's tale-tellers knew "Bur Rabbit" as a scoundrel, too, one who preyed upon his fellow animals. He "ain' got no conscience an' he mind jes fill up wid all kind er sport an' devilment." Like most trickster tales, "Bur Jonas' Goat" begins with a sense of harmony in the community. Bur Rabbit and Bur Jonas are friends. But then Rabbit steals Jonas's goat. "Bur Rabbit were such a scoundrel he ain' kin help stealin' an' he got sech low ways. He would steal from anybody, it ain' make no diff'ence if dey was he friend or no." Jonas's questions about his goat make Rabbit "oneasy" so he seeks someone else to take the blame. Rabbit and Wolf are "mighty close friends," too, "but dat ain' make no diff'ence, he been like lots er people we knows. Wuh he care ef he send Bur Wolf to de pen'tentiary? He would jes laugh an' make game at Bur Wolf for 'bein' sech a fool." He invites Jonas and Wolf to a dance. He then takes advantage of Wolf, who is "a shaggy ole fellow" trying to impress "de gals" by teaching him a song whose chorus is

> I stole Bur Jonas' goat
> I, by God, I stole Bur Jonas' goat.

Rabbit laughs at Jonas and Wolf while Wolf is put in jail.

"It is tempting to conclude," writes Robert Bone, that black lore's Fox and Wolf are "symbols of white power"; certainly they do serve as targets of the weaker ones' aggression and revenge. But it is also the case that as an institution slavery was set up to pit slave against slave ("wolf" against "wolf") in what all too often became "a fierce struggle to survive."[71] Nor is Rabbit simply a black wish-fulfillment hero, staking out secret advantages over and demolishing "white" dupes. It is true that in "Bur Jonas' Goat" Rabbit manipulates man and predatory animal alike. But in so doing he becomes not just the hero but the bearer of chaos, destroyer of community. His vanity, unscrupulousness, and greed for material and sexual prizes and sheer power make Rabbit seem closer to the powerful slave master than to the slave. Masters and overseers, as Frederick Douglass's Covey (the white "slave-breaker" whom the blacks call "The Snake")[72] makes clear, were often deceitful tricksters "with low ways," too. Douglass and Adams seem to agree that for the slave struggling for freedom or even mere survival, the fight involved trickster versus trickster, not just blacks against whites, but blacks against blacks, whites against blacks, blacks versus a hostile world.

We should recall here again that though Adams's animal tales cast reflections on the slave era, they were collected in the mid-1920s and tell us less about slavery than about Adams's view of life in black South Carolina more than a half-century after slavery ended. As in *Congaree Sketches*, the tales in *Nigger to Nigger* that are most forthright in their criticism of the political situation of Congaree blacks of this later era are those explicitly concerning the law. Here again these law sketches depict a cruelly unjust system in which whites, especially "crackers" but middle-class whites, too, scapegoat blacks accused of crime. They do so, it seems, with as much concern about what is right as Rabbit showed the wolf or the fox, "stretched like a string runnin' a race wid death."

So true to life were certain *Nigger to Nigger* pieces about blacks and the law that Adams feared legal action might be taken against him. The ballad "The Lynchers," mentioning the names of the killers in the much-publicized Lowman case, was one in which the facts were generally known. But "Just a Damn Nigger," which gave new information and judgments, prompted Adams to rush a letter to his editor at Scribner's:

> Before sending the sketch "Just a Damn Nigger" to Scribner's I showed it to a prominent lawyer here who advised me that there was nothing libelous in it. Last night another lawyer equally prominent read it over and advised me that it is actionable.
>
> The statement "A True Story" and the suggestion that "some of these mens have votes they control" seem to be the most undesirable parts. This murder was committed behind my lodge, and the facts of the case are well known.[73]

It turned out to be too late for *Scribner's Magazine* to change the story's text; the editors were reluctant to do so anyhow. But they did add the word "stories" in the table of contents listing several sketches. Sterling A. Brown for one praised "Just a Damn Nigger" as "one of the harshest stories to come out of the new realism."[74] The piece also had its expected detractors. After reading "Just a Damn Nigger" in *Scribner's Magazine*, a South Carolina judge made it known that he might get out an injunction against Adams if he had anything more to say about the courts.[75]

In the *Nigger to Nigger* sketches set in court we again meet Adams with his black mask on, speaking the facts of cases in black dialect and with so much force that it is no wonder he feared Judge Lynch might go gunning next for him. "Just a Damn Nigger" (renamed, in the book, "A Damn Nigger") is recited from a viewpoint that is decidedly black. It is a lynching tale that subverts the terms of the archetypal lynching "tale," Thomas Dixon's *The Clansman*.[76] Where Dixon saw a background of slavery that was sublimely ordered and serene in its peace and mutual good cheer, Adams saw slavery as a nighttown world of family disruption, secret plots, lies, violence, and counterviolence. Dixon viewed the multiplication of black rights during Reconstruction as the end of a golden era and the beginning of the good white people's captivity by "savage" blacks and their opportunistic northern white dupes and goads. In *The Clansman*, Dixon hailed the arrival of the Ku Klux Klan to rescue the white "prisoners" and to restore peace and order under white rule. In sequels to *The Clansman* the Klan would not be needed because white men were back in their rightful seats of power. As Adams underscores in both his books, but especially in *Nigger to Nigger*, it is the white lynch mob that brings disorder to the community. When the mob gets institutional power, chaos rules both with the gun and the gavel. With Judge Lynch (or "Foolbird") officiating in court, it is the blacks, not the whites, who, after Reconstruction, remain in the hell of latter-day slavery.

In "A Damn Nigger," Black Jake "been a great friend" to the white men who ultimately lynch him. He and the whites were "raise up together. Sleep in de same bed. . . . Jake wait on 'em an' follow 'em 'round like a dog." Here again liquor and lynching go together. The whites kill Jake when they are convinced he has stolen their bootleg liquor. Typical of the antilynching story, here the detailed, deliberate recitation of the process of Jake's mutilation and murder is incantatory, as if the language itself might exorcise the deed:[77]

> Dey say he stole dey liquor. An' dey find Jake an' put him in a automobile an' tooken him wey dey had de liquor, an' dey say 'fore dey kilt him dey fix him so he ain' neither man nor woman. Ef he'd er lived, he wouldn't been nothin'.
>
> Den dey took and lead him out in de woods an' beat he brain out, an' dey had hole in he head wey he brain was ooze out. Den, dey leff him, an' dey come back an' git him an' thowed him in a ditch.

Tad and Scip explain why the white lynchers escape severe punishment:

1. "In de first place, a nigger was kilt."
2. "An' de next place, dey say one of 'em had friend on de police force."
3. "Dem white mens . . . wored de uniform er dere country in war."
4. "Some of these mens have votes they control."

Hatchet speaks the sketch's bleak summary words:

> Dere ain' no nuse. De courts er dis land is not for niggers. Ain' nothin' for 'em but a gun an' a knife in a white man's hand, an den de grave, an' sorrow an' tear for he people. It seems to me when it come to trouble, de law an' a nigger is de white man's sport, an' justice is a stranger in them precincts, an' mercy is unknown. An' de Bible say we must pray for the enemy. Drap on you' knee, brothers, an' pray to God for all de crackers an' de judges an' de courts an' solicitors, sheriffs an' police in de land, for we must er been all er we livin' in sin. We stands in fear of de avengin' angel, for he's here an' we is surrounded.

In this chilling sketch the reversal of Dixon's mythic terms is complete: the southern white man, particularly of the middle and upper classes, having set himself up as "de avengin' angel" against crime and sin is himself the sinner surrounding and dismembering the innocent. "Mercy" on the part of the court hides complicity in lawlessness; "tender feeling" masks personal gain and white racial solidarity. In this instance, lynching becomes a powerful metaphor not just for unfairness toward black Americans but for national chaos.

Adams's tale "Thirteen Years" is what Sterling A. Brown terms a "brooding summary of the 'Ben Bess case' where a Negro, envied by white neighbors, was framed on a rape charge."[78] Here we get a slightly altered version of Adams's lynch tale in which not just the court's but the white criminal's motives and methods are explored fully. In this sketch, a companion piece to "Pick" in which a Negro guilty of owning too much money is shot dead, a black landowner who has rented land to whites decides "he want he land back for he ownt nuse." But the white tenants decide to stay put. So they arrange for a white woman to accuse the black man of raping her—the archetypal, deadly ruse. In deadpan language, Adams's narrator reports: they "have two trial 'for dey convict him, but dey was in doubt, so de judge guin him de benefit er de doubt an' guin him thirty years. Dey say dat kep' em from lynchin' him." He serves thirteen years before the white woman, who "were mighty sick" and fearful "she were guh bu's' hell wide open," decides to tell "de trute for one time in she life, an' she own up dat dis nigger ain' never done nothin' to her." In this tale the old bugaboo of "protecting white womanhood" is used to steal a Negro's land. (The situation recalls Walter White's statement that a southern white woman had about as much chance of being raped by a black man as she did of being struck dead by lightning. E. Franklin Frazer observed, too, that during this era to most southern whites the closer a Negro got to the ballot box the more he looked like a rapist.) In this case the white tenants need not gun down the black man in the way. In "protecting" the accused from the lynchers, the court plays into the lynchers' hands. Again, the "angel" white "protectors" are themselves the enslavers of the innocent and the deadeye authors of chaos.

Three years after the appearance of *Nigger to Nigger*, Adams published in *Scribner's Magazine* five sketches that brought home the message that white racism and violence against blacks were a threat to the South as a whole. Counterparts to the black Congaree tales, these later sketches, which Scribner's collectively titled "The Carolina Wilderness," record conversations held "cracker to cracker" among poor whites of the Sand Hills outside of Columbia, just northeast of the Congaree section proper. This Sand Hill area had been dirt poor at least since 1791, when George Washington labeled it "the most miserable pine barren" he had ever seen.[79] In the mid-1930s, Works Progress Administration writers described Sand Hill's "sandy troughs and crests, dunes of an ancient beach, overgrown with scrubby black jacks and pines, scattered with ponds fed by springs or wet weather streams. Unpainted shacks crouch in the hollows for protection against the winds that drive sand through every crevice. Here live the Sand Hillers, who lead a precarious existence and are often victims of pellagra. . . . To the Sand Hillers is attributed a song, each verse ending dolefully: 'I'm selling kindlin wood to get along.' "[80] Adams prefaces these *Scribner's* pieces with the following words about Sand Hill's "crackers":

> Settling in the Sand Hill belt with a soil unfertile, life for generations has been difficult. They are mostly poor, undernourished, and illiterate. Many undoubtedly have strains of Indian and Negro blood, and many are of as pure English blood as can be found in America. Mostly cruel, with a resentment toward society, they hate alike the successful white man and the more unfortunate Negro, whom they intend to keep in his place. However, there are exceptions, as there have come from these people some worth-while men who have made their way against all odds, and even among the untutored, one will find here and there a chieftain of strength and ability.

In these tales we get the poor white's view of blacks and the need to hold them down. According to Adams, these whites set up blacks as scapegoat murder victims and glory in attending chain gang parties at which blacks are "broke in" with whippings. They also sit on juries with set minds: "If they don't want 'em convicted they better not let me set on the jury," says Boze. "Cause I promised God that every chance I get I'll uphold the white race an' turn the juice on every damn nigger I ever gets a chance at." Pede's presence in these pieces modulates their tone by showing that every "cracker" is not a bigot and killer and also that prejudice is not an absolute blood inheritance: it is something men learn and thus can unlearn and reject in practice.

"The jury was meant to give justice," says Pede, the young "chieftain" held suspect by his friends for his funny ideas. Hate straightens him out: "Justice ain't got nothin' to do with it, not the way you means it. This country is over-run with niggers an' we got to pertect ourselves, our families, and our children." Elsewhere Boze informs Pede: "Jes bear in mind that we got to look out for ourselves; dat we got de nigger race against us, an' we 'gainst them." Then Pede and Boze reveal what for Adams and those of his class was a nightmare fear:

Pede: But you don't stop wid niggers. Dere is a lot er white men you' gainst, too.
Boze: Yes, I ain't got no use for dat class er white men dat's always tryin' to hold dey selves up better than anybody else. I'm jes as good as dey is, an' I wouldn't never miss a chance to harm one of 'em.
Pede: Some of 'em must have some good in 'em.
Hate: No matter what dey got, I hates 'em.
Pede: As bad as you hates 'em you don't slaughter 'em as bad as you do niggers.
Boze: We jes got to be a little more careful, but we sticks it to 'em when we gits a chance.

Thus depicted, the lynch mobsters were not only snipers in a race war but potential harbingers of class revolt.

Yet the general picture Adams paints is not one of revolution so much as it is of white solidarity across class lines and of white hatred of blacks. Still one principal point in these sketches is that even white men are not safe in this lawless realm of "rope and faggot." The final sketch in this sequence —and the last one Adams ever published—depicts a conversation about how easy it is to get away with murdering a white man. "If I has enough gainst a man," says a white Sand Hiller, "I'd set on de roadside at night an' pick him off jes like I would a bird." With ready cash and a vote for sale, a man accused of such a murder can buy lawyers who "stands in with the Governor and the judges"; he can fix the jury or get "the right kind of judge" to juggle things in his favor. "There ain't nothin' to the law, an' all this whoopin' an' hollerin' ain't nothin' but a lot of bluff." Here lynch law is no more than reversion to "wilderness law" in which raw force rules. These lawless "crackers," many of whom, Adams observes with wry irony, are "undoubtedly" part Negro and Indian themselves, will, to make a place for themselves in the American scene, undermine its institutions and crush all imagined enemies, of whatever color.

Clearly this was no simplistic class antagonism. Adams knew that if crackers were to blame for lynchings and for virtual lynchings in the courtroom, the blame stretched to the legislature and the governor's mansion. As in his earlier work,

Adams shows here that "things is gettin wusser" on a frighteningly broad scale. For problems of blacks and for whites, whatever their class, no simple answers were available.

Because of the presence of Pede, these Sand Hill sketches are not purely despairing. Nor, as we have seen, are the Scip and Tad sketches purely despairing. Like the heroes of blues songs—as defined by Albert Murray in *The Hero and the Blues*[81]—Adams's Tad and Scip face the troubles of the world squarely, head-on. They know that there is no hiding place down in the Congaree—not from the past, for its demons roam the swamp; certainly not from the present, for its flesh-and-bone demons roam the swamps—and they sit on juries and on judges' benches protecting one another. They know that no smart northerners can come down and save them. From beneath the bottom of the social hierarchy, from "wey down" in the Congaree, Tad and Scip have earned the tough "realistic" perspective on life from which they express themselves in these sketches. That perspective is close to the wryly comic and tragic perspective of the blues: these men hate that life is a lowdown shame, but they do see that it is, and they say so. Tad and Scip are resigned to a life of struggle, clear-visioned and poised for action when the time comes.

With his white mask in place to appease his white readers—and to avoid being sued—and with another mask behind that, the "black mask of humanity," Adams was able to do what American maskers before him have done: to stand before a predominantly white audience and, with a few concessions to those enamored of the truth according to Uncle Remus, with a few laughs and tears, to speak a much fuller, "blacker" truth than most of his white readers realized—to speak a truth close to the blues.

Like Jean Toomer, Langston Hughes, Sterling A. Brown, and Zora Neale Hurston, E. C. L. Adams recorded in art the Negro of the old country of the deep South who lived "wey down" "on the other side of the sun." Deep down in the Congaree, where the group's collective memory is stored, Adams made his notes among blacks who came to like and trust him. No Faulkner, Adams nonetheless found his best material in the community that he shared with blacks. Like Paul Green, Julia Peterkin, Eugene O'Neill, DuBose Heyward, T. S. Stribling,

Carl Van Vechten, and others—as different as these writers were from him—E. C. L. Adams was a white writer fascinated by his Negro neighbors. For him, as much as for the New Negro intellectuals and artists I have named, treating blacks as serious characters in serious literature—seeing the Negro, "old" and "new," with eyes unjaded by the conventions of minstrelsy and plantation fiction—was an exciting new literary calling. And no black or white writer publishing fiction in the 1920s comes as close to defining New Negroes like Tad and Scip: smart, tough, sometimes bitter, but nonetheless heroic analysts of the South they knew. Perhaps it is precisely because he wore "the black mask of humanity," and then, in deference to the Clarksons, Leveretts, Adamses, and other white readers, he wore a subtly wrought "white mask," Adams could bear to tell a great many unspeakable facts about a Carolina in shambles and to do more than that: to pierce the skin of fact and reach the "wey down" truth.

Notes

1. This formulation is Sterling A. Brown's.
2. Virginia F. Cullen, "Ned Adams of Columbia, Including a Few Sidelights on 'Tad' Goodson," *Sunday Record*, ca. 1931, reprinted from the *Savannah Morning News*; courtesy of Mrs. George C. S. Adams.
3. See Nathan Huggins, *Harlem Renaissance* (New York: Oxford University Press, 1971), pp. 129ff.; Sterling A. Brown, "Luck Is a Fortune," *Nation*, October 16, 1937, pp. 409–10; Ralph Ellison, "Recent Negro Fiction," *New Masses*, August 5, 1941, pp. 22–26.
4. A detailed study of white paternalism during slavery is Drew Gilpin Faust's *James Henry Hammond and the Old South: A Design for Mastery* (Baton Rouge: Louisiana State University Press, 1982).
5. Langston Hughes, *I Wonder as I Wander* (New York: Hill and Wang, 1956), pp. 49–50.
6. See Faust, *Hammond*, pp. 72, 103–4, 319–20.
7. See John Dollard, *Caste and Class in a Southern Town* (Garden City: Doubleday, 1937), pp. 8, 212; and Hortense Powdermaker, *After Freedom: A Cultural Study in the Deep South* (New York: Russell and Russell, 1939), p. xix.
8. This phrase comes from Zora Neale Hurston, *Their Eyes Were Watching God* (1937; rpt. Urbana: University of Illinois Press, 1978), p. 85.

9. Adams to Hughes, January 19, 1934, Hughes Correspondence, Beinecke Rare Book and Manuscript Library, Yale University. Adams replied that he would like to contribute but he had given so often in such cases that he would pass this time.

10. Ralph Ellison, *Shadow and Act* (New York: Random House, 1964), p. 55; and Ellison, "It Always Breaks Out," *Partisan Review* (Spring 1963), p. 128. Here I am indebted to Robert A. Bone's *Down Home* (New York: G. P. Putnam's Sons, 1975) for ideas about black Americans and the tradition of masking.

11. See Robert C. Toll, *Blacking Up* (New York: Oxford University Press, 1974).

12. See Laura Jervey Hopkins, *Lower Richland Planters: Hopkins, Adams, Weston and Related Families of South Carolina* (Columbia, S.C.: R. L. Bryon, 1976); David Duncan Wallace, *South Carolina: A Short History* (Chapel Hill: University of North Carolina Press, 1951); the Columbia *State*, March 18, 1934, p. A3, E. C. L. Adams Papers, South Caroliniana Library, University of South Carolina.

13. Nor was this inspiration a one-way affair. Padriac Colum credited Adams with the anecdote that inspired his play *Balloon* (1929). See G. C. S. Adams's "A Source for Padriac Colum's *Balloon*," *Eire-Ireland* 10 (Spring 1975): 95–98.

14. *Dublin Magazine*, January–March 1926, p. 1. Colum favorably reviewed *Congaree Sketches* in the *Dublin Magazine*, July–September 1928, pp. 82–84.

15. Conversation with Stephen Adams, June 1983.

16. Conversation with Stephen Adams, June 1983.

17. Conversations with Mrs. Mamie Blakeley, June 1983.

18. See, for example, Adams's letters to Teresa Helburn, November 17, 1929, Adams Papers, South Caroliniana Library.

19. Cullen, "Ned Adams of Columbia."

20. For example, see the *State*, July 29, 1922, p. 3.

21. See ibid., August 18, 1916, p. 6.

22. Ibid., March 18, 1934, p. A3.

23. *Reviewer*, April 1925, pp. 97–99; October 1925, pp. 64–67.

24. Paul Green, "Introduction," *Congaree Sketches* (Chapel Hill: University of North Carolina Press, 1927), pp. 10, 12, 15.

25. Interviews with William Terry Couch, October 22, 1970, November 11, 12, 21, 1970, Columbia Oral History Collection, p. 135, Columbia University Library.

26. William T. Couch to Nell Lewis Battle, June 8, 1927, University of North Carolina Press Archives, Chapel Hill.

27. Couch interview, p. 135.

28. Couch to Battle, June 8, 1927.

29. David Singal, *The War Within: From Victorian to Modernist Thought in the South, 1919–1945* (Chapel Hill: University of North Carolina Press, 1982), pp. 266–67.

30. Telegram from Adams to Couch, May 26, 1927, University of North Carolina Press Archives.

31. *State,* June 5, 1927, p. B5; Adams's lines come from a letter to George Coffin Taylor, May 30, 1927, Adams Papers, South Caroliniana Library.

32. Quoted by Singal, *War Within,* p. 217.

33. Mary White Ovington, NAACP Press Release, September 30, 1927, University of North Carolina Press Archives.

34. Adams to Taylor, May 30, 1927.

35. As a result, the holders of the copyright to *Congaree Sketches* have withheld permission to include Green's essay in this edition.

36. See, for example, the New York *Independent,* July 25, 1927.

37. *Saturday Review,* June 25, 1927, p. 929.

38. *Boston Evening Transcript,* November 10, 1928, p. 6.

39. *Columbia Record,* October 7, 1927, Adams Papers, South Caroliniana Library.

40. *State,* March 18, 1934, p. B4.

41. Zora Neale Hurston, "You Don't Know Us Negroes," unpublished manuscript, James Weldon Johnson Collection, Bienecke Library, Yale University; Sterling A. Brown, *Negro Poetry and Drama and the Negro in American Fiction* (1937–38; rpt. New York: Atheneum, 1969), pp. 122, 124.

42. Maxwell Perkins to Adams, February 1, 1928 and March 7, 1928, Adams Papers, South Caroliniana Library.

43. *Ibid.*

44. See the unpublished sketches, Adams Papers, South Caroliniana Library.

45. See Lilia MacKay-Cantell to Adams, July 19, 1929.

46. Ellison, *Shadow and Act,* pp. 24–44.

47. See Robert Hemenway's Introduction to Joel Chandler Harris, *Uncle Remus: His Songs and His Sayings* (1880; rpt. New York: Penguin, 1982), pp. 7–31.

48. Bone, *Down Home,* pp. 32–41.

49. See Sterling A. Brown, "Negro Characters as Seen by White Authors," *Journal of Negro Education* 2 (April 1933): 179–203.

50. Ibid., pp. 186, 192.

51. Ovington, NAACP Press Release, September 30, 1927, University of North Carolina Press Archives.

52. Harris, "As to Education," *Uncle Remus,* pp. 215–16.

53. Thadious M. Davis, *Faulkner's Negro* (Baton Rouge: Louisiana State University Press, 1983), p. 4.

54. Ibid., p. 26.

55. See Richard M. Dorson, *American Negro Folktales* (Greenwich: Fawcett, 1956), pp. 178–80; Ralph Ellison, "Flying Home," in Edwin Seaver, ed., *Cross Section* (New York: L. B. Fischer, 1944), pp. 469–85.

56. Bernard Wolfe, "Uncle Remus and the Malevolent Rabbit,"

Commentary 8 (July 1949): 31–41. For ideas about bracketing tales and the audience, I am indebted to Robert B. Stepto.

57. E. C. L. Adams, "Congaree Sketches," *Dublin Magazine*, January–March 1927, p. 26.

58. In *Nigger to Nigger* (and in the present volume's glossary) this same definition is given, with this sentence added: "There is also a community called Congaree."

59. John R. Swanton, *The Indian Tribes of North America* (Washington, D.C.: U.S. Government Printing Office, 1952), p. 93.

60. "Congaree," *Encyclopedia Britannica*, 15th ed., 1975.

61. This reference is to the early, *Dublin Magazine*, version of this sketch.

62. See Adams's gloss for "purtty" or "pritty."

63. William Faulkner, *Requiem for a Nun* (New York: Random House, 1951), p. 92.

64. See Powdermaker, *After Freedom*, pp. 20ff.; and Dollard, *Caste and Class in a Southern Town*, pp. 47–48, 75ff.

65. See Allen W. Trelease, *White Terror: The Ku Klux Klan Conspiracy and Southern Reconstruction* (Westport: Greenwood, 1971), pp. 189, 282, 305, 331.

66. W. J. Cash makes the point in *The Mind of the South* (New York: Vintage, 1941) that blacks were often employed by white bootleggers as deliverymen and salesmen. The liquor trafficking in hotels often meant that these blacks in bootlegging also pimped, using white prostitutes to ply their trade. Thus was illegal liquor part of a deadly combination involving white women and black men—who, Cash specifies, demanded the usual pimp's fare: most of the money and sexual intercourse with the prostitutes.

67. Sterling A. Brown, *Negro Poetry and Drama and the Negro in American Fiction*, pp. 122–23.

68. Note to the editor from Robert Farris Thompson, September 6, 1983.

69. Bone, *Down Home*, p. 35.

70. In "Song, Sermon and the Spoken Word" (*Sagala* 1 [1980]: 6–8), Sterling Stuckey says that the tale "Bur Rabbit in Red Hill Churchyard" shows "the prefiguring of jazz."

71. Bone, *Down Home*, p. 36. I have modified Bone's overstatement of the case. His claim is that "slavery creates a situation where every black man is a wolf to his neighbor. For slavery abrogates community, destroys solidarity, and pits each slave against his fellows in a fierce struggle to survive." Lawrence Levine and, especially, John Blassingame, have been among those historians whose work has stressed the slave's ability to resist slavery's pressures against his or her community, family, and sense of humanity: the determination to survive without becoming self-destructive.

72. Frederick Douglass, *Narrative of the Life of an American Slave* (1845; rpt. New York: Signet, 1968), p. 73.

73. Adams to Maxwell E. Perkins, May 9, 1928, Adams Papers, South Caroliniana Library.

74. Brown, *Negro Poetry and Drama and the Negro in American Fiction*, p. 123.

75. See Adams to Perkins, May 8, 1928 and July 3, 1928, Adams Papers, South Caroliniana Library.

76. I am indebted to Richard Slotkin for the idea of *The Clansman* as the archetypal work about lynching.

77. See Trudier Harris, *Exorcizing Blackness* (Bloomington: Indiana University Press, 1984).

78. Brown, *Negro Poetry and Drama and the Negro in American Fiction*, p. 123.

79. Quoted in *South Carolina: A Guide to the Palmetto State* (New York: Oxford University Press, 1941), p. 340.

80. Ibid., p. 341.

81. Albert Murray, *The Hero and the Blues* (Columbia: University of Missouri Press, 1973).

CONGAREE SKETCHES

Scenes from Negro Life in the Swamps of the Congaree and Tales by Tad and Scip of Heaven and Hell with Other Miscellany

Contents

The Big Swamps of the Congaree

Tad: Gentlemens, how is you-all?

Voice: Howdy! how you been?

Second Voice: Tolerable.

Tad: I been down in de big swamps on de Congaree.

Voice: Tell us, brother?

Tad: I been down to de Congaree in de big swamps, where de trees is tall an' de moss long an' gray, where de Bullace grow, an' where I hear de tune of de bird in de mornin'; down wey de wild turkey gobbles, way down on de Congaree; wey God's mornin' leads to de devil's night; down on de river, where night make her sign, where owls on a dead limb talks of de dead, talks wid de dead and laughs like de dead, way down in de big swamps of de Congaree; down where de blunt-tailed moccasin crawls in de grass, where de air is stink wid he smell; where de water is green, where de worms is spewed out of de groun', where de groun' is mud, where de trees sweat like a man; down in de home of de varmint an' bugs, down in de slick yallow mud, de black mud an' de brown, way down in de big swamps of de Congaree; down in de land of pizen, where de yallow-fly sting, in de home of de fever an' wey death is de king. Dat wey I been, down in de big swamps. Down in de land of mosquito, way down in de big swamps, down on de Congaree.

The Hopkins Nigger

"Is any of you niggers ever heared the tale 'bout the Hopkins nigger? One time a Hopkins nigger died and atter he dead he clumb up that long hill what lead to heben. When he got to de top he knock on de door wid he hat in he han', jest like a nigger, persisely like a nigger. En ole Peter cracked de door an' peep out an' say, 'who dar?' and de nigger say he er Hopkins nigger, like dat been sumpen great, an' ole Peter say he 'ain't like no Hopkins nigger nohow. Wait here, an' I'll fine out can you come in,' en he closed de door an' he left de nigger standin' dere an' atter while he come back and he open de door and tell de nigger he can come in. Time dat nigger hit heben he hit it a throwin' them foots an' shouting. Peter walk up to him and say, 'Hole on, nigger, the Lord want to see you.' An atter he git the nigger quiet de Lord come up to de nigger an he fasten pair of pearley whings on him and guin him silver feathers and gold claws and a gold bill and he said, 'nigger, you is an angel, fly!' An' when de Lord say dat de nigger stretch hisself and flop he whing three or four times an' create a dust, den he riz up an' he fly an' he flewed and there never been seen such flyin' since heben been heben an' de Lord look on an' was 'stonished at de way dat nigger flew and he call Gabel and Michael to him and he say, 'go git dat nigger' and dem white angels lit out atter dat nigger and dey flyed and dey flewed and dey ain't done nuttin. Dat nigger circled around heben like a buzzard. Atter while he got tired playing wid dem white angels and he lit on a dead snag and set dere pluckin' he feathers and running he bill down he long feathers in he whings. Atter while dem white angels come up dere an' suade him to go back wey de Lord and his Son was an' 'fore dey git dere dem buckra angel done plan a tonement. Ain't you see dat nigger done done. He got hot for de tonement. You know he been hot for it when he fuse a tater annudder nigger han' him, but he done done. De course of de tonement lay 'cross de west end of heben where two ole gate posts been stan' right in de course eber since heben been first build. Ain't you see dat nigger done

done? An' when de tonement start a whole lot of buckra angels been put in an' dey put Gabel to one end of de line and dey put Michael to de udder end and dey put de tall angel in de middle by de nigger, and de Lord and his Son stood on a high hill and de Lord's Son guin de sign for de tonement to start. When dey start dat nigger flop along kind o' careless like, tryin' to suade dem buckra angels to light out. Atter while he fine out dey ain't doin' nuttin and he lit out hisself and Gabel and Michael and de tall angel helt dem young buckra angels down, so dey ain't none of dem gur git hurt, but dat nigger lit out and he flyed and he flewed to such a rate he couldn't stop hisself and he flewed into dem gateposts. Atter while de Lord and he Son and de white angels come up and dere lay de nigger, he pearley whings broke, he silver feathers scattered on de groun', he head twist one side and he gold claw curl up and de Lord look at him an' say, 'jest like a nigger, persisely like a nigger,' an' de las' time dat nigger been seen ole Peter have him in a wheel-barrow rollin' him down a hill on de back side of heben to de grand trash pile, and he was murmurin' and a mutterin'. This comes from bein' like a nigger.

"Jest like a nigger! Persisely like a nigger!"

Jonas

Voice: Way you been Scip?

Scip: I been to de trial.

Voice: Who trial?

Scip: Un' Fed boy, Jonas.

Voice: When dey guh finish?

Scip: Dey done finish.

Voice: Wha' dey do wid him?

Scip: You talk like a fool. Axe me what dey guh do wid him. Ain't I tell you dey try him? Ain't I tell you dey done finish try him? You axe me wha' dey do wid him. Ain't you know who set on de jury?

Voice: White folks.

Scip: Yes, white folks, and dat ain't all,—poor white folks, poor buckra, cracker,—ain't dat 'nuf? Dat what set on de jury.

Voice: But Jonas ain't do nuttin'.

Scip: Dat ain't make no difference. I done tell you who set on de jury.

Voice: Is he pa fret much?

Scip: No he ain't fret. He know dey ain't no nuse to fret. He raise he chillun right and he ain't fret. He got sense. He know wha' guh be, guh be, en he ain't fret.

A Freshet on the Congaree

Leck: Gentlemens!

Voice: Sorter slow. Wuh's de time, Ber Leck?

Leck: Time ain't so much.

Voice: Wey you come from?

Leck: Jes come out of de Congaree swamp.

Voice: How come time ain't so much, Ber Leck?

Leck: Jes come out de Congaree swamp and de ole river sho' is ragin'. I never is seen a wusser freshet. De logs spin 'round a hundred feet long and roarin' 'gainst de big trees like dey guh tear de heart out de earth wey de go,—varmints a settin' on limbs and ridin' on logs, and I seen er drove er cow swimmin'. Each one had a head a restin' on de tail of de other cow. Den de call come and de first cow sink and all de other cows sink. After while I see 'em whirlin' over and over. Sometime day feets in de air, sometime dey horns, and de river been mess up de cows' horns and foots and it th'owed 'em every which er way, and I see hog cut dey own throats tryin' to swim out of dis torment and de river, and it look like God Almighty must a wrop he arm 'round de flood and whirl it back in He anger. Every which er way I look I see 'struction. I see sturgeon tangle up in a wire fence and de birds quit singin' and went to hollerin', and I look down on de yaller water and I see wey buzzard cast his shadow. Everywhere I look I see buzzard. I been prayin' to God to help me and I been fightin' de angry waters and 'struction been rollin' at me and I been lookin' death in de face. And God save me dis time, and I reckon I'll stay 'way from de big swamp and try and don't do nothin' to defy Him.

Brother, when de Congaree gits riled, it mighty nigh look like Jesus hisself forgits de poor critters, it look like he stan' back and give de devil a chance to do he do. And if your heart ain't right, my brother, de big swamps will 'stroy it. Dey 'stroy your body and if dey ain't 'stroy it, look like dey' 'stroy your soul.

Voice: Did you hear Ber Leck? He ain't tell no lie. I see a heap of mens come out de big swamps. If dey stay dere long enough, when dey come out, dey look more like beasts or varmints dan dey does like mens. Brother, God ain't make dem swamps for mens. Dey de home of de devil, de home of 'struction; dey de home of serpents, de home of buzzards, and if you put mens in dem swamps, de only way dey can live is to be like de critters dat live dere, and take on dere ways. Yes, my brother, stay 'way from de big swamps.

Hell Fire

Scip: Is you hear 'bout dat Congaree nigger wuh act so miserable in this worl', and have so much weeked ways an' how he dead, and slip down dat long hill into hell, an' how he act when de devil start puttin' de fire to 'im?

Voice: Tell we, Bur Scip.

Scip: Well, one time dey been a Congaree nigger an' he went on terrible in this worl'. He cuss, an' steal, an' make game at God's work, an' do everything de Bible say he ain't mus' do. He act like he been one of de devil's own chillun. When he dead he hit dat broad steep road dat leads to hell, an' it been slick as axle grease, it been used so much. Time dat nigger hit it, he hit it slippin' an' scramblin' an' tryin' to git back, so he ain' doin' nothin'. He was slidin' at such a rate till he was smokin' 'fore he git half way down, but dat little heat ain' nothin' to wuh he goin' git. The gates of hell been wide open, look like de openin' to a railroad tunnel, an' smoke an' fire was jumpin' out of it every minute. 'Twus a terrible lookin' place, an' when dat nigger hit hell he hit it so hard he parted de flames. He cut a road through dat fire for about two mile, an' everywhere he looked he see folks from Congaree. White folks an' niggers, all both of them, an' all lined up 'side of de road, an' all un'um war smokin'. Dey was jumpin' 'round' ever minute, look like every time dey get settled a new fire would bus' out. Dere was mens, a plenty of them, an' Jesus! De wimmens! Hell was jam full of them. Dat nigger when he did git on he foots clam up on a rock an' started lookin' aroun' when de old devil come up to him an' axed him wey he come f'um. An' he say, he a Congaree nigger. Time he say it de devil git so close to him he can smell de burnin' hair on 'im. He git close to de nigger, an' look in he face wid he red eye, an' he nose look like a big red hot fish hook. He had horns on 'im wuss dan a cow, an' he tail look like it war some kind of a red hot snake, an' he switchin' it ever which a way, an' everything he tech with it he raised a blister. He had foots like a goat but dey was diff'unt, an' was scortched from jumpin' 'roun' on red hot rock. When de devil come up to dat nigger an' look down in he face dat nigger act just like a 'ceitful Congaree nigger. He say, 'Boss, you sure God is a good-lookin' man.' Time he say it de devil start grinnin' an' laughin' an' winkin' he eye at he chillun', makin' sign to 'um, an' he says to de nigger 'You think hell a hot place, but I guh show you wuh a hot fire is, 'cause I got back logs in here an' brush-heaps I just been savin' for you. I always has trouble wid dem low down Congaree nigger, an' I is had a heap of experience wid 'em, 'cause hell is full of 'um.' Well suh, he had dat nigger in a sweat. Ever time dat nigger clam up on a safe lookin' place fire an' smoke would start creepin' out f'um somewhere, an' de nigger git kiner onrestless, at first, but atter while he started to takin' long steps, skippin' 'roun', an' jumpin'. Look like he was cuttin' the buck. You know hell ain' no lonesome place. But dat nigger been so busy he ain' had time to make compersation wid nobody. De big Devil sho' is a busy man, but he got plenty of help, an' 'em chillun of his'n he sho' is raisin' 'um in he own way. He called some un 'um, an' he tell 'um to pay particular attention to de Congaree nigger, like he think so much on 'im he ain't want to neglect 'im. Great God, dat nigger was havin' a hot time. De first part of de time he spend hoppin' 'roun'. Den he step on he toe, an' he jump up an' down, but dem chillun ain't luh 'im res' while dey Daddy set up dere on a high red hot rock an' laugh like he guh kill he' self, an' egg 'um on. He say he always have a Circus every time anybody come f'um Congaree. He say it one time he ain' grudge nusin' a little extra fire kaze Congaree furnish hell wid all de clowns an' animals too an' only pleasure he 'low 'um in hell is to 'low he subjects to see how de sinners f'um Congaree, white folks an' niggers, act when dey is gittin' broke in, an' he say dey sho' ain't fit fer nothen' but hell. He say he sho' is wase' up a lot of hell fire on all both un 'em, an' been doin' it ever since dey been a Hell. Dat is one of he main business. Well, suh, dem chillun had dat nigger stretched. He was jumpin' ditches an' canals an' tearin' theu red hot briar patches like he ain't never done nothen else an' dem chillun was stretched out behind him like a pack of houn' dogs atter a rabbit. Dey was runnin' at such a rate till Hell ain' been nothen but one big dus' cloud of sparks. He passed de place where Dives were an' he seen Annias, an' de high Priest, but he ain't stop to axe 'um no questions. He look like he ain' goin' have nothen to do wid compersation. He ain't run 'roun' nothen. He jumpin' 'cross everything. He cleared ever obstacle in he path an' de last time he been seen he been makin' for de big Gulf an' he look like he guh tackle dat.

The Rattlesnake

Tad: Spencer, is you hear 'bout dat big rattlesnake back in slavery-time?

Spencer: I ain't know what you talk 'bout, Tad?

Tad: You know de white folks had a chile, a little chile, 'bout four or five years old, an' ever day at dinner time, 'fore dinner was over, dat chile take he dinner an' go out de house an' set down on a pile of rock out in de yard. He do it ever day, an' one day dere was a ole Uncle July say he curious, an' he watch dat chile, an' he say he see de chile go out in de yard an' climb up on pile of rock, an' he see de chile take a piece of bread in he han' an' put in he mout' an' bite it, den put it down side him an' rub an' pat, jist like he rubbin' an' pattin' somethin'. Ole man July he say he get a little closer an' he seen a rattle-snake come out of a hole in de rock an' he put he head up dat high,—stick he head out 'bout a foot, just sway back an' forth, an' he head been wide as a man han', an' rusty, an' he little eye been shinin' an' he poke he tongue out, jist lick it out, and the chile put another piece of bread in he mout', an' bite it, den he put he han' back down 'side of him, an' dat snake done take it and eat it out of he han'. An Ole July said he so scared he mighty nigh faint, lookin' at dat chile an' at dat snake. An' he went in de house an' tell de people in de house 'bout it an' fore dey got out dere dat snake done gone an' de chile settin' dere on the rocks by hisself.

Sunning on the Golden Stairs

Sam: Is you hear wuh sa preacher say how de nigger is guh prosper? He say dey is guh be great rulers an' big bosses, dat heben is full on 'em an' God got 'em crowded 'roun' de throne an' nigger angels is flyin' ever which a way an' dey got great 'thority. Dey settin' 'roun' de foot-stool an' roostin' all 'round on de bannisters an' sunnen dey self on de golden stairs.

Scip: Yes, Brother, I hear him. I ain't pay too much 'tension to da preacher. Dat ain't nuthen but nigger talk. If niggers in heben act like dey act in dis worl' dey sure got heben ruint up.

Jube: They must be ain't no white folks dere.

Sam: Wuh make?

Jube: You know white folks ain't go hab niggers sunnen dey self on de stairs an' roostin' on de bannisters.

Scip: Brother, you spoke. God ain guh have a passel of niggers messen up in he business. Niggers got dey place an' dat ain't on top. Has you ever see a tumble bug roll he load? He ain't never satisfy wid it any way he got it. He always try to roll up a hill. He gits up a piece and then he roll down again, 'en that's a nigger.

Judge Foolbird

Perk: I been over to see de Jedge pass on Noah.

Voice: Wha' Noah do?

Perk: He been in ole man Hall Store, an' he say 'God-dam' to a nigger standin' dere, an' ole man Hall say he a Christian gentleman an' don' 'low no perfanity in he place of business—'git out!' An' Noah say, he ain't mean no harm, an' he walk out an' cross de big road. Atter while ole man Hall walk out an' follow him up an' he walk up to Noah an' bus' him over de head wid er axe halve an' beat him up an' de Police 'rest both 'un 'em, an' Jedge Foolbird axe ole man Hall what de nigger do when he follow him up and ole man Hall say 'He ain't do nuthin', but he look like he goin' say sumpen,' and Jedge Foolbird fined Noah one hunnerd dollahs.

Voice: What did he do wid ole man Hall?

Perk: He fine him fi' dollahs.

Voice: 'Fore God! What make he fine ole man Hall fi' dollahs? Ain't he white folks?

Perk: Jedge Foolbird is de law, an' he goin' do what he goin' do. He de law, and de law is de law.

Old Sister

Bruser: Dey show is been a turn-over down to de old street; every kind er mix-up, niggers fighten every which a way.

Tad: Wuh de matter ail em?

Bruser: Ole Sister start sompen.

Scip: Dat's what Ole Sister good for. Carrying news and putten pizen out.

Bruser: She done put de pizen out up de street, den she pass on she look dat satisfy.

Scip: Pass on to put pizen out some wey else.

Tad: You ain't think all dat 'bout Ole Sister, is you? She look so Christian. Ain't I see her in church and meeten look like she always prayen and beggen God to forgive poor sinners.

Scip: She tongue forked just like a snake, one half on it drips prayers and tother half turns loose ruination, and den she talk so sweet 'bout God and how she give agvice and do everything she kin do to save her friend.

Voice: She wouldn't live long if she ain't been able to ring de heart strings loose from some er dem people she say she friend to, I done watch Ole Sister.

Scip: Ole Sister's business is other folks' business; she are a upright 'oman; she ain't never do no wrong; she know how to pray in de public place.

Voice: Dey tells me it was folks like Ole Sister 'casion Christ to be crucify.

Scip: Well, Christ pick out two thieves to go wid him, you ain't see no Ole Sisters hanging on de cross wid Him.

Voice: Wuh you reckon he do dat for? You think he ain't been able to die right if he had anything wusser than them thieves?

Scip: I ain't say nothin' 'bout that.

Tad: I reckon she so satisfy, she rub she self 'bout de way she and God live.

Tad: Ole Man Daniel tell we dat way back in slavery time dere been a nigger dey call him Gabel. He say Gabel been a kind man, double jinted and soft talking; everybody come to

Gabel when 'struction start. He ain't luh no man beat he wife, ef de 'oman come to him for pertection. He pertect everything in trouble, mens and womens, but other times he ain't take nothing to do wid nobody. He were always a peace-maker, less some-body push him too far, and he ain't have to larn many un em. Ole man Daniel say Gabel been courtin' a pritty gal, and one day one ur dem ole sister spile her name, and run to her wid all kind er tales 'bout herself, and run to she friends and tells tales to everybody, she just strew dat little innocent gal's name, and claim she only talkin' in friendship, but she kept on talkin' and Gabel mighty nigh loss he mind, he fret so. Atter while dey torment de little gal so till one day she swallow a handful of bottle glass, and Ole Sister had her time moanin' at de settin' up and de funeral, she walk 'round lookin' as pious as a buzzard hoppin' 'round a carcass.

Voice: Hell must be full of Ole Sisters.

Scip: Dey got a particular pen in hell for em, and when a sinner is too weeked, dey throws him in de pen wid dem ole sisters, and dey picks de smoke off he bones and chats 'round him like a bunch of blackbirds.

Voice: Hell must be a bad place.

Scip: Brother, you know hell is a bad place when dey got generations of ole sisters pen up together, for de punishment of poor sinners.

Voice: It must be worse than bad, de fire is wusser nuff.

Another Voice: Dat must be de bottomless pit I hear so much talk 'bout wey all dem ole sister.

Tad: I reckon we better pray.

Bruser: Who dat comin' yonder?

Voice: Dat's Ole Sister now.

Several Voices: We best be leffen.

Tad: Less we pray.

Scip: Set still, brothers, prayin' and leffen neither one guine to stop Ole Sister's tongue. Set still, brothers, and take your honey and pizen now. Dey is only one way out and dat's ter cut your thoat from year to year, and ef you do dat, it will be Ole Sister's pleasure, all you do is to fill Ole Sister's pizen sack again and start her fresh on her road of 'struction. Set still, she only talks to her friends 'bout her friends, she is a good ooman, she prays and shouts, she got two worlds, dis world and hell and she mighty nigh done turn dis world into hell, it's wusser dan hell sometimes.

Tad: Less we pray.

Scip: I done tell you prayin' ain't guh help you wid Ole Sister, wey dey is most prayin' dere is most Ole Sister. Set still and let de ole moccasin whisper in your year.

Ole Sister: Brothers, how is you?

Several Voices: How is you Sister?

Tad: I just been sayin' ef everybody was like you, Sister, dis would be a good world to live in, but people is so weeked, ain't nobody can control em.

Voice: Ain't dat de truth Tad spoke?

Another Voice: Jesus knows.

Tad: Sister, what's de news?

Scip: Sister's heart is heavy, Tad, she try so hard to bring peace and good behavior. Sister too busy tryin' to save sinners to have news.

Ole Sister: Brother Scip, you knows my heart, it is weary wid tryin' to save people. I mighty nigh done talk my heart out geeing agvice to dat gal of Riah's. I talk to her and ain't never say a word 'bout her to nobody. She my friend and I wants to save her. I stand by my friends, and I sets example for dem.

Tad: Do Jesus, less we pray.

Voice: Amen.

Several Voices: Amen.

Tad: God loves Ole Sister.

Scip: Ole Sister are a blessed ooman.

Old Sister's Friends

Old Sister: Well, my brothers, I tries to live right, but my trials is heavy. Ain't nobody can tell who dey friend. Now, dere's dis here gal Ellen. I seen her walkin' wid Mensa two time an' havin' compersation. Her an' me is good friends. We go every wey wid one another, an' I axe her wuh she see in Mensa, an' wuh de whole compersation 'bout, an' she say, "Is I broke any law? If I wants to talk wid Mensa, wuh make I ain't can talk to him?" Ain't you see how her mind run? An' I ain't never say a word 'bout her, cepen I went to Pooch an' Big Daughter an' Sister Janie an' Rachael an' I tell dem 'bout it an' axe dem to intercede an' I tell dem not to breath it to nobody. Wha' more kin I do? I is Ellen's friend, but I got to stan' by my Jesus too. Ain't none of we can serve two masters.

Scip: Sister, I ain't see where you can do no more dan you has done. Ellen oughts to love you.

Tad: Here comes Mensa. Sister, is you talk to Mensa?

Old Sister: No, I ain't said nothin' to Mensa, an' I ain't say nothin' 'bout Mensa. He so curious an' he so vigus he ain't never had no reason, an' he ain't got no conscious. He ain't got no right to run wid Ellen. He run after too much women. Well, I must tell you all good day. Mensa so 'spicious, if I stays here he mought think I been talkin' 'bout him an' Jesus know I ain't never called he name to nobody. Good day, my brothers.

(Mensa comes up)

Mensa: Gentlemens!

(Several voices acknowledging salutation)

Howdy! wha's de time? Ber Mensa.

Scip: Brother, you is a little 'lated. Dat ole gal of yourownt is jes lef' we.

Mensa: I seen Ole Sister lef' here. You ain't mean her, is you? er ole two face-ed wench.

Tad: Brother, you ain't ought to nuse them hard words 'bout er Christian ooman that gits down on her knees and prays to God to save your soul.

Mensa: I ain't axed de ole she-rat to pray for me.

Scip: Calm ye-self, my brother. Ole Sister ain't say nothin' 'bout you. She jes tell we she ain't never call your name, neither this here gal Ellen. You know she Ellen's friend, an' Ole Sister take so much interest in she friends.

Mensa: It looks like dat's de kind er people God got all 'round here prayin' for Him. Jesus! If I could fasten my hand on her th'oat one time, I'd make her eye-balls jump out. But dere ain't no nuse, dere is so much hypocrite in dis world, dey all got low-down minds. You can do anything ef you doos it in de name of God, ef you don't do it to a Christian hypocrite. Some time it seems to me I could naturally set in de chair to git my satisfaction.

Voice: Be patient, brother.

Tad: My agvice is to go on your way rejoicing, 'tend to your own business an' don't pay no 'tention to Ole Sister. Time she find out you guh hab your own way, she luh you 'lone. Ole Sister got a kind er mind dat don't dwell long on sompen she can't hurt. She got a selfish mind, she so stucked on she self, she ain't nobody's friend; she think she are a friend, but she ain't no friend. Her hide is thick as a ox hide, an' she don't belongs to 'sociate wid no other kind er mind.

Mensa: Tad, you is right.

(Ellen comes up. Greetings exchanged)

Ellen: Is you all see Ole Sister?

Scip: Yes, she ain't so long lef'.

Ellen: Wey she gone?

Mensa: De ole devil is gone on de devil's business. She been servin' de devil 'tendin' to he business an' other people's business.

Tad: Don't say dat, Mensa, think wha' you has a mind to think, but don't let no evil thoughts run out on your tongue.

Ellen: Shut your mouth, Mensa, Ole Sister my friend; she say she my friend.

Scip: She you friend, she say she you friend. I heared her say it.

Mensa: Come on, Ellen I'll walk a piece er de way home wid you.

Ellen: You can walk a piece er de way.

(They leave)

Ellen: Mensa, I thinks a heap er you, but I can't stan' for Ole

Sister an' all un 'em talk. She my friend an' I loves you more'n all un 'em, but I can't gee up my friends for you, an' Ole Sister tell me she an' she friends ain't guh have nothin' to do wid me ef I don't drap you, an' I ain't able to fight all un 'em. She say you is a bad man, an' course dey will stan' by me but dey ain't like it.

Mensa: Dey will stan' by you long enough to cut your th'oat.

Ellen: Dey has already done cut my th'oat. Long as dey kin keep me whipped, dey ain't guh lef' me.

Mensa: I'll try an' be friend wid 'em.

Ellen: Dat ain't no good, ef one un 'em were drownin' an' you save 'em, dey would say you done it jes so you could see me.

Mensa: Ellen, I is all broked up. I guh lef' you now. Honey, don't forgit me. I ain't no worse dan you friends.

Ellen: God be wid you, Mensa. Ef it do you any good, jes 'member I belongs to you. I love you an' I got friends an' I ain't never guh forgit how dey sting me. Good bye.

Mensa: Honey, good bye.

Old Sister in Heaven

Tad: Scip, is you all ever hear 'bout de big sturbance dey have in heaven?

Scip: Wuh kind er 'sturbance? Look like dey have nuff 'sturbance here. Dey ain't gone to havin' 'sturbance in heaven, is dey?

Bruser: Tell we, Tad.

Tad: I ain't know for certain it de trute, but I heared an' it soun' kind er pamelia to me.

Voice: Less we hear it, Ber Tad.

Tad: Well, one time one er dem ole sister dead an' slipped into heaven duenst a big storm. She ain't hit de bottom er de stairs 'fore she start sompen.

Voice: How you reckon she slip in, Tad?

Tad: Everything git so rough ole man Peter lef' de gate wid one er he chillun an' went to help Gabel close de windows. De wind was blowin' at such a rate it look like it were guh blow all de shutters off, an' rain was comin' so fast it was spilin' de carpet. It blowed some of de angels out er de trees. Angels was mess up all over heaven. Dere been so much feather scatter 'round it look like all de angels in heaven was moultin! It 'stroy some er dey nes', an' little angels was layin' all 'round on de ground cryin' an' hollerin'. A turn er dem been out in de garden playin', some un 'em was jes larnin' to fly. Some of dey wing feathers ain't start to sprout yet. Most of de chillun out in de garden ain't been ole enough to fly, dey was layin' all round under rose bush an' tangled up in vine. Gabel been so busy he ain't know he head from he foots. Part er de time he was workin' at de windows wid Peter, and den he would quit an' run all 'round an' blow he horn for help. It look like dey never was guh git dem chillun back in de mansion. Some er de chillun flewed up on de window sill. Dey'd hang dere a little while wid dey claws an' flop dey wings an' drap back on de groun'.

Voice: Tad, wey de Lord been? Ain't He kin stop all dat?

Tad: He been worryin' so 'bout He carpet, he forgit He got other things to 'tend to.

Voice: Wey Ole Sister all dis time, Tad?

Tad: You axe so much question, you turn my min' from Ole Sister. Dat storm blowed de gates open an' scared dat chile of Peter's so bad he run off an' Peter ain't find him for a week. An' when he is find him he been in a ole shed settin' down 'twixt two ole angels eatin' spiled manna. He mighty nigh loss all he feather.

Voice: Dat sho' must er been a storm.

Tad: It like to ruint heaven, an' it mighty nigh ruint de carpet, an' it spiled so much manna till de Lord had to put de angels on short rations.

Bruser: Wey Ole Sister been all dis time?

Tad: Well, she slipped into heaven when dat no 'count chile of Peter's lef' de gate. She creep 'round a while watchin' everything an' everybody. She kept quiet for one or two days, but she ain't shet she eye an' she mind been workin'. She'd sneak around an' watch de angels an' it ain't been long 'fore a man an' ooman angel dassent to set on de stairs, or walk in de garden together. She gee agvice to Peter, she worry Mikel an' she had de tall angel worried up so till he spend most er he time settin' on de top of a barn by he self, an' Gabel say he mind tangled up so he mighty nigh forgit how to blow he horn. He say he don't reckon he never will git a chune out'n it again, an' Peter say de Lord guin him de devil 'bout lefen dat gate open. He say a storm kin blow heaven in half, but he'll never lef' de gate no more.

Voice: Ole Sister!

Tad: Dat ain't all. Ole Sister had de angels, mens an' womens, so 'sturbed up dey was feared to go to roost at night. Things got so bad an' ole Sister got such a start on 'em,—you know dey ain't nuse to seein' nothin like her in heaven,—she had Delilah so excited she cut off Aaron's beard, and she got so worse she started to carryin' tales to de Lord on He son. She mighty nigh create a fuss 'twix 'em.

Bruser: Dat sounds jest like our Ole Sister. I always is say you can't dodge 'em. I wonder wha' kind er lookin' whings she got.

Scip: I ain't know. I reckon dey is lousy jes like her mind wid ambier drippin' off her bill jes like it drip off her tongue in dis world.

Voice: Tad, did dey ever git rid on her in heaven?

Tad: Yes, dey git rid on her. One day de Lord an' He son went off on a piece of private business, an' took Gabel and Mickel wid Him, an' he lef' de mansion in charge of de tall angel. Dey ain't lef' good 'fore Ole Sister flewed up on de throne an' set herself dere to watch. While she was settin' dere three or four of dem rough angels what Ole Sister been pickin' at sneaked up behind her an' jerked her off de throne. She tried to holler an' flutter, but it ain't no nuse, dey put her in a crocus sack an' dragged her to de back door of heaven an' th'owed her out de door an' down de hill an' de last of dat ole sister seen from heaven she was rollin' an' bouncin' down de hill to hell where she b'long. She been so hard she been knockin' sparks out de rocks.

Voice: You reckon de Lord an' He son schemed dat er way to git rid on her?

Tad: I ain't know.

Scip: It ain't look like it safe to die an' it look like it dang'-ous to live.

Old Sister in Hell

It were a wicked day in hell when Ole Sister come slidin' and bouncin' through the gates. Hell was full of moaners and prayer leaders and deacons from all the churches and there been a drove of preachers there and you could hear ever kind of sound comin' from the ole sister pen. The devil had generations of ole sister pen up in their own perticular pen and he dassen' turn 'um out dey act so wuss. He say if he ain't keep them ole sister pen up they will torment him more'n he can stan'. He say he punishment is great but ef he ain't careful wid dem ole sister hell won't be a fitten place even for him and dey will always be tryin' to spile he reputation and undermine he authority. When our Ole Sister hit hell the first thing she do been to try and make sheself satisfied. She start messin' in everybody business, carryin' news on dis un and dat. Shadrach, Messach, and Abed-ne-go tooken to de fiery furnace, thought dey would escape there, but dat old gal went right on in and run 'em out. She put de serpent to makin' de crookedest track he ever make tryin' to escape. Everywhere she pass all dem old hell buzzards would scratch de feet and rise up. Dey had hot cinders and ashes sprinklin' everything in hell. De angels in hell would rise up in droves. Dey get so excited dat dey mighty nigh bust deyselves open flyin' into one another, an' all 'un 'um was cacklin' and screechin' and flyin' all through de flames from de mountains of hell right on down into de deep valley. De devil say she had 'im so nervous he can't sleep. He say he think he nerves is 'stroy. Dat old ooman done every kind of devilment, sneakin' 'roun' wid her eye skinned and her tongue hangin' out. She act just like she act 'roun' de churches and people in dis worl'. She alarm everything. She run into a drove of Philistines and like to run dem out of hell, and she worried Judas Ascariot till he went to de devil and tell him he know he done a heap of wrong but he know he don't deserve no such punishment as this. He say he betray Christ kase he thought Christ was so powerful he could pertect hisself, and he done it for thirty pieces of silver, but he say Old Sister do she devilment for nothin'. He say she betray Christ and everybody else in de worl'. Dats her nature, and he tell de devil if he lef' her alone she'll betray him and everything else in hell, and de devil own up how worry he been. He say one of the main troubles 'bout all dem ole sisters is dey is so tough he never is had a fire in hell hot enough to burn one of 'em and he said dis particular ole sister were extra bad. He say dey could not stan' her in heaven and dey threw her in hell. He say dey ain't as fair in heaven as dey makes out dey is and dey ain't treat him right. He say he don't mess up wid heaven and it look like all de angels in heaven will have a sin for throwin' dat old huzzy into hell unbeknownst to him. He say he will have to study up some scheme and trap her and get her in de pen. Dat Ole Sister got after Annias so hot till he like to lied heself out of hell, and when she spied Dives she made him flee and ever time he stop for breath old sister been dere. She run him up on de banks of de great Gulf and he looked across wid a longin' eye at Lazarus restin' in Father Abraham's bosom and he seed he could'nt make it, an' he cast he eye back one time at Ole Sister and jumped on in de Gulf. She got after Lot's wife and Lot say he wife ain't never looked back since she got a glimpse of Ole Sister. He say ef he'd had Ole Sister atter he wife when they left Sodom he believes dey would of made it, all two un 'um. He say he mighty nigh believe de pillar of salt would of moved. But one of de men's who was havin' a wuss time and been mighty unrestless were King Solomon. He went to de devil wid tear in he eye an' axe 'im for de sake of he poor old father who been at dat very moment walkin' through de flames of repentence singin' psalms, and for de sake of he own peace of mind to he'p him get shet of Ole Sister. King Solomon had a long compersation wid de devil, and he tell him dat King David was a old man now and can't do no harm and he mine in sech a state he ain't know he suffer, but he feared Ole Sister would be carryin' some kind of tale on dat ole man and get him kilt, and den King Solomon say he would like to aid de devil wid some of he wisdom. He would like to he'p him get Ole Sister fasten' up. He say he can't rest he so feared she might git in dere amongst he numerous wives, and he tell de devil wid he knowledge of women it would be hell shore 'nough. He say it were well known what trouble Ole Sister could create wid one wife an' he have to be very careful wid he six hundred; dat it takes great wisdom to rule 'um. He say when he look at all dem wimmen he ain't shore he wise as he reputation, and dere is time when dey is a great strain on him. Ole Sister rumpussed around hell so till complaints was comin' f'um ever which er way. She 'stirbed up the Moabites and she had the Malakites and de Hittites all gettin' ready for war. She been ever where, in ever place, high and low, wid dat scandal lovin' tongue of hern. She like to uh ruint dem poor little foolish virgins, tormented dem 'bout dere lamps and oil and other things and started all kind of scandalous tales on 'um. Her righteous mind always was runnin' on all kind of righteous things and so was her tongue. Brother, lem me tell you, you sees her kind ever day, in churches and frolics, wid dey eyes skinned meddlin' in other people's business, carryin' news. Well things war in a terrible fix in hell and de las' news been dat de devil on de advice of Solomon had set a trap and baited it with a innocent lamb, and I reckon it will be have mercy on de lamb.

The Settin' Up

Dere was a fellow that went to one of he fren's settin-up, and dis fren' was laid out dead on de coolin-board, and in some shape he wanted to go an' relieve him, an' he got down to prayer. Had a crowd of people there, too. He was prayin' dere wid he eyes shut, and he say, "Lord be wid dis deceased brother, he gone, he is dead; if it be thy will raise him; if it is not thy will, God, save his soul. God, he leaves all he sisters, he brothers, he companions here behind him. God, be wid him, have mercy on him, save his soul. Father, it is within thy power to raise him, it is within thy power to save him. Lord, go with his bereaved family he leff behin'."

An' as he was down dere prayin', wid he eye shut, de man on de coolin' board raise up, an' set up, an' de people saw him an' slipped out an' sneaked out, an' he still prayin' an' he raise up an open he eyes an' sawed no people but de dead man in front of him an' he backed off de dead man an' grabbed up a ax, an he say:

"If you don't wait till I git out of here I'll finish killin' you."

An' ever since den mens has been more perticular 'bout what dey axe God to do.

The Little Old Man on the Gray Mule

Tad: Wuh you run in here like you guh bus' your brains out fer? Is anything atter you?

Bruser: I see sumpen en it frighten me.

Tad: Wuh you see?

Bruser: I have been passin theu the Big Pea Ridge woods en I seems to hear the leaf cracklin'. I ain' know if I hear um ur no, but I sho I see sumpen, en I ain' know how I feel, en when I look I see a man runnin', wid he clothes tored mighty nigh off him en he eye red en he tongue hang out like dog. He look like he all tored up. And while I look he pass out of sight. Before I can get myself straight I seen a houn' dog wid he nose to de groun' trailin', and he pass on. And I see a pack of dog en dey pass me en dey all look like dey barkin' on a trail, but dey ain't make no soun'. And atter while here come a little man wid he long hair on his shoulder, yaller, ridin' a gray mule, and he bent over he mule en he look like he whoopin' to he dog, and he pass on, and de moon look brighter, and de tree shadder look darker, and de frosts on de leaf look like snow. And I ain' move for a while and it look like my heart guh froze I been so frighten. And den I lef' and I ain't want stay no longer, and I ain't wan' go dere no more.

Voice: Who you reckon it been?

Bruser: I ain't know.

Old Daniel: Is dis de fust time you hear about de old man wid he gray mule and he houn' dog, and de runnin' nigger?

Tad: Tell we.

Old Daniel: Way back in slavery time old Marster's Daddy had a little yaller nigger. De old folks says he had heap uh nigger. He had nigger he raise, and he had wild nigger, and when dese niggers been unruly and git punished some of dem run off and de little yaller nigger wid de gray mule's business been to run um wid he dog. Dat been he juty and dat been he pleasure, to say he ain' love nothen but he mule and he houn' and he old marster. And dey say dey ain' certain he love he old marster but he want to be friend wid him so he can have he pleasure. And in dem times in all de hours in de cold nights of winter and in de hot nights of summer and when de flowers is bloomin' or when de leaves is fallin' you could hear de little yaller man wid de gray mule whoopin' to he houn'. You could hear de dog trailin' and you knowed a nigger was in 'stress. And when he horn blow you knowed de race was done. And de little yaller man look kind and talk easy, and he look like he wouldn't harm nothen, but he heart, if he had a heart, been cruel as de teet' of de houn'.

Tad: Wuh make runnin' nigger wid houn' and punishin' 'um give him pleasure?

Old Daniel: Jesus knows. I ain' know. Ain't nobody know, but it is mighty hard to understand the minds of mens.

Voice: Un' Daniel, wuh he runnin' nigger now fer?

Old Daniel: Dat he sperrit. And all you see, de nigger wid he tongue hangin' out, de little yaller nigger wid de gray mule, all dem is de sperrits of dead mens and beasts and dey'll never git no rest. Dey punishment is to keep on runnin'. Dey run in slavery days. Dey's runnin' now, and dey'll be runnin' when you is kivered up in de groun'. And dey can be seen in de dark woods when a bright moon is shinin' and de frost is on de leaf, and de people and critters of de worl' is asleep. Dey 'pears as a warnin' to mens.

The Lake of the Dead

Tad: De big swamp draws people like a trap draws flies, an' people dies in de big swamps like flies dies in traps. Dey's all kind o' unknown critters an' varmints an' trees an' herbs an' pison, an' you meets unknown men an' ain' know wey dey come from an' you ain't know wey dey gwine. Dey ain' right an' dey takes on de ways of things dat ain't nat'ral.

Kike: Dey is dang'ous. Ole man July tells me dere is one place in de big swamp ain' nobody know wey it is, but if you wanders far enough an' long enough, you is sho to fin' it an' you don't come back.

Tad: I is heared 'bout dat place. It's a lake o' water wey all humans an' beasts perish on its shores.

Kike: Tad, you sho is heared 'bout it. When I been chillun, de ole folks ain' 'lowed we to talk 'bout it, it was so fright'nin'. I heared it were a place wey nothin' can live, an' if it do live, it ain' never come back nat'ral. Humans loses dey minds, an' beasts never does act like other beasts, an' dey says its shores is strewed wid de dead, a hog one place an' a cow, here a little bird an' sometime it ain' nothin' but a bug. An' dead men lie dere, an' ain' nobody ever sees life cepen dreadful things.

Dey say dey is always one an' sometimes two or three buzzards walkin' through over an' 'round de dead. Sometimes a buzzard will be settin' on a log, an' sometimes dey will be slowly walkin' 'round like dey ain' dere for no purpose but to make de place look more dreadful. Dey don't seems to have to eat de food dat's put 'efore 'em, an' dey looks like some'n dat's dead wid de power to walk slow an' dey walks like dey counts dey footsteps, an' dey footsteps is de footsteps of de dead. Once in a while dey shake dey self an' streches out dey neck an' makes a sound dat makes your blood creep like dey was tryin' to make things as worse for your hearin' as it is dreadful for your eyes.

A beast will walk to de edge of de water an' raise his head an' poke he head way out an' look 'cross de lake, an' den he sinks down. Some beasts draws back, an' all seems to have de feelin' of another world creepin' on 'em. An' mens is de same way, but dey mind takes 'em wuh dey nature tells 'em to go back. Why it is an' wuh it is ain' nobody know, but don't seek it, my brother, don't seek it.

Voice: Who guh seek such a place, Un' Kike?

Kike: My brother, mens seeks many things an' strange places way dey got no business seekin', an' many falls into danger an' mens an' beasts stumble on hard things an' de big swamps breaks men. Some places is worser dan other places. Stay 'way, my brother, stay 'way from de path of de buzzard; for ef you walks in dey path an' wanders too far, you'll land on de shores of de Lake of de Dead, an' men has walked on de shores of dis lake.

Aunt Dinah's Cat

Bartchy: Dey shore been a tangle up in de old street an' Aun' Dinah look like she done loss her mind, she been raisin' such a rucas.

Tally: Wuh Aun' Dinah raise a rucas about?

Bartchy: Toodney kill Aun' Dinah cat.

Joe: Wuh he kill Aun' Dinah cat for?

Bartchy: I ain't know, but he say he been catchin' he Ma chicken an' killed him, an' all dem nigger mout' been runnin'. Soun' like a passel of frogs, night birds and varmints wey dey been hollerin' an' guin' on. I done hear so much talk 'bout cat my years is ringin', an' if dem niggers do wuh dey say dey guh do wid Toodney he in a wus fix den dat cat. The ole people always say bad luck will follow a man if he 'stroy a cat. The ole people says a heap of thing and some of them is wise. I ain't know.

Willis: If I been Toodney I ain't worry myself wid no cat. Some people looks like dey all de time sarchin' fer trouble an' cat look like dey mix up wid evil. Is your hear 'bout dis here boy, Jube, ole man stutterin' Jube grand-chile?

Tally: I is hear some kind of talk. Ain't he dead?

Willis: Un' Beve tell we Jube tooken he Ma cat an' throwed him in a big open fire. Dat cat scramble around in dat fire hollerin' an' when he git out he dash out de house wid all de hair burn off him, he eye burned an' he run off an' he cry like a chile. An' Jube tooken sick, an' he cry like a chile. An' he ain't got no res'. An' in a week from dat day Jube war dead. An' dat night at de settin' up an' all de time de people was moanin' dey hear dat cat cryin', cryin' and moanin'. An' next day when dey buried him de cat git right in de big road an' follow de funeral, follow de funeral to de grave hollerin', wid all de hair burned off him an' he eye burned out. An' Un' Beve say, everybody look at de cat. An de cat been kiver wid sore. An' when dey throw de dirt in de grave dat cat disappear an' ain't nobody see him since.

Murder vs. Liquor

Scip: Well, things is gettin' wusser.

Tad: How come?

Scip: White folks been havin' such a time killin' niggers in self defense dey gettin' a taste fer killin' white folks de same way.

Tad: Wuh you talkin' 'bout, Scip, hush!

Scip: My mind has been runnin' on de law and de cotes. I just been ramblin' a little.

Tad: Wuh law and cotes, dey ain't never ought to have a law 'gainst killin' niggers.

Scip: Dey claims to have a law against killin' both white folks and niggers, but sometimes de law protects 'em an' ain't l'um be try.

Tad: Dey send ole man Reuben to the penitentiary fer seven months fer a little liquor.

Voice: Dey got to broke up liquor.

Scip: Reuben were a nigger an' hab liquor an' dat were de jedge in de big cote. Ain't he de law?

Tad: How come you say ain't he de law, and wuh you talk 'bout liquor for? You started off talkin' 'bout murder, now you gone to liquor.

Scip: Dey always punish fer liquor, an' de law 'lows killin', an' I ain't been talkin' 'bout no murder.

Tad: How come you say dat. You better hush your mout'.

Scip: Ain't I hear de jedge tell de jury to bring in a verdict of not guilty. He tell 'em dey can't try dis man. He guh pertec' him kase de law got de right to go in anybody house, day or night, rouse him out, and kill him if he try to 'fend he-self. All de officer got to do is to tell de jedge he were huntin' liquor.

Tad: Ain't he got to find it?

Scip: He can say he find it. He can say wuh he have a mind to say.

Tad: Scip, you ain't talkin' 'bout de big cote, is you?

Scip: No, I ain't talkin' 'bout de big cote. I jes sayin' de jedge is a great man and he can go against God if he got a mind to. He helt up de law, and de law is de law!

Tad: Have mercy! Jesus!

Scip: De jedge guh say wuh he guh say, an' he guh do wuh he guh do, an' he guh broke up liquor.

Tad: How 'bout murder?

Scip: I ain't say nothin' 'bout murder. I been talkin' 'bout liquor, an' de jedge is de law. When de jedge say dey ain't no murder, I ain't guh say dey is. De jedge know he business, an' I know mine, an' my business is to keep my eye wide open an' to keep my mout' shet tight, else if I got to open it I guh let my chune be he is a hones' jedge. He guh kill liquor! He guh kill liquor! He guh pertect everything in he cote from de louse in de witness box on uppass heself. He de law an' he guh broke up liquor. I ain' say nothin' 'bout no murder. Is killin' a man in he house at night murder when dey's huntin' liquor? It ain't matter how dey kill him if dey is huntin' liquor.

Tad: Scip, you is right. Murder is one thing, and liquor is another.

Scip: An' de jedge is de jedge, an' de law mus' be helt up. De jedge is a great man. He is a hones' man. He know he business an' he guh broke up liquor.

Old Dictodemus

Leader: Brothers and sisters, Brother March will preach to you tonight, and he words is always full of meanin' and dey ain't no fool words. Dey got dey meanin' and if you listen good, you will see he p'int. He tell you wuh he tell for de understandin' of colored folks. Brother March speaks our language and he speaks in words of wisdom.

Brother March: 'Way back yonder when Paul and Jesus and other great mens was in de world and was tryin' to save sinners from a burnin' hell, dere was men dat thought dey self bigger dan anybody else. Some un 'em had heared of Jesus, and some un 'em ain't know nothin' 'bout him, and if dey is know, dey try to discount him. But, my brothers, Jesus ain't been a man for nobody to discount. He were a man ain't never git mad; he was such a man he could grab a lion by de head and wring it off jes like you would wring a chicken's neck. He was such a man he could reach out one hand and grab de top off a mountain and throw it 'cross de world. Dat's de kind er man Jesus was.

And dere was a man in dem times dey called him Dictodemus. He were a great bad man. He defied God and Man, all two un 'em, and laugh 'bout it. He was a man was always fightin' and beatin' up people but one day ole Dictodemus, dis great bad man, run into de wrong man,—he met he match. He tried to put his self up against Capt'n Jesus. He ain't know it was Jesus, but it ain't take long to find out.

Well, Jesus ain't waste much time on Dictodemus, he had so much other things he was 'tendin' to. Ole Dictodemus got so humble he start to slippin' 'round at night tryin' to creep up to Jesus' tent, but Jesus run him off, he wants to git him when de right time comes. He wants to tes' him out.

One day he met Dictodemus in a lonely spot on de big road, and he stopped and had a talk wid him. Jesus been ridin' a little mule ain't no bigger dan a mouse, and he dismount and he say to Dictodemus, "Mount." And Dictodemus look at de little critter and sorter hold back, and Jesus say, "Mount." And

Dictodemus mounted and rode a long distance into de holy city of Jerusalem, and when he git dere, de little mule stopped right in de heart of de city in de front of de temple, and Dictodemus say to de little mule, "Go on." And de little mule shake he self two or three times and started to buckin' and jumpin', and he th'owed Dictodemus clean out er sight, and when he landed he were on de back of sompen, he ain't know wuh it were. It had horns like a goat, but it ain't no goat; it had years like a cow, but it ain't no cow; it had a mouth like a hog, but it ain't no hog. And Dictodemus' mind been all angled up, he ain't know wuh it were; he ain't know wuh happen, he ain't know he self when Jesus appeared and hold up he hands and say, "Let dere be peace." And den he stepped back on he little mule and rode out to Jerusalem wid Dictodemus followin' behind on he foots tame as a dog.

Excited Sister: (Shrieking at the top of her voice)
Oh, Lord! Oh, Lord! Oh, Lord, My Jesus!
It must a been a mule!
It must a been a mule!
It must a been a mule!

Congregation: (Chanting)
It must a been a mule!
It must a been a mule!
It must a been a mule!

Jeff's Funeral Sermon

Reverend:

Oh, Lord, dis man was born in sin, an' he died in Christ.
He sold his lot in Egypt, an' he bought a lot in Paradise.
Watch wey you put your foot-steps,
Don' put 'em in de mud.
Kiver up your tracks,
'En look out for de serpents dat's lyin' all 'bout.
Don' tell your secrets.
Don' put your trus' in mens,
But put your faith in Jesus,
He is de only fren' you got.
Keep your eye upon your foot-steps,
Kiver up your tracks,
Don' walk in de mud.

Old Lucy: (Walking up and down the aisles, waving her hand and hollering at the top of her voice)

Great God, Reverend, hold your holt! I'm gwine to my Jesus! I'll bus' heben wide open wid a trail of light leading to my Lord. Great God, Reverend, hold your holt!

Jeff's Son: (Standing by the coffin, bending up and down and hollering)

Pa, Oh, Pa! Pa gone. I de last one talked wid Pa. Pa tell me, he say tear down dis shed an' buil' a better one. Pa, Oh, Pa! Ain't you hear me? I goin' do what you say.

Feminine voice in back of congregation, shrieking:

Jesus, Jesus, gone to Jesus!

Reverend:

Oh, Lord, dis man was born in sin an' he died in Christ.
He sold his lot in Egypt, an' he bought a lot in Paradise.
For he watch where he put he foot-steps.
An' he kiver up he tracks.
He place his faith in God, an' he walk aroun' de serpents that was lyin' all 'bout.
He put his faith in Jesus, an' he trusted in he God.
He kept his eye upon he foot-steps.

He kivered up he tracks, an' he never put 'em in de mud,
For he put he faith in God.
Oh, Lord, he born in sin, an' he died in Christ,
He sold he lot in Egypt, an' he bought a lot in Paradise.

Old Lucy: Great God, Reverend, hold your holt!
I'm goin' to bus' heben wide open wid a trail of light leadin' to de throne.

Voice: (of sister, in middle of congregation)

Lead us, Sister Lucy,
Lead us to de light.
Lead us from de darkness,
Lead us from de night.
Lead us toward de throne,
Where all is snowy white.

Reverend:

Our deceased brother was born in sin, an' he died in Christ.
He sold his lot in Egypt,
An' he bought a lot in Paradise.
He has placed his foot-steps on de golden stairs,
He never put 'em in de mud.
He has kivered up his tracks.
He's up in heben.
He is on his way to Jesus.
He has throwed away his crown of thorns.
He has shunned the path of serpents.
He steps beneath the silver lights,
He is walking on the golden stairs,
He is climbing to the pearley throne.
He'll set up a foot-stool at the feet of Jesus.
He'll tell to him the secrets
That he didn't tell to mens,
For he is walkin' up the golden stairs,
He is climbing to the pearley throne,
And he will set upon a foot-stool in spotless white,
Beneath the bright and shining lights of heben.
And he will tell his troubles to his God,
For he was born in sin,
An' he died in Christ.

He sold his lot in Egypt,
An' he bought a lot in Paradise.

Old Lucy:

Great God, Reverend, hold your holt!
I'm goin' to bus heben wide open,
I'm goin' to the throne of Christ.
I'm goin' to make a trail of light.
I'm goin' out of darkness,
I'm goin' to lef' behind de night.
I'm on my way to Jesus,
I'm goin' to my Christ,
I'm goin' to shout my way theu Paradise,
Great God, Reverend, hold your holt!

Fragment of a Negro Sermon

Our Brother is dead,
He rests from he labor
An' he sleeps,—

(Shrill voice of Sister)	He sleeps, Oh, he sleeps!

Wey de tall pines grow,

(Another voice)	On the banks of a river.

On the banks of a river.

(Several voices)	On the banks of a river.

He trouble is done,
He's left dis world
On the wings of glory.

(Voice)	On the wings of glory!

Out of life's storm,

(Another voice)	On the wings of glory!

Out of life's darkness,

(Several voices)	On the wings of glory!

He sails in the light,
Of the Lamb.
Away from his troubles,
Away from the night

(Congregation)	In the light!

In the light!
Of the Lamb.

He's gone to the kingdom above,
In the raiment of angels,

(Voice of Sister)
In the raiment!
In the raiment of angels!

To the region above,
An' he sleeps,—

(Voices chanting throughout congregation)
Oh, he sleeps,—
Oh, he sleeps!
On the banks of a river.

Way de tall pines grow,
On the banks of a river.

(Congregation)
With the starry
crowned angels,
On the banks of a river.

An' the flowers is bloomin'
In the blood of the Lamb.

(Shrill voice of Sister and taken up by congregation chanting and swaying)
The blood of the Lamb!
In the blood of the Lamb!

An' the birds is singin'
Wey de wind blows soft,
As the breath of an angel,
An' he sleeps!
Wey de tall pines grow,
On the banks of a river.

(Voice)
An' he sleeps!

(Another voice) Wey de tall pines grow.

An' his sperrit is guarded,

(Several voices) On the banks of a river.

By a flaming-faced angel.

(Sister) Yes, Jesus, of a flaming-faced
angel
On the banks of a river.

Standing on mountains of rest.
An' he sleeps way de tall pines grow,
On the banks of a river.

(Congregation) Oh, he sleeps!
He sleeps!

His Day Is Done

His day is done,
His work is over,
And he is riding through the sky,

(Shrill voice of Sister) He is riding, Oh, yes, he's
riding, through the sky.

To his home in the heavens,
Just above the thunder,

(Another voice) Just above the thunder.

In a golden chariot,

(Another voice) In a chariot,
In a chariot.

Just above the thunder.

(Other voices) In a golden chariot,
Just above the thunder.

Jesus waits for him,
At his home in the sky,
There's wings on his chariot,

(Sister) There's wings on his chariot,
on his chariot,
on his chariot,

And a light around his head,

(Another voice) A light, a light, a light around
his head

Just above the thunder,
In a golden chariot,

(Other voices) In a golden chariot,
Just above the thunder.

Just above the thunder.
His life was weary,
But he's done his duty,
And now his road's beyond the clouds,

(Several voices) Beyond the clouds,
Beyond the clouds,
Beyond the clouds.

In a golden chariot,
Just above the thunder,
In a golden chariot,

(Another voice) In a golden chariot,
In a golden chariot.

Just above the thunder.

(Congregation) Just above the thunder.

He does not dread the lightning,
From sin his soul is free,

(Several voices) His soul is free, free,
Oh, his soul is free.

He sweeps across the skies,
With Jesus as his guide,
Just above the thunder,
In a golden chariot,
Just above the thunder.

(Congregation) Yes, Jesus is his guide.
Just above the thunder,

In a golden chariot,
Just above the thunder.

And he looks with pity upon the world,

(Voice) Pity, pity, he looks with pity upon the world.

That he has left so far below,
He's flying in a chariot,

(Another voice) He's flying in a chariot.

And angels is his horses in the sky,

(Shrill voice) And angels is his horses, in the sky.

Just above the thunder,

(Sister) Angels is his horses.

In a golden chariot,
Just above the thunder.

(Congregation)
Just above the thunder
In a chariot,
A golden chariot,
Just above the thunder.

Ole Man Rogan

Balti: Ain't had so much luck since we been fishin' here. Dis here place done fish out.

Tunga: Less we lef' here and go to Boggy Gut. Ain't nobody fish much dere.

Old Bill: I rudder stay here and don't have so much fish. I never is think too much of Boggy Gut.

Tunga: How come you ain't want to go to Boggy Gut?

Old Bill: Is you 'member hearin' 'bout Ole Man Rogan name call?

Balti: I hear Ole Man Rogan name call, but I ain't know nothin' 'bout him. Tell we.

Old Bill: Ole Man Rogan nuse to sell nigger in slavery time. Dat's wey he nuse to fishin', and every time he come for res' he come to Boggy Gut. Ole Man Rogan a man wid curious ways. He ain't beat a nigger much, and he guin him plenty to eat, and he bring 'em here in drove and he have 'em chained together, but he have curious ways and he ain't have but one pleasure,—settin' fishin'. He always buy ooman wid chillun, and ooman wid husband, and ain't nobody can buy from Ole Man Rogan mother and chile or man and ooman. He great pleasure been to part. He always love to take er baby away from he ma and sell it, and take he ma somewhere else and sell her, and ain't luh 'em see one another again. He love to part a man and he ooman, sell de man one place and sell de ooman another, and dat look like all Ole Man Rogan live for, and when he ain't 'casion 'stress dat er way, he been onrestless. He love to see a man wid he head bowed down in 'stress, and he love to see chillun holdin' out dey arms cryin' for dey mother, and he always looked satisfied when he see tear runnin' down de face of er ooman when she weepin' for her chile.

And Ole Man Rogan die on Boggy Gut, and ever since den he sperrit wander and wander from Boggy Gut to de river and wander 'cross de big swamps to Congaree. Whether it be God or whether it be devil, de sperrit of Ole Man Rogan ain't got no res'. Some time in de night ef you'll set on Boggy Gut, you'll hear de rattle of chains, you hear a baby cry every which er way, and you hear a mother callin' for her chile in de dark night on Boggy Gut.

And you kin set on de edge of Boggy Gut and you'll see mens in chains bent over wid dey head in dey hands,—de signs of 'stress. While you sets you see de sperrit of Ole Man Rogan comin' 'cross de big swamps. You see him look at de womens and mens and chillun, and you see him laugh—laugh at de 'stress and de tears on Boggy Gut, and he laugh like he satisfied, but he ain't had no res'. And when he stayed a minute on Boggy Gut, to de river 'cross de big swamps and back again he wanders, on de edge of Boggy Gut.

Big Charleston

Tad: All dis compersation 'bout hot suppers, dances, womens and funerals brings a heap of diff'ent things to my mind. One thing I been thinkin' 'bout been Big Charleston and he doin's, and dat ain't one thing neither. It er range of things kiverin' diff'ent things in life,—a laugh one place and a tear another.

Barchy: I jes is 'member Big Charleston. He create a lot of 'sturbance in he time. Some folks says he was a human, and some says he were a beast and dey say he was double j'inted.

Scip: Well, deys all kinds of diff'ent roads to de grave, and Big Charleston ain't been too long findin' out he road.

Voice: Tad, tell we de tale 'bout Big Charleston.

Tad: De first time I see Big Charleston been at a dance and hot supper over to de ole street. Dem niggers been havin' some time eatin' hash and rice, drinkin' liquor, singin' reels and dancin' and gamblin' and fightin'. You could hear 'em laughin' and talkin' a mile. Dey come to de road jumpin' to de drum and steppin' as high as a man's head. And as de night wored on you ought er seen some of dem niggers cut de buck and de buzzard lope, and sidin' 'round dem sisters like er rooster 'round er hen. Everything been lovely till dis gal of Potee's from de bluff come. She been pritty, but my brothers, I is here to tell you she been one little devil, and she 'casioned more'n one funeral. When she hit dat floor, niggers got to movin' and de fiddlers made dem fiddles talk and sing and cry. And dat little gal she was dartin' up to one nigger and leffen him and dartin' up to another. Back and forth she was swingin' and swayin', flyin' 'round dere like some kind of little bird. She dat pritty and sweet she set dem niggers crazy. And den she picked out Silas for her man, and Big Charleston come up and walked 'round de room, den he fasten he eye on de little gal and he lean over and snatch her from Silas like some kind of great hawk takin' a chicken in he claw right out de flock. And when he do dat, de little gal pull back and say she guh stay wid Silas. Den de trouble start.

All dem niggers been 'gainst Charleston. Charleston picked Silas up and th'owed him 'gainst de wall. Den dey started crowdin' him, and he looked like a boar hog wid a passel of fice dogs 'round him, and every time he twis' he self some of dem niggers was drapped jes like fices draps when a boar hog rips 'em up wid he tushes. Every time Big Charleston hit a nigger, a nigger hit de floor. When he'd reach out and grab a nigger, it look like he guh broke him in half, he'd pick de nigger up and slam him down and de nigger would tremble a little bit and lay still. Big Charleston been bleedin' all over wey dem niggers stucked him. He reached over and wring a stick out of a nigger's hand, and den he clean up. Niggers was th'owed all over de place, and Silas was dead, and dat little gal th'owed herself down and weep and moan over Silas, and she promise herself and she promise God dat she were guh make Big Charleston travel de same road he send Silas.

And Charleston walk out wid he head up and walk to de boss, and de doctor 'tend him. Den dey 'res' him, and de boss say he'll be tooken care of, and he been tooken care of. He been a favor-ite wid de boss.

And dat night at de settin' up dem niggers been talkin' 'round, moanin' and weepin', and dat little gal of Potee's been leadin' de singin' and she were prayin' and moanin'. And de followin' Sunday dey bury Silas and dere was great moanin' and weepin' from de sisters, and I ain't know whether dey weepin' for Silas or for Big Charleston. And dat little gal look like she guh bus' her heart out de way she holler. Her voice ring out all over de place and dat preacher tried his self, and brothers and sisters was swingin' and swayin', and shoutin' and singin', and it look like all of 'em had forgit everything but de sperrit, and de sperrit lifted 'em from de earth. When dey started comin' out wid de box to take Silas to de grave, dat little gal th'owed herself 'cross it and called on Silas and beg God for Jesus' sake to take her along and lay her in de same grave wid Silas. And de sisters lif' her up, tored her loose from de coffin and dey buried Silas.

Barchy: And wuh dey do wid Big Charleston?

Tad: Dey ain't do nothin' to Big Charleston, jes take him to de cote and dey try him, but de boss he been behind him, and when he lawyer git up and tell dat jury wuh kind of hand Big

Charleston been and how much work he can do, he say he ain't never been in no trouble wid white folks, and he say, "You all ain't got nothin' 'gainst Charleston, wuh he do? He kill one nigger in self defense, and he broke up two or three others. Wuh harm is Big Charleston do?" And dat little gal of Potee's been dere. Instead of her being agin Big Charleston, she help him, and when de jury turn Big Charleston loose, wuh she do? She set dere and wait. When she come out de cote house, she been wid Charleston and she been recognize as he ooman.

Scip: You sho' never is know wuh er ooman guh do. De bes' thing you kin do is to figger out wuh dey guh do, and dey is more'n apt to be contrary and do de other thing, and den your mind is more'n apt to have you wrong. You never is know wuh er ooman guh do.

Tad: Well, I figger out womens dis er way. When it comes to mens heap er time it ain't matter wuh er man do or wuh kind of man he be. Look at all de womens. All un 'em atter Big Charleston, and dey know wuh kind of man is Big Charleston, and most generally dat's womens.

Voice: Wuh come of him, Tad?

Tad: Well, him and dat little gal live together, and she been crazy 'bout Charleston, but atter while he lef' her and tooken up wid another ooman. Dat's de way he started travelin' on he las' road. Dat little gal mighty nigh tored de other ooman up, and she stick er knife in Charleston and he die, but 'fore he die he grab her and twis' her over and broked her neck on he knee, den he fall back and she fall 'cross him and when dey find 'em dey both been kivered wid blood.

Scip: All you got to do is follow womens.

The Yellow Crane

Jube: Limus dead back in de swamp on Crane Lake.

Sandy: Wuh ail him?

Jube: Him and Saber been seinin' back dere wid a gang of dem Free Issues, and dey all come out of de water. Limus stan' up on de edge of de lake and look out dere and look like he froze; he looked and stiffen he self and nod he head like he geein answer to somebody out in de water. Saber say he look like he git a call to come on and he ain't got to go less he gree, and he nod he heard and stiffen he self like he see sompen ain't no human ever see 'efore, and den he shake all over and drap dead. And Saber say he ain't see a God's thing in dat lake but a monster big crane, a yaller crane.

He say it were a natural crane, but he been yaller wid eye like a goose, and he been taller dan a man and he had a bill longer dan de handle of a blacksmith's tongs. He say he noticed dat good, kase when Limus drap he seen him open he bill and work it like he were laughin'. He twis' he head dis way and dat and he ain't make a sound, but he wink he eye and ain't never shet it, but he half close it. It look like some kind of evil sperrit lookin' through a crack in de side of he head. He said dat ole bird guin him de ague.

Den he say dat crane rumple up he feather and shake he self. He start walkin' straight to wey Limus lay. He say he look at him good. He look like a crane and he look like a man, like a ole man yaller wid a beard, and he look evil and he look like de father of death. And he walk up to wey Limus lay and stoop down 'side him and put he head close to Limus' head like he listenin' to sompen. Den he twis' he head one side and look at him careful and laugh widout makin' a sound. Den he step 'cross Limus and put he foot on him like he scorn him, den he reach 'round his self like a man pullin' a cloak 'round him and walk out 'cross de big swamp wid he head drawed up. He look more sinful dan sin. He look satisfied and he look like he were in misery. Saber say he ain't know wuh to make of how he look, he look so much diff'ent kind of way.

Sandy: Wuh de ole Issue do?

Jube: I axe Saber and he say he look and he seen all dem Issue walkin' off through de swamp, and dey ain't say nothin' and dey ain't look like humans. He say he ain't call 'em and ain't wan call 'em. He say de swamp look evil wid de yaller mud from de high water up on de trees higher 'an a man's head, and shadows from de trees and flies and things flyin' 'round. And up in de air a hawk been sailin' 'round and a buzzard way up dere in de sky; and through de yaller swamp de yaller crane and de goose eye yaller Issue was passin' in de distance mixin' wid everything else dat were yaller, and passin' dis way comin' into sight one minute and fadin' de nex' till dey all was swallowed up and everything were like it were not in a human world.

Saber say it were dreadful, and ef it had er las' much longer, he would er drap down dead like Limus done. He say he ain't know how he git home, and he know he days is shortened.

Kike: You all ain't got no sense. You ain't heared 'bout de yaller crane of Crane Lake? Wuh you reckon dey call dat place Crane Lake for?

Voice: Wuh?

Kike: It been Crane Lake way back in slavery time when my grand-daddy's pa been chillun, and it ain't never been no place for crane, scusin' de big yaller crane Saber see, and dat ain't been no crane.

Back in slavery time dey been a ole Issue who daddy sent him off to a furrin lan' for schoolin'. He sent him when he were chillun and he brung him back when he were a man. And dis here Issue been mighty smart wid heap er book and heap er larnin', and when he come back to de Sand Hill he been a doctor, and he live by he self. He had more sense 'an white folks and niggers both; he scorn everybody, nigger and white folks; and dey tells tales 'bout how he nuse to 'casion niggers to die. Dey say he ain't never miss a chance, and ain't nobody ketch him. White folks was feared on him wusser 'an nigger, and he look like he ain't got no nuse for Issue, but dey sey he ain't harm 'em.

And he nuse to walk in de big swamp, and de ole folks says he would stan' on Crane Lake and laugh at he own weeked ways, and he were satisfied when some folks died; and he been full of misery for he self and everybody, but a real nigger were pison to him, and he were pison to de nigger. He hair were straight and he been goose eye and he look like a crane and he wored a long black cloak. He died on Crane Lake and many slavery time niggers die on Crane Lake, and dere is certain times when de yaller crane is seen, and a nigger always die and dey is enticed dere by Free Issues wid one excuse or another.

Voice: Un' Kike, you done guin me a chill. Wuh he have 'ginst niggers?

Kike: I ain't know. De ole folks says dat de way dey come to be Free Issues dat white womens were dey mammy and niggers were dey daddy, and de law ain't 'low de chillun of a white ooman to be a slave; and a new lookin' race of goose eye niggers was created, and dey had minds of dey own and ways of dey own. Dey was discounted by white folks and dey was scorned by niggers.

And now I done tell you de first start of Issues and dey creatin'. I ain't know no more and I ain't guh say no more.

Tad: Wey all dem niggers?

Preb: Dey down dere.

Tad: Down dere wey?

Preb: Down dere to de fire on de creek.

Tad: Wuh dey do down dere?

Preb: Hab heap er compersation an' tellin' a passel er lies.

Spencer: Preb, you ought to be shame on yourself scusin' people er tellin' a passel er lies. You ain' got no 'casion to say dat.

Preb: How come I ain' got no 'casion to say wuh I say? Ain' I see all dem niggers together? Ain' I got my two good eye?

Tad: Your eye ain' hear 'em tell no lie.

Preb: Trute, my eye ain' hear 'em, but my eye see a passel er niggers, an' more en that I been where dey is an' my years heared 'em. Wey dey go to wid all dat compersation if dey ain' lie? Tad, if I ain' knowed you, I'd think you wuz a fool. Wuh dey hold so much compersation about?

Spencer: Tad, you ain' ought ter axe Preb dat. You fixin' to make Preb lie.

Tad: Luh him lie. It ain't hurt nobody when he lie. I an' you an' him all know he guh lie. Luh him lie. He ain' fool no nigger, an' if he keep in practice hit will help him wid de white folks.

Spencer: Tad, I ain' guh jine you an' Preb in your lowness.

Preb: Brother, I ain' tell no lie, Un Scip boy been off an' he tell dem niggers ef dey jine togedder dey can rise up an' take dey own place in de worl', an' he been talkin' 'bout schoolin' an' 'bout respect dey self an' how dey will be respected. He say dey got a long road to travel, an' it's up hill all de way, dat dey's down in de valley of darkness now, but bright lights is shinin' at de top. He say de road is long over high mountains an' dat dey will fall in deep gullies; dat dey got to keep on climin' to reach de Promised Land. He tell 'em to gird up dey lines an' git de scent of guano off 'em; hit ain' 'lowed on dat road. He say dere will be storms an' worser storms, an' some will drap on de road side, but dey must keep dey eye on de light at de top of de hill; dey must climb out of de mud an' 'stroy de briers dat tangle dey feet. He tell dem to take up dey bed an' walk. If dey don't show dey own manhood dey ain' nobody goin' to show it for them. He say niggers lives today an' does today an' don't study 'bout tomorrow.

Tad: Wuh you say to him, Preb?

Preb: I done say wuh I guh say. I lisen to wuh he say.

Tad: Dat ain't nothin' but nigger talk.

Spencer: A nigger's a nigger. If he tempts to be better'n a nigger a nigger pulls him down an' a cracker pushes him down. Down is de nigger's cry. He's got two main enemies—crackers and niggers. White folks is white folks, crackers is crackers an' niggers is niggers.

Wild Goose Nest

Brother Hickman: Brothers and Sisters, we come before the Lord this day with prayer. Dear father, look down from the throne on high and view these children of yourn. Look into dey hearts and see if dey's pure. Jesus, if dey ain't make 'em repent and don' lu'm tell no lies dis day, Amen.

Congregation: Tell us about it, Brother.

Brother Hickman: Sister Peggie, what is your experience? Has you reached a determination in your travels?

Sister Peggie: Brother, I is. I travel a long distance and de road been rough and mighty dark, and at a long distance and at a great height and nigh de end of de road I find a wild goose nest, and all the eggs but one is white, and it were black.

Brothers and Sisters: (Chanting)

Wild goose nest,
Wild goose nest,
Wild goose nest.

Brother Hickman: Sisters, go back in de wilderness and pray some more. Go seek again till all de eggs in de wild goose nest is white.

Shrill voices from Sisters in different parts of the congregation:

Wild goose nest,
Wild goose nest,
Wild goose nest.

(Sister Peggie goes and returns)

Sister Peggie: Brother Hickman, I traveled to de wild goose nest, and de road been long and de road been rough, and I come to de wild goose nest.

Voices in congregation: Tell us, Sister.

Sister Peggie: Wild goose nest,
Wild goose nest,
Wild goose nest.

And de nest been soft with
Feathers, from de wild Goose' breast

Wild goose breast,
Wild goose breast,
Wild goose breast.

An' all de eggs been white but one,
And it still were black.

Brother Hickman: Go back, Sister Peggie! Go back in de wilderness and seek again for a determination. There still is work to be done. Go, and pray and seek, sister, till all de eggs in de wild goose nest is white.

Congregation: Wild goose nest,
Wild goose nest,
Wild goose nest.

(Sister Peggie goes, and returns for the third time.)

Brother Hickman: What you find Sister Peggie?

Sister Peggie: Brother, I have been to de wild goose nest and all de eggs is white. All de eggs is white.

Brother Hickman: My Sister, you has reach a determination in your long travel and your labors is done. Rise, Sister, your journey is done.

Congregation: Wild goose nest,
Wild goose nest,
Wild goose nest.

Frank: Seems to me I hears sompen comin'.

Scip: 'Tain' nothin' but Tad.

(Tad walks up)

Tad: Yes, it ain' nothin' but Tad, and that ain' nothin'.

Scip: Wuh make you say dat? Ole Taddy! Nigger, you does sometimes tell the truth, even ef you ain' means to; but watch out, a lie is comin', I'm tellin' you, my buddy.

Voice: Tad, where you been?

Tad: I lay down back there in de swamp wid my head on a log and drapped asleep, an' I ain' wake up 'till I hear somebody laughin' and talkin', an' when I open my eye, one of dese here owls been settin' on a limb of a dead snag right by me, an' he look right down in my eye and laugh an' say, "Brother, is you restin'?" and I say, "I is been restin', but I done wid res' now. I is leffen' here." An' he say, "Brother, hole on a minute." An' I look at him good, an' I see he ain' no owl, but he been people, an' I get more intent on leffen. But dat old bird look like he helt, an', my brothers, he looked dried up and weeked, an' then he say he been a friend of my grandpa way back in slavery.

Voice: Great God, dat's when I would er tored out.

Tad: You thinks you would er tored out. You wouldn't er tored out no more en I done, an' I had a mind to, but I ain' been able to. Dat ole bird tell me when he been in dis world, he been ole man Smart Daniel' daddy, en he say he don't res' none. He spen' he time flyin' aroun' in de night an' talkin' most of de time wid other spirits, an' sometimes he makes heself known to humans. He say he ain' live right in dis world, an' he an' none un um can stand the light of day, an' he main pleasure is meetin' de chillun of he ole friend and dey chillun, when dey pass out of dis world an' take on de same shape he take on. An' he say some un um takes on other shapes an' lives in de form of different birds and animals, an' when dey is 'stroyed dey changes dey shapes. He say one shape don't recognize nobody in a different shape, an' he ain' know when he catch a bird or a snake ef he eatin' he friend or no.

Voice: Great God! You reckon all dat true, Tad?

Tad: I ain' know, but it sound like de truth, an' every time he say sompen, he'd laugh an' cold sweat would bust out on me, an' den he tell me he guh look for me, in he world a little later, an' dat we guh have some time laughin' an' talkin' 'bout different things, an' ef he can, he guh see some more.

Voice: My God!

Another Voice: Do Jesus!

Tad: I reckon I los' my life now tryin' to keep from goin' to sleep.

Frank: You say he put a spell on you, Tad, an' you ain' been able to lef'? How come you is here now?

Tad: Brother, I ain' linger wid dat ole spirit no longer than de law 'low. All of dat compersation of hisn ain' create no enjoyment in my min'. I jes naturally ain' been able to move 'til he say, "Son, I guh put sompen in your year you always will 'member. I guh gee you a spirit world sign so we can recognize one 'nother when you time come." Well, I say, "Wuh it is?" An' he say, "I can't say it out loud. I guh whisper it to you." An' when he say dat, he hopped down off de snag and started walkin' to me, laughin' de worse he know how. Dat were when I busted de spell. I ain' want no spirit world sign, an' I ain' want no ole mens whisperin' in my year, 'specially weeked ole dead mens, an that's when I broke loose. An' you know dat ole spirit float along behind me laughin' an' hollerin' an' makin' de worse sound I ever is hear mighty nigh all de way to dis camp.

Frank: You can look for anything in dis swamp you ain' wan' to see.

Voice: I never wus too much for dis swamp in de day-time, much less de night.

Scip: Well, Tad and ole man Smart Daniel' daddy ain' de onliest ones guh pass out of dis life an' take on de looks of birds an' beasts. Some un um takes on dem looks an' ways in dis life, an' I ain' 'sputin' nobody when dey says it b'longs to em.

Voice: I reckon it's time we bes' be lef'in' here.

Belton's Spirit

Tad: Well, Buddy, I am mighty nigh finished wid de big swamps.

Voice: Why is you say dat, Tad?

Tad: Las' week I been 'way back in de swamp on Hen-House Gut an' when I was comin' out I had dis here boy of Crappos wid me an' heared a lim' fall and the bark tored off an' sumpen' scramble up a high pine, an' I had my gun an' start to the tree an' thought it were a varmint, when dat boy ketched me by the sleeve an' he ain't say nothen, an' pull at my sleeve, an' I say, "Wait a minute" an' den he say, "Come on! Les we lef' here!" An' I start off agin' an' he spring on my back an' like to th'owed me down. An' I say, "Wuh ail you?" an' he say, "come on!" I see a man clam' up dat tree, an' I look at him, an' he ain't look natural, an' my min' tell me it were best we lef'. An' when we get on the edge of the swamp I axe him wuh make he act that-a-way, an' he say, "I see a man clam up dat tree," an' he ain't say nothen else, an' my mind tell me don't say no more.

Voice: Wuh reckon it been, Tad?

Tad: I see Cott next day, an' I axe him 'bout it, an' he tell me, "Tad, ain't you know dat de tree they lay Belton out under?"

An' I ain't say no more.

The Animal Court

Rab: Wuh ail you, Israel, how come you tored up so bad?

Israel: I got tored up in dat cane-brake.

Voice: Wuh make you go through cane-brake?

Israel: I been back on de bee-tree track, down by the big sand-bar, 'en I see all kinds of thing walking around on sand-bar, an' dey ain't look natural, 'en I took de shortest course an' I ain't luh no cane-brake an' brier patch an' gut stan' in my way, 'en I got tored up.

Voice: What kind of thing you see, Israel?

Israel: God knows, I ain't know. Wuh I see frighten me.

Kike: Dat sand-bar always been a frightenin' place. I been talkin' to ole man Robbin way back in slavery-time, 'en he tell me 'bout one night he been los' on de bee-tree track, an' when he find heself he been in de bushes on the aige of de big sand-bar, an' he set down on a log to res' heself, an' de moon been shinin' bright, an' while he settin' dere he look out on de sand-bar an' he seen a drove of owl walk out dere like a set of men, one big owl been wid dem. When dey got out a piece in de sand-bar dey all stan' up dere together, an' ain't move, an' atter while he seen a fox, seen a coon, seen a possum, an' seen a rabbit, all of 'em comin' dere an' get together nigh unto dem owl, 'en crow, jay-bird, snake, crawl out de water, all kinds of varmints been gathered around, an' while he settin' dere he say he see two woodpeckers come in wid a turkey buzzard an' dey march up dere in front of dem owl an' he set der an' watch 'em, an' dem owl helt a cote, just like people, an' dey 'scused de buzzard of eatin' Bur Rabbit brother. Bur Buzzard been a undertaker an' went to de settin' up dat night all night long, an' he look like he guine shed tear an' stan' roun' dere an' look mournful, an' bow he ball head, like Bur Rabbit brother ain't been nobody brother but he own, he look like he fret so. Next mornin' all de animals lef' to go to dey work an' lef' Bur Buzzard to bury Bur Rabbit brother, an' when dey come back dey fine out Bur Buzzard ain't bury him, but eat him. An' dey had a jay-bird 'scusin' Bur Buzzard, an' dey had varmint, an' had snake all for one kind of witness or anudder, an' lyin' every which-a-way, an' dey convict Bur Buzzard, an' dey pick out Bur Fox to execute him he got so much sharp ways an' he do so much low trick, but Bur Fox mighty perticular 'bout what he do an' what he put he mout' on. Bur Fox he start to lef' an' dey axe him wuh he guine, an' he say, "ain't you hear dem dogs out dere in de woods, dat is wuh I guine."

An' nobody didn't do nuthen to Bur Buzzard, an' ain't never done nuthen to Buzzard. Dat's why so much buzzard. Dey always gits off.

Ole Man Tooga's Chile

(A Tale of the Chain Gang)

Josey Mammy: Is you hear 'bout ole man Tooga?

Scip: Wha' ail ole man Tooga?

Josey Mammy: Ain' nothin' ail he health, but he mine mighty sick wid worryation.

Voice: Wha' he worry 'bout? Worry ain' no nuse.

Josey Mammy: He worry 'bout he chile.

Voice: Wha' chile?

Josey Mammy: He worry 'bout Wash.

Tad: Wha' de matter ail Wash?

Josey Mammy: Nuff ail Wash. He done cross de path of de law an' de poor buckra got him.

Voice: How come de poor buckra got him?

Josey Mammy: De chain gang is he home now. Is you know wha' I mean?

Tad: Ef he ain' larn how to pray, now he time, for he show God guh wear suppen sides clothes.

Scip: Prayin', wha' he guh pray for? Mercy, he bes' save he breath. When God drap him in de han' of er cracker, he done wid him, he done quit noticin' prayer, Him an' he Son an' all un um. Dey got too much else to 'tend to. He mought pray to de cracker ef he wants to create a laugh an' game makin'. Luh him pray.

Josey Mammy: Son you knows a heap but you ain' know wuh ole man Tooga do an' wuh he say an' how he act wid dem cracker. Ole man Tooga full o' worryin' an' he ain' loss he mine yet an' he ain' loss he scheme.

Scip: Is you ever see a mice when de cat's got him? Schemin' helps him.

Tad: De cat know he business jes' a leetle better dan de mice.

Scip: An' de cracker know he business.

Voice: Josey Mammy, tell we.

Josey Mammy: When ole man Tooga visit de guard, he carry

a fryin-size chicken to de head boss an' gee it to him, den he axe 'bout Wash, an' he tell ole man Tooga Wash is goin' to make a good prisoner. He say when he lef' de gang he goin' to be a good nigger or a dead nigger. He say Wash 'tend like he got de fever, but ain't nothin' ail him. He guh show him how he brokes em in. He say ole man Tooga ought to handle him dat a way when he raise him an' he would a been some service to him.

Voice: Wha' ole man Tooga say?

Scip: Wha' he kin say?

Josey Mammy: Ole man Tooga say he ain' nothin' but a nigger an' he never is been in no trouble an' he ain't set his self up to be equal wid white folks, an' he said he ain't know wha' to do to keep he chillun out o' trouble. He says he do he bes' an' he thankful for agvice from good white folks.

Scip: Well, he in de right place to git it.

Tad: Is he git it?

Josey Mammy: I ain' know 'bout agvice, but I know dem cracker brung Wash out an' chain he foots, shackles an' all to a stob in de groun'. Tear been runnin' down Wash' face an' sweat was bust out all over he fore head, an' he axe for mercy.

Scip: He axe for mercy?

Josey Mammy: He axe for mercy, an' dey throwed him down an' twis' him over so he can't move he foot an' one man put he foot on he neck an' de other man work on him wid a strop thick as a man's hand. Wash moan an' beg so hard he had tear in he voice, he prayed to he God an' call on he Pa an' he holler for he Ma, he cry like a sucklin' chile. He make a noise like a hurted beast, but it ain' do no good. One o' dem cracker kick him in de face an' de side two or three time, den ram he foot in Wash' mouth an' say, "Holler ef you wants to, gee him twice as much." Den he call a trusty an' tell him to rub salt in he cuts an' atter dat dey put him back on de chain.

Voice: Wha' ole man Tooga say?

Tad: You talks like a fool. Wha' he kin say?

Josey Mammy: Ole man Tooga tell de guard he know bes' an' axe him please for God' sake don't cripple him kaze he want dis boy to work for him. He all he got to 'pend on, den he thank de boss an' tell him guh bring him another chicken, he think so much on him.

Voice: Wha' de boss say?

Josey Mammy: He say he guh turn him back a good nigger, an' ole man Tooga bow an' scrape an' guin him heap o' thanks an' tell him he's a white man an' he knows bes' an' he know he guh turn him back a good nigger.

Scip: He guh turn him back a nigger.

Voice: Ain' he already a nigger?

Scip: All I says is he guh turn him back a nigger, an' I ain' guh say no more.

Fine My Chile

Voice: You ain' got no manners. Is you seed me today?

Hezekiah: See you today, en I ain't see you. I ain't know nothen 'bout no manners tonight, an' I ain't no manners, an' I ain't care nothen 'bout no manners.

Voice: How come, brother?

Hezekiah: I come from Dry Branch to Pea Ridge, and when I come against the Barrs Field by Miss Jimmie Crossin', a little ooman, with a check gingham dress, with a red handkerchief 'roun' her head and a big bunch of key hang from her apron, stan' in front of me an' I hail her, an' she say "Wey my chile?" An' she look at me, an' she act like she guine jine me. An' she ain't look natural, an' I move to walk and she walk 'side me an' she say "Wey my chile?" An' she ain't say nothen but "Wey my chile?" An' I walk fas', an' I run an' she run, an' I turn off Pea Ridge Crossing an' she riz' up 'afore me, an' she ain't tech de groun', an' she say, "Fine my chile!" an' she float way off in de air, an' atter she gone I hear in de bush, in de field an' in de air, in de cloud an' in de sky, I hear "Wey my chile?" "Fine my chile!" An' it ain't been natural an' it ain' been life, an' she ain't holler, an' she ain't cry. She just moan, "Wey my chile? Fine my chile"! It ain't been life, an' it might have been death, but it ain't been natural. My ears is bustin' an' my head is full, an' I ain't hear nothen' but de moanin' of de ooman, "Wey my chile? Fine my chile!"

An' I done hear it in de night when de sun is shet out, on de dark night and on de moon-lit night, dis ooman walk, an' dey ain't no ooman, an' dey ain't nothen but de onrestless sperrit, an' it walk from Pea Ridge to Dry Branch, an' she always moan, an' the soun' of her voice an' de rattle of her key, an' her gingham dress an' her red handkerchief, an' de light of her eyes could be seen on de earth, an' de soun' of her voice could be heard in de skies, an' in de dark bushes, an' in de air, an' out in de night de sinful will hear, "Wey my chile? Fine my chile!"

Over de fields and across de woods, from Pea Ridge to Dry Branch, "Wey my chile? Fine my chile!"

Purtty Little Folks

Old Rhody: Mornin'.

Voice: Good mornin' Aun' Rhody.

Old Rhody: You up soon, Bubber.

Voice: Yes, Aunt Rhody, I been up since fo' day.

Old Rhody: Wuh you see?

Voice: I see de sun rise.

Old Rhody: Is dat all you see? If you look close you see more'n sun rise.

Voice: What you talk 'bout Aun' Rhody, tell we?

Old Rhody: If you look close at dat time, 'twixt darkness an' daylight you see de purtty people an' curious little folks what's so perticular 'bout what dey do an' wey dey steps.

Voice: Who is dey, Aun' Rhody, tell we?

Old Rhody: I ain't know who dey is, but dey is de little folks of de sperrit-world, de purtty little folks an' dey don't do no harm, an' you see 'em 'twixt night an' mornin' an' dey walks on de leaves, an' if you look up in de tree you see 'em step from leaf to leaf, an' dey walk down de limbs on de leaf an' dey steps on dey toes like dey's dancin' an' like dey ain't know nothen but joy, an' dey come out of heben, an' dey walks on dey toes, an' dey steps from leaf to leaf, an' dey steps so light till dey walks on de spider webs an' de swings dey-self from stran to stran.

Fuh dey is de purtty little folks an' dey don't do nothen ugly an' dey don't walk on nothen ugly. Dey walks on de jue-drops, an' dey dances on de blossoms, an' dey ain't do no harm an' dey looks like dey come out of heben; for dey is de little folks, de purtty little folks, an' dey comes 'twixt night and mornin'; an' dey walks on de spider-webs an' dey home's in heben. Dey comes 'twixt darkness an' dawn an' 'pears for a short time, an' dey pass in de mist.

Fuh dey is de purtty little folks.

The Falling Star

There is a superstition among the negroes of Lower Richland County that it is a great offense to point your hand at a falling star, the idea being that they come from heaven. I was walking down the road between Pea Ridge and Pine Bluff, and pointed my hand at a falling star and called an old negro's attention to it. He caught my hand, pulled it down, and said:

Brother, don' pint your han' at a fallin' star.

Jesus sets on he throne in heben, an' he watch all de night theu, an' he watch a sinful world, and den is de fallin' stars, an' Jesus weeps on he throne in heben, and dem is de tears of Jesus, fallin' for a sinful world.

Dem is de sparks of heben, dem is de fallin' stars, and dem is de tears of Jesus, fallin' on a sinful world. Don' pint your han' brother, don' pint your han', for dem is de tears of Jesus, fallin' on a sinful world. Dem is de lights from de throne in heben, dem is de tears of Jesus.

Don' pint your han' Brother, don' pint your han' at a fallin' star.

Jay-Birds

Sam Leck: Bubber, where you been?

Boy: I been back in de woods wid my tap-stick, trying to kill a jay-bird.

Sam Leck: You ain't want kill no jay-bird, ain't you know jay-bird bad luck to kill?

Voice: Tell us about it, Leck?

Sam Leck: Jay-bird is a mighty busy bird. When you see him in dis worl' he here fer rest and fer git wood. Every Friday jay-bird fly to hell and carry wood fer de devil. If it ain't been fer jay-bird dey ain't been no room in hell fer sinners. Jay-bird keeps de fires of hell burnin', and you know he totes a heep of wood as sinful as dis worl' is. No Bubber, you ain't want kill no jay-bird. It is bad luck! It is bad luck! Is you hear how stressful jay-bird holler? Is you know wuh make he holler' stressful? Case he see so much stressful sights. When jay-bird fly to hell atter he t'row he wood on de fire he fly up on de high rocks and rest he-self, an' pleasure he-self, lookin' down on de burnin' sinners, set and laugh, and make game. Jay-bird like a man wid blood on he hans'. Dey ain't no rest fer him. Man got blood on he hans', jay-bird got blood in he heart. Jay-bird a 'stressful bird an' he see some 'stressful sights. No Bubber, don't kill no jay-bird! Don't kill no jay-bird, fer it's bad luck.

Jay-bird is a 'stressful bird, an' he see some 'stressful sights. He see some 'stressful sights.

Jack-Ma-Lantern

Jake: Who you reckon dat walk up and down dat ditch an' 'bout dat mash?

Bruzer: I ain't know.

Jake: Ain't you see 'em wid dat light bob up and down like dey lost sumpen?

Bruzer: I ain't know who dey is, dey must be sumpen perticular make 'em walk all around in de rain an' brier. I see 'em but I ain't know wuh ail 'em.

Hooten: You sure God ain't know. Dat ain't no people. Dat's a Jack-ma-lantern an' you best l'um 'lone. You ain't know what kind of danger dey lead you in if you follow 'em.

Jake: Wuh make dey lead you in danger. Ain't you kin stop follow 'em when you see danger.

Hooten: If dey gits a holt on you and you follow 'em, it don't lead you to no good. When you starts to follow, one mind will tell you l'um 'lone and turn back, and another mind will tell you follow 'em, and you follow 'em.

Jake: What's a Jack-ma-lantern?

Hooten: A Jack-ma-lantern is a sperrit. It is a evil sperrit. It is ole folks. Sinful ole folks. It is folks wuh ain't 'lowed in heben and can't get in hell, and dey punishment is to wander in de bad places and on de bad night, and dey business is enticing mens to follow 'em, an' dey ain't got no res', les' dey entice mens to lef' de right road. Is you 'member Ole man Lunnen? Well you know he been a ole man, and he been wise, and ole man Lunnen tell me, he say, one time he been walking down de road and he been wid dis same ole man, July Uncle, dey call him "Hock," and say, him and Hock walk down dis road and dey see a light walking right out in dat dere mash and Hock say he guh see who it is and ole man Lunnen say he try to 'suade Hock to stay in de road. Hock say he ain't scared he guin dere and ole man Lunnen say he ain't guh have nothin' to do wid it, and Hock left him, and ole man Lunnen say de last time he see Hock dat night Hock been fallin' in de hole and scramblin' in de brier, and dat night Hock ain't come home and den dey search for him and dey find him that night back in de high grass and brier on Hog-Pen-Gut, and he stan' in de mud up to he knee, and he reared back wid he head pulled back holdin' both han' out in front of him like he tryin' to 'fend hisself and he look in he face and he eye wide open and de look on he face were terrible, like it were froze, and he put han' on him and he war stiff dead.

Ole Man Rouse

Cricket: Fishin' ain't seems to be right. I been fishin' all day and catch heap of fish 'en I try to catch coota but I ain't ketch 'em. Everything look wrong and everything been wrong. The water ain't look right, an' the sky ain't look right, an' I ain't like the soun' in the trees, soun' like de win' come theu de tree, soun' like I hear a voice, an' dey ain't no voice an' dey ain't no win', an' everywhere I go, everywhere I look I think I see sumpen an' dey ain't nuthen. Every cypress tree look like it guin raise up an' walk off or say somethin'. Dey is all kind of noise everywhere, an' dey ain't no noise. De sky look yaller an' de water look yaller. Everything look yaller an' it ain't yaller. Everything look like a sturbance an' it ain't no sturbance. I ain't know wuh it is, but it feel like sumpen guin bus' loose an' I look over on a log an' I see a lot of yaller bellies, an' while I look I see a man put he han' up out de water an' lif' hesself up on de log. Look like he stoop over an' he head ben' down, an' I see him stretch heself an' draw heself up, an' I get a little closer, an' I look and it ain't a man, it a coota, an' I know a yaller belly don't get dat big, an' it ain't no other kind of coota sets on a log, an' I gets closer an' de big coota steps off de log an' wey he steps in de water he don' make no stirbance an' he don't make no soun'. He don't make no riffle, an' de water smooth as glass, an' I looks at de little yallow bellies an' dey ain't dere, an' I turns roun' wid my boat an' as I pass out I see a lizzard run in a hollow tree an' he turn roun' an' peep out an open he mout' and laugh, an' I ain't know if he a lizzard, an' I ain't know if he laugh, en I come out, an' I feel like I ain't livin'.

Peter: I ain't never think too much of fishin' here in de Big Cypress.

Voice: Wuh make?

Peter: Everything you see here ain't sumpen. Everything you hear ain't sumpen. It ain't natural. Cricket ain't see no coota, but Cricket see a man. Dat man was ole Man Rouse. Ole Man Rouse wuh a white man, an' he live in slavery-time. He ain't had no heart when he sober, en when he drunk God knows what he had. When he git mad at a nigger heh wey he punish him. He punish him in slavery time, an' he punish him in freedom, an' here in Big Cypress is wey he punish he niggers, wey he drown 'em, en one time he come here fishin'. He been out on dat log an' de niggers push him off, an' he clim' back, an' dey kept on pushin' him off till he ain't clim' back; an' he sperrit live in Big Cypress.

If You Want to Find Jesus

A preacher in Charleston was holding a revival and he had one text he preached. Every night he said his text, "Well, Sisters and brothers, my subject tonight as before, I usually preaches every night one thing, I preaches one chapter about gainin' sinners, and it is my work to go out sinner hunting and devil driving."

And the Sisters say to him, "Yes, Buddy, that is what we want, to drive the devil. God send you here." "Yes," he says, "I want to gain sinners for the Kingdom of God, and my subject will be tonight my stan-by as before, 'sinners, ef you wants to find Jesus, come on the Lord's side.' "

And he was preaching that way every night, and a little boy got to studying devilment. They had a little glass on the altar where the preacher drank to clear his throat. And the little boy went and set a glass of whiskey up there. And he start his text that night. And after a while he went to clear his throat, and he missed the water and got hold of the whiskey glass, and he got to feeling good and commenced to preach sure enough then, and he said, "Sinners, ef you wants to find Jesus, come on the Lord's side." The Sisters moaning over there in the corner, "Um-m-m-m, um-m-m-m, tell it, Brother, tell it. If you wants to find Jesus, come on the Lord's side."

He felt like a drink again and he took that same glass and drank it about half way, and he start sure enough, "Sinners, I says, if you wants to find Jesus come on the Lord's side, come on the Lord's side." And the Sisters started to moaning. And the little boy went over in the corner where he had a banjo, and he saw the preacher had took about half of it and he took his little banjo and he hit it, tum, lum, tum, lum, tum, lum. And the preacher listened over there, and that sounded good when he was drinking, and he reached back and he got that glass and dreen it, and the sisters got to moaning sure enough and the little boy thought he had the preacher about right and he started to picking right. Tum, lum, tum, lum, tum, a lum tum and turned the church into a dance and they all got to dancing with the music.

Tad: Paul, where do you live now?

Paul: I stays up at de old street.

Tad: What old street?

Paul: The old street up to 'Elm Savannah.'

Tad: Buddy, I thought you ain't been stayed up to de big house.

Paul: Wuh make?

Tad: No, my Jesus. No, Buddy, I ain't want nothen to do wid dat place. No my brother, I done got my belly full on it.

Paul: Cap'n Bob stay dere, 'en he say he fare mighty well, 'en he been here a long time. Coase I ain't know too much 'bout de big house. I ain't visit there too frequent, 'cep' in de day-time.

Tad: My Brother, dat what I talk 'bout. I visit there in de Big Day, 'en dem white folks was standin' on de front piazza shooten' people's cows on dey oats. Dey been shootin' cows and drinkin' liquor en tellin' tales 'en cussin' scandalous. Great God! Dem sure is bad folks. And when I been standin' there everything been still and dey ain't been a breath of air stirrin' 'en I see de front gate open. It opened slow and wide, like a man han' been on it, en' I ain't see de han', 'en it stay open long 'nuf for somebody to walk in, an den I see de gate close, 'en a man han' close it, an' I ain't see de man, an' I ain't seen he han', an' I tell Cap'n Bob 'bout it, an' he say, "go 'way fum here an' shet you lyin' mout'. I'm tired you niggers come 'roun' here an' create stirbance an' tell lie" 'en I say 'I ain't tell no lie. Jesus my Judge. I seen 'it. 'En Cap'n Bob say, "Bubber, you seen it, an' I seen it, an' I see it all de time, an' I see more'n it, an' it ain't nothin' to talk 'bout. It ain't been nobody but ole Marster, an' he visit here frequent."

Paul: How much time you see dat gate open?

Tad: I seen it one time, an' I lef' Buddy, I lef', 'en I ain't tarry.

The Crow

He set to preaching a text every night 'bout gainen sinners. And he was preaching several years and preaching one text, and said to the congregation, he says, "Sisters and brothers, dey come an' remark, 'some people say you preach one text all of de time,' but when John was preaching on de river Jerden he didn't have but one text, and his text was, Repent and be baptized, an' dat was his one subject. Atter dat John would go preachin' and preachin' until Jesus, the Master, come to him to be baptized. An' my subject is one text, I don't preach but one text, Sisters and Brothers, and that is, Sinners, you want to find Jesus; go down below. My subject is, you want to find Jesus; go down below." Old Sister answered him in the corner, "Yes, Buddy, dat is de way I fine him I went down below. Dat is what I say. My standpoint is if you want Jesus, go down below! Go down below!"

And while he was preaching every night dere was a crow got familiar with de text, an' he flewed up in the loft over de pulpit, and he heard him preachin' his text dat night, "Sinners, if you want to find Jesus, go down below! Go down below!" After the crow got familiar with it the crow flewed out de loft of de church an' lit on de altar and turn he head one side an' look up at de preacher, an' say, "Go down below," an' de preacher went right down below. He jump over de altar and de people screamed an' crowded one another, and in getting away dey jumped out of windows, so dat dey got all mixed up under de quire in front of de door, an' de crow got frightened hisself and flewed across de church an' lit on a old lady's shoulder, who could not get out, an' he look up in de old lady face an' say: "Go down below!" An' she said, "Do Bubber, I jest come here on a visit. Dis ain't my church."

An' atter that he change he tex'.

Primus

Scip: Dey put the fixings on Primus today.

Voice: Wuh he do?

Scip: Dey scuse 'im of stealin' two automobile tires.

Voice: Tell we.

Scip: Primus see a automobile in de ditch' side de road an' stole two tires off en it. He ain't steal 'em good 'fore he sell 'em. De police ketch 'im an' de judge fine 'em twenty fi' dollahs.

Voice: Who tire dey been?

Scip: Ain' nobody know.

Voice: Primus show is lucky. How come de judge luh 'im off dat easy? Look like he headed for de gang.

Scip: De judge is a good man. He say he temper he justice wid mercy, but he got to broke up stealin'.

Voice: Wuh dey do wid de tire ef dey ain' know who dey b'long to?

Scip: De judge put one on he car, an' de police put one on he car.

Voice: An' Primus pay de twenty fi' dollahs?

Scip: Ain't Primus stole de tires?

Jumping-Gut

Scene: Mt. Moriah Church.

Rev. Lowman: Brothers and Sisters, I is here today before God an' he chillun to pronounce de death of Yandy Yow.

Voices in Congregation: Yes, tell us, Brother.

Rev. Lowman: Yes, Brothers and Sisters, Yandy die, and he die wid a 'ooman in he mine an' eagle flop in he face.

Congregation: Flop in he face,
Flop in he face, yes,
Flop in he face.

Rev. Lowman: An he met a eagle on Jumpin' Gut.

Voices: Jumpin' Gut,
Jumpin' Gut,
Jumpin' Gut.
An' a eagle flop in he face,
Flop in he face,
Flop in he face,
On Jumpin' Gut.

Rev. Lowman: Yes, Sister, a eagle fly in he face on Jumpin' Gut.

Sisters, on Jumpin' Gut! on Jumpin' Gut.
Flewed in he face on Jumpin' Gut!
An' he fought on de road from Jumpin' Gut, an' he fought wid a eagle, an' he died on Jumpin' Gut,
An' a eagle flop in he face.

Sisters: Yes!

Voices from Various parts of the Congregation:
Flop in he face!
Flop in he face!
Flop in he face!
On Jumpin' Gut!

Oh, Lord, a eagle flewed in he face,
Flewed in he face,
Flewed in he face,

On Jumpin' Gut,
On Jumpin' Gut,
On Jumpin' Gut.

Jube: Wey Mensa?

Sam: You ain' know Mensa, is you? If you is know him you know he ain't gur set round here in dis swamp an' waste he time wid a passel er mens. He gone to er entertainment.

Jube: Wuh kind of entertainment?

Sam: Dey got a party for de preacher, him an' he young wife.

Jake: Buddy, I'm wid you. Wuh fuh kind er man is Mensa? He ain't look to me like he bus' he heart out runnin' atter preacher.

Sam: He ain't lossin' no time runnin' atter preacher. He ain't lossin' no time wid no mens. Mensa's a hawk, swift as lightnin', wicked as pizen, sure as death. Mens likes him an' wimmen b'longs to him wid he soft way, an' he bad ways. He ain't look like a panter for nuthen. The Bible say God make us, but when I see Mensa sumpen tell me maybe de debel have he han' in it. I ain't know but he sure is got some frightenin' ways.

Lias: Wuh make you all back-bite Mensa? Ain't you say he gone to er church entertainment? He mought be seekin' for de light.

Sam: Brother, he mought be seekin' for de light. I done tell you who de entertainment for. I done tell you Mensa gur be dere, an' my advice to dat preacher is you better skip. Bur Rabbit, de ole field is a fire and de hawk is here.

Preb: (Enters scratched and bleeding, clothes torn, muttering:) Huh, pup, huh! Huh, pup, huh!

Voice: Wha' ail you, Preb?

Preb: Ain't nothin' ail me. You must be ailin' yourself. Is you blind? Can't you see dem dogs?

Second Voice: Preb must be lossin' he mind.

Preb: What make I loss my mind?

Voice: How come you to call dog when dey ain't no dog? How you say you see dog when dey ain't no dog, how come?

Preb: Brother, if you been wid me you see dog, 'en you see more'n dog? You see snake, an' hear 'em bark, bark like dog. I come out 'er mill pasture an' I hear dog bark, an' I look, an' heap 'er little dog an' snake all tangled up 'twixt my feets an' hit look like I guine step on 'em, an' I ain't step on 'em, an' all down mill-dam dem dog bark and snake tangle up 'twixt my feets, an' I lef de mill-dam an' I to'd out theu de brier an' dey kept wid me, an' dey tangle up 'twixt my feets an' dey bark, an' dey come here wid me, an' you ain't hear 'em bark, an' you ain't see 'em. Ain't nobody see 'em but me. Ain't nobody hear 'em but me, an' dey tangle up 'twixt my feets.

Spencer: Brother, you see 'em an' I see 'em. Dem is sperrit dogs, an' dey run dese woods an' dey run wid de barkin' snakes, and dey run on certain night an' dey wait dey own time an' dey run in mill-pasture an' Black Lake, an' dey home is God knows way, an' dey is a sign, a onlucky sign, which pass dis way 'afore de earth-quake, an' dey come here wid de storm, an' 'afore death, an' 'afore war, and it is a sign of 'stress. Dey is de barkin' snakes an' sperrit dogs, an' dey travel in de night of storm, an' dey travel in de night of 'stress, an' dey tangles 'twixt de feets of men, and all men is feared ur de sperrit dogs an' de barkin' snakes. Dey come 'afore death an' in time of 'stress, an' dey tangles 'twixt de feets of men.

Death Owl

Long Jim: Hush your fuss.

Voice: Wuh fuh we hush we fuss?

Long Jim: You ain't hear dat det' owl, is you?

Voice: We hear him. What dat got to do wid we fuss? Det' owl got he mout', we got we mout', det' owl holler, we laugh.

Long Jim: Dis ain't no time to talk about det' owl got he mout' and you got you mout', when det' owl holler you laugh, when you laugh det' owl holler.

Voice: How come, brother, you ain't want we laugh when det' owl holler, tell we.

Long Jim: You make fuss, you ain't know wuh fuh you make fuss, det' owl know wuh he do. When det' owl holler somebody guh dead, somebody sperrit guh enter de sky, somebody sperrit guh pass in de night. Don't you laugh and don't you holler, an' don't you make game at a det' owl, fuh when det' owl holler it's a warning, somebody soul guh enter de sky, somebody guh flap he wings across de burnin' lake. It ain't no fun, and it ain't no joke, and it ain't nothin' fuh make game. Det' owl ain't no owl, and he ain't no bird. Det' owl de lost sperrit of a lonesome soul. He de scarified sperrit. No, Bubber, don't kill no det' owl. Don't kill no det' owl fer it's bad luck. Det' owl 'stressful bird, and he see some 'stressful sights. An' he ain't got no fren' an' he ain't got no company but de partin' sperrits, an' he fly wid 'em to de far shore. He rest in de hollow tree, an' he live in de night, an' he visit on de far shore. He de voice of de onrestless sperrit, he de soun' of death, an' he ain't nothen fer ter make game at. He de onrestless sperrit an' he fly with the partin' sperrits to de far shore an' de soun' of he voice is a notice of sorrow an' it's answer is weeping. He ain't nothen fer make game at. He ain't nothen fer pleasure, for he voice is de soun' of sorrow, an' de answer is tears.

De Law Got Simon

Scip: Gentlemen's!

Voices: How do, Scip?

Scip: Sorter slow.

Voice: Is you well?

Scip: Middlin', is you hear de news?

Voice: We ain't hear no news, tell us, brother?

Scip: Well, de law got Simon.

Voice: Who got Simon?

Scip: De law got him.

Voice: How come, what he do?

Scip: Kilt a white 'ooman.

Voice: How come he kilt a white 'ooman?

Scip: I ain't know, and if I know I ain't say. All I say Simon kilt a white 'ooman an' de law got him. I see him an' he face twis' an' swell up, an' he eye red, an' he ain't say nothin' an' de law got him. He ain't say nothin' kaze he heart black an' he mind white an' de law got Simon.

Voice: Have mercy!

Second Voice: Dey ain't no mercy.

Third Voice: Jesus!

Fourth Voice: God have mercy!

Scip: Ain't I tell you de law got Simon?

Old Daniel: Simon ain't nothin'. He ain't bird-dog an' he ain't houn'. He ain't nothin'.

Voice: How come Simon ain't nothin'?

Old Daniel: Simon Daddy white, Simon' Mammy black, Simon ain't nothin'. He got a nigger heart an' a white man head, an' dat's a mighty poor mixtry. What Simon head say Simon heart ain't know, an' what Simon heart say Simon head tangle up. He ain't white an' he ain't black, an' he ain't nothin'. White man spiles the nigger in him an' nigger spiles the white man. He born tangle up an' he guh die tangle up, an' all I can say is God forgive he Daddy and God love he Mammy an' God have mercy on Simon. He ain't nigger, en he ain't white, an' he ain't nothin'. He born tangle up.

Scip: Well, all I say is, de law got Simon.

A Fool Nigger

Harriet: Tad, wey you been?

Tad: I been over to de mill.

Harriet: Who you see dere?

Tad: A passel of niggers. Is you hear de news?

Harriet: Wuh news?

Tad: Blake an' Louisa done part. Blake is such a fool. You ain' hear de fun, is you?

Harriet: Wuh fun?

Tad: Dat one twis' horn cow of Blake's hook Louisa, an' she been moanin' an' groanin' an' Blake, a ole fool, send for a Doctor, a nigger, an' when he come instead of he axe Louisa how she feel an' 'zamine her, he went out in de yard an 'zamine de cow, an' den he went to de pizer where Louisa been layin' on a pallet an' he say, 'Sister, I think your cow'll git all right. She don't seems to have nothin' serious,' an Louisa all swell up an' git so hot about it she run de Doctor off, an' Blake tried to 'suade her he send for a cow Doctor kase a cow hook her, then she run Blake. A fool nigger show is a fool.

The Two Ducks

Dere was er ole man, you know, he had a daughter, and he tell he daughter he had invited a preacher to he house, and he say, "Daughter, I guine down to de train to meet de Reverend, and bake two ducks and leave 'em dere for him, don't tech 'em." And she said, "No, I ain't guh tech 'em." And he go to de train to meet de Reverend, and de gal taste de ducks, and dey taste good, and she taste 'em till she taste 'em all up.

And atter de ole man come, he never look in de place wey he had he ducks, and he went in de other room to sharpen he knife on the oil stove, and de preacher was settin' in de room wid de gal. She knewed her papa was guine to whip her, and she started to snifflin' 'bout it, and de preacher say, "What is de matter, daughter?" And she say, "Dat's all de fault I find wid papa,—papa go invite preachers to he house and go and sharpen he knife to cut off both dey years." And de Reverend say, "What is dat, daughter?" And de gal say, "Yes, papa invite preachers here all de time and cut off both dey years." And he say, "Daughter, han' me my hat quick." And de gal guin hem he hat and he run out. And she call her papa and say, "Papa, de preacher got both de ducks and gone." And he run to de door and holler to him and say, "Hey, hey, wey you guine? Come back here!" And de preacher answer him and say, "Damned ef you'll git either one of dese."

And he raise a dust de way he flewed down de road. And de ole tales tell you dat womens has always been sharper dan mens.

The Mule and the Ox

A ox and a mule was workin' together in de same wagon. One day de mule say to de ox, "Look here, Ber Ox, you got to do better, you let me do all de work. If you ain't do better, you guh be kilt, kaze I heared de butcher talkin' to our boss today, and he say, 'Dat ox would make mighty fine beef, I would like to buy him from you.' Ox, if you don't change your ways, you guh be kilt."

And de ox say to de mule, "I ain't guh change my ways for nobody. I'm guh keep on jes like I always been doin', and you jes 'member dis, if I is kilt, my hide will be a terrance to you de balance of your days."

And ever since den mens have been whippin' mules wid ox hides.

That Quart Kept on Beckoning Me

Tad: I done laugh till I mighty nigh bus open.

Scip: Wuh make you laugh?

Tad: Jim.

Scip: Wuh Jim?

Tad: Ole Crazy Jim wuh works for de white folks, an' be ain' so crazy nuther.

Voice: Tell we 'bout it.

Tad: Well, de white folks come down to Congaree wid striped pants on an' a jim swinger coat dat wouldn't take a lick off'n him, wid a red flower in he button hole. He look so good he look like he guh git married or serve God, or like he guh do sompen you can't put no 'pendence in, an' he called Jim an' he said, "Jim, you been a faithful servant to me an' I wants to show you my 'preciation by presenting you with this little token of my esteem," den he hand Jim a quart of liquor, an' he says, "Jim, I want you to take charge of my kitchen tomorrow. I has some distinguished ladies and gentlemens comin' as my guests. I want you to cook breakfast an' prepare my Christmas dinner." Jim thank him an' tell him he look like the president of the Nunited States and tell him he guh do some cookin' ain't nobody never see nothin' like it 'efore, an' dey both went off perfectly satisfied, 'cept I ain't blame Jim for looking satisfied.

Tad: When breakfast come, ain't everybody satisfied.

Voice: How come?

Tad: Jim been in dat kitchen at sun-up. He 'larmed de neighborhood singin' hymns. He woked up everybody in de big house, an' de boss was rollin' 'round so uneasy he look like he have fleas on him. He act like he scared to git out er bed. Ole Miss ain't been able to stand it; she jump out er bed an' dash down to de kitchen, an' when she git dere Jim been makin' batter cakes on de kitchen shelf an' tryin' to turn 'em over. He say dey look like dey won't brown, an' Ole Miss been hot, she say, "What are this? I ain't goin' to have no such doings. What will de Bishop think?" An' she run Jim off. But dat ain't all.

Dere ain't nobody dere can cook no Christmas dinner. An' de boss say he very much disturbed dat dis is a most unfortunate state of affairs.

Voice: Wuh he do?

Tad: De white folks git so unrestless till dey went down to see Jim an' axe him can't he git he self together an' cook dat dinner an' wuh make him act so bad.

Voice: Wuh Jim say?

Tad: Jim say he wants to do he duty an' keep he promise, an' when he sing hymns he serves God, an' de Missus hurt he feelins when she say he ain't know nothin' 'bout makin' no batter cakes an' he ain't fitten to cook for a bishop. Atter while him an' de white folks make it all right, an' he say wuh make him act dat er way he tooken dat liquor home an' teched it two or three times, an' every time he tech it an' went to 'tend to he business dat bottle er liquor beckoned him, an' time he go an' tech it an' lef' it would beckon him again, an' atter he touch it four or five times more, it kept on beckonin' him, an' he got to studyin' 'bout it, an' he say he make up he mind he guh let nothin' beckon him an' keep on beckon' him dat er way widout he geein' answer, so he just went back dere an' finish drink up dat quart.

Scip: Brother, he ain't de onliest one a quart er liquor beckons to, an' most un 'em gees answer.

Don't 'Sturb a Houn'

Don't 'sturb a houn' when he is howlin',
When he is howlin' at the moon.
Fer he sees sumpen, and he knows sumpen,
An' it mought be the face of God, shinin' in de moon.
Fer he sees sumpen, an' he knows sumpen!
An' he can't tell it.
Don't 'sturb a houn' when he is howlin',
When he is howlin' at the moon.
Fer dey's sumpen on he mine,
An' dey's sumpen in he heart,
An' dey's sorrow in he voice.
Don't 'sturb a houn' when he is howlin',
When he is howlin' at de moon.
Fer he is lookin' in the face of God,
An' he can't tell it,
An' der is trouble in he soul,
An' der is sorrow in he voice,
An' he can't tell it.
Don't 'sturb a houn' when he is howlin',
When he is howlin' at the moon.
Fer he sees sumpen, and he knows sumpen,
An' he can't tell it,
When he's howlin, when he's howlin' at the moon.

Don't You Play wid Married Wimmens

Don't you play wid married wimmens,
For dere's 'nuff of other wimmens, willin' wimmens, in de worl',
For de worl' is full of wimmens, willin' wimmens.
If you has your wimmens, don't have 'em roun' your home.

For de worl' is full of wimmens, willin' wimmens,
Anywhere you go.
Don't play wid chillun,
Take 'em when dey's grown,
An' take 'em 'way from home,
For de worl' is full of wimmens, willin' wimmens,
An' take 'em far from home.

Keep your business in your mine,
An' don't tell it to your fren',
For de worl' is full of wimmens, willin' wimmens,
An' if you take 'em, take 'em far from home.

Don't take 'em in de daylight,
Fine 'em in de night,
An' lef' 'em where you fine 'em,
For de worl' is full of wimmens, willin' wimmens,
An' you better take 'em far, far from home.

Tad's Advice to His Son

Don't trust a 'ooman,
She's a curious thing,
When she's right she'll die to save you,
An' when she's wrong she'll die to git you.

There's danger in de trut',
When a lie will do de work,
Tell it to a 'ooman,
Tell her what she loves to hear.

Tell her she's de only 'ooman,
Tell her dat your heart is bursting,
An' your head is swimmin',
An' dere ain't no other wimmens.

What a 'ooman loves to hear is soft and sweet,
Dere's danger in de trut',
An' a lie will do de work.
A lie will do de work wid a 'ooman,
An' de trut' is sure to hurt.

When you're talking to a 'ooman,
Talk as soft as a breath of air creepin' t'ru a crack.
Be as calm as a mouse crawlin' on a carpet.
An' when you're breakin' loose from her,
A lie will do de work.
Take her in your arms, and whisper in her ear.

Be gentle as a ray of moon-light fallin' on a flower.
Be tender as a mother's song, floating on de air.
If you know'd it you'd be careful in a bed of rattle-snakes,
So be careful when a 'ooman's near.

Soft talk is cheap,
It ain't cost you nothen

An' when you dealin' wid a 'ooman,
Dere's danger in de trut',
An' a lie will do de work.

Old Sister's Advice to Her Daughter

Don't trus' mens,
But keep your feets flat,
Flat upon de groun'

Don't listen to no easy talk,
Don't l'em 'suade you,
For de worl' is full of lying mens,
Just keep your feets flat,
Flat upon de groun'.

De Bible says dey all is liars,
And Jesus knows 'tis true,
De more fair dey talk,
De worse dey is.
Sister, keep your feets flat,
Flat upon de groun'.

Don't l'em 'suade you,
Don't listen to no easy talk,
If dey axe a unfair question,
Keep your feets flat,
Flat upon de groun',
For dey is devils,
An' dey is atter you,
So keep your feets flat,
Flat upon de groun'.

Don't you risk 'em,
An' don't you trus' 'em,
For if you listen to dey honey
You might not keep your feets flat,
Flat upon de groun'.
For dey'll kiss you and dey'll love you,

An' talk as soft and pretty as de jue
  upon a flower,
But dey'll lef' you wid a laugh,
If you don't keep your feets flat,
Flat upon de groun'.

Jesus Had Trouble All over the World

Jesus had trouble all over the world,
With Adam and Eve, Cain and Abel,
Jesus had trouble, Jesus had trouble,
Trouble all over the world,
 Oh, Lord! Save my soul.

Jesus had trouble all over the world,
With the flood, Noah and the Ark,
Jesus had trouble, Jesus had trouble,
Trouble all over the world,
 Oh, Lord! Save my soul.

Jesus had trouble all over the world,
With Shem, Ham and Japhet,
Jesus had trouble, Jesus had trouble,
Trouble all over the world,
 Oh, Lord! Save my soul.

Jesus had trouble all over the world,
With Abraham, Isaac and Jacob,
Jesus had trouble, Jesus had trouble,
Trouble all over the world,
 Oh, Lord! Save my soul.

Jesus had trouble all over the world,
With the children in the wilderness,
Jesus had trouble, Jesus had trouble,
Trouble all over the world,
 Oh, Lord! Save my soul.

Jesus had trouble all over the world,
With Absolum, David and Joab,
Jesus had trouble, Jesus had trouble,

Trouble all over the world,
  Oh, Lord! Save my soul.

Jesus had trouble all over the world,
With the high Priests in the temple,
Jesus had trouble, Jesus had trouble,
Trouble all over the world,
  Oh, Lord! Save my soul.

Jesus had trouble all over the world,
With Jezebel, Jonah and Judas,
Jesus had trouble, Jesus had trouble,
Trouble all over the world,
  Oh, Lord! Save my soul.

Jesus had trouble all over the world,
With Delilah, Saul and Samson,
Jesus had trouble, Jesus had trouble,
Trouble all over the world,
  Oh, Lord! Save my soul.

Jesus had trouble all over the world,
With Herod and his avenging angel,
Jesus had trouble, Jesus had trouble,
Trouble all over the world,
  Oh, Lord! Save my soul.

Jesus had trouble all over the world,
With John the Baptist and Salome,
Jesus had trouble, Jesus had trouble,
Trouble all over the world,
  Oh, Lord! Save my soul.

Jesus had trouble all over the world,
With Lazarus, Dives and Pilate,
Jesus had trouble, Jesus had trouble,
Trouble all over the world,
  Oh, Lord! Save my soul.

Jesus had trouble all over the world,
With the Philistines, the Gentiles and the Jews,
Jesus had trouble, Jesus had trouble,
Trouble all over the world,
  Oh, Lord! Save my soul.

Jesus had trouble all over the world,
At the wedding with the water and the wine,
Jesus had trouble, Jesus had trouble,
Trouble all over the world,
  Oh, Lord! Save my soul.

Jesus had trouble all over the world,
With Peter and the Cross on the Mount,
Jesus had trouble, Jesus had trouble,
Trouble all over the world,
  Oh, Lord! Save my soul.

Jesus had trouble all over the world,
On the Cross with the thieves and the thorns,
Jesus had trouble, Jesus had trouble,
Trouble all over the world,
  Oh, Lord! Save my soul.

Jesus had trouble all over the world,
With the liars, Annanias and Sapphira,
Jesus had trouble, Jesus had trouble,
Trouble all over the world,
  Oh, Lord! Save my soul.

Jesus had trouble all over the world,
With the virgins, the wise and the foolish,
Jesus had trouble, Jesus had trouble,
Trouble all over the world,
  Oh, Lord! Save my soul.

NIGGER TO NIGGER

To

The Sportsman, Humorist, Fatalist, Philosopher

THADDEUS GOODSON

The Tad of These Sketches

Contents

Foreword

These sketches are typical of the negroes of lower Richland County and the great swamps of the Congaree. This section is in the heart of South Carolina and within a few miles of the capital city, Columbia. It is remarkable that so definite a survival of the negro of Africa as modified by white relationships should be maintained in such purity in the very midst of so exclusive a white culture.

These stories show the influence of slavery, the dread of the overseer—escapes and capture—things that have lived and will always live in the memory of the negro. These memories, combined with superstitions brought from Africa and terror created by the canebrakes and jungles of the Congaree, with its lakes, streams, guts, mysterious shadows, and yellow waters, with its old fields and dikes, relics of slave days, all make up what may be called the psychology of the negro of these sketches.

The dialect is of course English shot through and influenced by the traditions and sentiments of the African slaves. Very few genuine words are distinguishable, but there is a marked influence of the African sense of melody and rhythm. This gives to every word, even if otherwise good English, a peculiar dialectal sound and significance.

It needs to be remembered that this particular dialect, while pure nigger, is neither the dialect of the coast nor of the northern part of the Black Border, but is absolutely distinct, and is the product of the soil, race, and environment. In other words, it is English as adapted to the needs and knowledge of these primitive peoples. Sometimes a word that is pronounced correctly has several dialect meanings, and several sounds of the same word may be found in a single sentence. There is no rule.

Some of the poems are fragments of sermons in which the preacher or prayer-leader has worked himself into a chant and in which he swings and sways, and members of the congregation repeat words or lines that impress them.

Many of the negroes themselves are of an unusually high type. Some are black and many have white and Indian blood.

—E. C. L. Adams

THE SWAMPS

Evil Sperrits

Tad: I seen a frightenin' thing dis evenin'.

Voice: Wuh is you see?

Tad: I ain' know exactly, but I know it ain' gee me no desire to go in de swamp.

Voice: Wuh it is?

Tad: I been standin' on de bluff lookin' out over de swamp jes as de sun was settin'. It was a great, big, red sunset. Look like a ball er fire. An' right 'gainst de sun dere was a dead snag wid de top broke off, an' one or two broke-off limbs leff on it. It were outline so clear I could er seen a hoppergrass ef he had er lit on it.

An' while I been lookin', I seen sump'n look like a varmint crawlin' 'round—crawlin' 'round sorter slow—an' I look good an' I see it ain' been no varmint but a man, hollow-eyed, grey-faced wid grinnin' teet'. He crawl all 'round slowly an' twis' he head dis er way an' dat. He ack like sump'n dead dat was movin' an' crawlin' over dat snag, more like he were draggin' he self.

An' while I watch, I see a buzzard lit on de snag an' den him an' de man went to fightin'. It were frightenin', my brothers. An' dey fought back an' forth. Some er de time it were one an' den de other dat looks as ef he was gittin' de best on it. An' as de sun fade, I see 'em fasten dey self to one annudder wid dey teet' an' bill an' claw, an' seem like I zern sump'n drap as de sun an' de snag all on 'em pass in de darkness from my sight.

Voice: You ain' find out wha' it were?

Tad: No, I ain' wan' find out.

Kike: It ain't de first time dat man an' dat buzzard fight. Dey ain' natu'al, an' been seen 'fore dis. Dey ain' natu'al, dey is evil sperrits put here to frighten mens an' womens. Dey is a notice an' a warnin', an' dey come from de place er evil sperrits. Ef you ain' serve you' God an' git to heaven, you'll go to dat land wey dem ole things is waitin' for you at every turn. Dey is a warnin', my brother, an' my agvice is: don't seek to know too much 'bout 'em. Put you' mind on other thing an' serve you' God, for dem ole evil sperrits will crowd out everything else 'fore you know it, an' dey will be in full control an' you' place on earth an' in hell will be to do dey business.

The Swamps

Tad: Is you hear de news?

Voice: Wuh news?

Tad: White folks loss in de swamp.

Scip: Wuh white folks? Us white folks?

Tad: No, my Jesus! Mighty good white folks, but ain't us white folks.

Voice: Wuh de diff'ence?

Tad: Heap er diff'ence, an' ain' so much diff'ence neither. Dey expresses dey self diff'ent—jes de diff'ence 'twix' "Do Jesus!" an' "God damn!"

Scip: Brother, 'tain't no diff'ence. All two de same when it's white folks.

Tad: I ain' guh argue wid you.

Voice: You all done ramble off. Wuh de news?

Tad: We ain' ramble off. It were white folks ramble off, an' Simon say he done some ramblin'.

He say he look at him good. He pass him several time, an' he ack like he loss he mind; he run all 'round wid he shirt tail hang out hollerin' for Jesus. He say any time anybody run 'round dem swamp hollerin' for Jesus, he know sump'n wrong. Dat ain' no place to look for Jesus. He say 'tain't none er he business, but white folks mought er been a revenue or he mought er been makin' liquor. Anyway, he ain' messes wid nobody what look wild an' hollerin' for Jesus in dem swamp. He say he 'tends to he business an' Jesus 'tends to He business; an' any time Jesus luh He business git down in dem swamp, it look like He wants to loss it, an' he ain' never guh put his self up to interfere wid de hand er God.

So he luh dem white folks wander on. He say several niggers seen de white folks, an' dey say he was a strange white folks; an' ef you wants to go in dem swamp an' live, it's best don't meddle wid nobody. So he luh him wander.

Scip: My brother, Simon been here a good while an' strange things is common in dem swamp. Dat's wey a mice looks like a deer an' a rabbit looks wuss 'an a bear, but de baddest thing in dem swamp is mens. Dere ain' no law dere.

Tad: Simon say dat de loss white folks been follow every wey he been, an' dere was other white folks dere seen him, but dey wouldn't harm him long as he ain' come too close to wey dey been cookin' dey mash.

Scip: I seen a dog in dem swamp, an' dey ain' got much sense as a loss man. All dey does is to set down an' howl, an' it is much as you kin do to bring 'em to dey senses wid a stick, dey gits so fool.

Voice: You all hab so much side talk. We ain' never guh git de full news.

Tad: Well, dat white folks wandered 'round for two days an' thought it was a hundred years, but he kep' on in de true faith an' were saved.

Voice: Wuh is de true faith?

Tad: Some say he had dis kind er religion an' some say he had another, an' one on 'em claimed he was a Methodist.

Scip: Well, ain' none er dem religions guh help him. He must er been a Baptist. Dat's de moest hope. Dere ain' but one religion can stand de mud an' briar an' de water, an' dat is de true Baptist. Dat ain' no place for sprinklin' Christians. It ain' no place for nothin' much, but varmints an' Baptists is better suited for dem dangers.

Tad: Well, I ain' guh jine you in dem ideas, but ef my judgment ain' wrong, you better put you' mind on gitten out when you is loss. You ain' got no time for prayin', de thing to do is to git out, an' it ain' matter how you git out. When you is safe, go to prayin' an' offerin' up thanks. You can't fool God wid no prayers. He got sense 'nough to know you thinkin' 'bout gitten out. You ain' thinkin' 'bout Him. He mought listen to prayin' when de danger is over, but it's too late to pray when you is lost. My brother, you better be prepared.

Scip: Tad, I ain' guh jine you in everything you say. It helps a man to pray sometime. He ain' foolin' God, but it helps him to fool his self, an' it sounds good when he gits out. Course, I knows a man ain' thinkin' 'bout no love er God when he's all tored up in a briar patch an' canebrake, an' he heart in he mout' where he has to swallow every now an' den for fear he guh injure it wid he teet'.

Scip: Dem swamp wid dey briar patch an' canebrake an' tall trees wid vine wrop 'round 'em ain' never been nothin' to create no joy in me. In de daytime dey is dark when de sun is shinin', an' night is wusser. All de night birds an' varmints starts to movin' an' makin' diff'ent sounds. Some on 'em whispers, some cries, an' dem ole owls makes you cold from one end er you' backbone to de other.

Voice: Dey tells me men's bones has been found in dem swamp all whiten up from de elements. Dey ain' hardly can tell human bones from hog bones cepen dey head an' some er dey bones is a little diff'ent shape.

Scip: Dere's a heap er humans in dem swamp wha' looks more like hogs when dey is livin' dan when dey is dead.

The Lonesome Hunter

Does you hear de hunter's horn?
I hear it ring across de swamp;
De lonesome hunter,
De lonesome hunter's horn.
For he hunts in de night
In de lonely river swamp;
De lonesome hunter.
I hear de ringin'
Of de lonesome hunter's horn.

Up an' down de river bank
An' across de river swamp,
From flat lake to de river,
When de water's low,
He rides across de swamp;
De lonesome hunter.
I hear de ringin'
Of de lonesome hunter's horn.

An' when de water's high,
De drippin' of his paddle
An' de river's water's swishin';
An' far across de river swamp,
De lonesome hunter.
I hear de ringin'
Of de lonesome hunter's horn.

His home de trees an' vines,
De canebrakes an' de briar.
An' when de river's high,
All around de yellow waters,
De angry river waters,
I can hear de ringin' of his horn;
De lonesome hunter.

I hear de ringin'
Of de lonesome hunter's horn.

Who's de lonesome hunter?
Dat I ain't guh tell.
He's roamed dese swamps
For twenty years.
He killed a man, he killed a man,
An' he roams dese swamps.

I ain't guh tell.
I goes in dese swamps;
It's here I has my hogs;
I hunts an' fishes,
An' I ain't guh tell.
He killed a man, he killed a man,
He's roamed dese swamps
For twenty years.

He change he name
An' he lives alone,
He killed a man, he killed a man,
An' he's roamed dese swamps
For twenty years.

His rifle is sure
An' my mout' is shut;
He's de lone hunter
An' he hunts alone.
He killed a man, he killed a man,
An' he's roamed dese swamps
For twenty years.

The King Buzzard

A group around the camp-fire

Tom: I wonder wey Tad.

Cricket: I ain' know. Look like he wants to git out er draggin' dis here seine. He leff here ever since 'fore day. Say he guh see kin he kill a turkey.

Voice: Who wid him?

Cricket: Ain' nobody wid him. He leff here by his self.

Tom: I sho' ain't loves to wander 'round dese here swamps by my lonesome.

Cricket: Tad is a ole swamper. I reckon he know wuh he doin'.

Voice: He ain' tooken nothin' to eat wid him, an' it atter midnight. I reckon he must er had some kind er trouble.

Cricket: Looks to me like I hear sump'n comin'.

(Tad approaches, his clothes badly torn. He is wet and covered with yellow mud.)

Tom: Tad, wey you been? You sho' looks like you loves to wander 'round dese here swamps by you'self.

Tad: Look at me. Is I look like I been enjoyin' myself?

Tom: You sho' is tored up. A bear must er had you.

Tad: I seen sump'n wuss 'an a bear.

Voice: Wuh it been?

Tad: I been walkin' 'long on de edge er Big Alligator Hole, an' de air been stink; an' I walk on an' I see sump'n riz up in front er me bigger 'an a man. An' he spread he whing out an' say, "Uuh!" He eye been red an' he de nastiest lookin' thing I ever see. He stink in my nostrils. He so stink, he stink to my eye an' my year. An' I look at him an' see he been eat a dead hog right dere in de night time. I ain' never see buzzard settin' on a carcass in de night 'fore dis. An' he look so vigus, he look like he ain' care ef he stay dere an' fight or no.

An' I been so oneasy an' frighten, till I ain' kin do nothin'; an' 'fore I knowed it, I jump at him. An' he riz up—makin' dat same dreadful sound—an' start flyin' all 'round me. Look like he tryin' to vomick on me. An' I dodge, an' dere in de moonlight dat ole thing circle 'round—look like he guh tackle me. An' he spewed he vomick every which er way, an' I see de leaf an' de grass wuh it fall on dry up. All de air seem like it were pizen.

An' I turned to leff, an' it keep on gittin' nigher an' nigher to me. An' I ain' know wuh would er happen, ef I ain' git in a canebrake wey he ain' kin fly. An' I crawl 'round for God knows how long, an' when I find myself, I been lost. Jesus know I ain' never wan' see no more buzzard like dat.

Cricket: My God!

Voice: Wuh kind er buzzard dat?

Tad: God knows.

Tom: Dat ain' no buzzard. I hear 'bout dat ole thing 'fore dis.

My pa tell me dat 'way back in slavery time—'way back in Af'ica—dere been a nigger, an' he been a big nigger. He been de chief er he tribe, an' when dem white folks was ketchin' niggers for slavery, dat ole nigger nuse to entice 'em into trap. He'd git 'em on boat wey dem white folks could ketch 'em an' chain 'em. White folks nused to gee him money an' all kind er little thing, an' he'd betray 'em. An' one time atter he betray thousands into bondage, an' de white folks say dey ain' guh come to dat coast no more—dat was dey last trip—so dey knocked dat nigger down an' put chain on him an' brung him to dis country.

An' when he dead, dere were no place in heaven for him an' he were not desired in hell. An' de Great Master decide dat he were lower dan all other mens or beasts; he punishment were to wander for eternal time over de face er de earth. Dat as he had kilt de sperrits of mens an' womens as well as dere bodies, he must wander on an' on. Dat his sperrit should always travel in de form of a great buzzard, an' dat carrion must be he food.

An' sometimes he appears to mens, but he doom is settled; an' he ain' would er hurt Tad, kaze one er he punishment is dat he evil beak an' claw shall never tech no livin' thing. An' dey say he are known to all de sperrit world as de King Buzzard, an' dat forever he must travel alone.

An Escaped Convict

Nothin' but a convict
Loosed from de chains,
Wid shackles left behind me,
Wid shackle scars upon me,
Wid a whip an' a chain
Waitin' ef dey ketch me,
Wid bloodhounds an' bullets
On my trail,
An' de dangers er de swamp
In front er me.
I'll take my chance, brother,
I'll take my chance.

De rattlesnake an' moccasin,
De mud an' de briar,
An' de pizen vine ain' nothin'
To de danger
Dat is left behind me.
Dere is striped clothes
An' double shackles
An' a rawhide whip
All behind me.
So I'll take my chance, brother,
I'll take my chance.

I know dere's a hard, hard road
Behind me,
An' dere ain' no road in front;
Dat de mud is heavy,
An' dere ain' much food
To separate my backbone
From my belly.
For I ain' nothin' but a convict,
Wid de scars to prove it.

I'll take my chance, brother,
I'll take my chance.

Goose Pond

Voice: Tad, is you ever fish in Goose Pond?

Tad: Goose Pond wey de white folks loves to camp in de big swamp? Cap'n Bob tell me he nuse to go dere 'way back in slavery time, long time 'fore a railroad were ever built an' when folks travel in wagon an' carriage. He nuse to go dere wid he marster. He say all de swamp in dem times was full er game: deers an' bears an' all kind er wild thing. He say Goose Pond been a favor-rite place wid de white folks. Dey say it were beautiful, an' Cap'n Bob say he always jine 'em when dey say dat, it ain' make no diff'ence wuh dey think. He say course he have he own thought 'bout it. He say it were not sech a bad place when you have a heap er comp'ny, but it were no place for him when he been by he self; dat dere has always been many strange an' cu'ious thing in dem swamp, an' Goose Pond look to him when he by he self like it been de headquarters. All 'round de shore you kin see diff'ent thing come out er de bush. Some is beast an' some on 'em is bird an' some on 'em is shapes er thing nobody ain' know wuh dey is, but dey is not live thing—dat one thing he sho' of.

An' dere is a ole tree dat stand out in de water dat all you got to do is to watch it an' you kin see ha'nts come out er de moss an' see 'em make sign to one annudder. Sometime dis here tree is kivered wid 'em, but most time dere is jes two on 'em settin' on a limb. Ain' nobody know wha' dey say, but dey voice will rise up an' creep to you' years on de night air, an' it come like a wail or a moan. An' de moonlight gits cold in de hot summer time an' fog rise up an' all kind er thought comes to you' mind: people dat is long since dead an' gone, both white folks an' niggers, ole time slavery folks, niggers dat he nuse to know, white folks—fine white—buckra an' overseer, mens an' womens dat nuse to work in de swamp fields an' hunt an' fish in Goose Pond. He say dere was people dere he knowed an' he ain' know.

He say one night he marster send him back for some fishnin tackle an' he seen a man—a white man—ride down to de pond an' stop he horse jes on de edge er de water an' look up an' down de pond, den ride in an' swim he horse to de other shore. Them kind er strange thing make it a place dat were not create in he mind for humans.

He talk 'bout de wild night bird an' de big sturgeon leff by de high water an' ain' kin git out, an' how dey plunges from one end er de lake to de other. An' when a big bull alligator would bellow, de whole swamp would tremble an' you would mighty nigh crack you' teet' tryin' to steady you' self. He tell how he hear a alligator clack he teet' on de bank an' a pig squeal.

I ain' never forgit all wuh he say, an' has a onnatural feelin' when I passes dis pond in de big day. I ain' got no heart for fishnin an' huntin' dere.

Voice: White folks say dey oughter call dis Beautiful Lake. It's hard sometime to onderstand a white folks' mind.

Bannister Bridge

Bannister Bridge
Wid its moss-kivered trees,
Dark waters
An' dark ways,
Big gums an' pines,
Lighted by a million fireflies
In summer,
Horrid wid de sound er owl,
Dang'ous wid de pizen
Er de moccasin;
Wey rattlesnake,
Older dan slavery time,
Wid moss on he back,
Creep up an' hum a chune
Wid he tail,
A warnin' dat danger is near.

Bannister Bridge,
Restin' place er de guards;
Hidin' place er de convict;
Here wey dey enter de swamp
An' here wey dey gits help.
Dis bridge
Is de place
Of murders an' tales,
Live men an' spooks,
De law an' de outlaw.

For here is wey de swamp
An' de hill meets up,
Here is wey crimeals enters an' leaves.
Guards wid dey guns,
Convicts, wid stripes
An' bu'sted shackles
Still hangin' on, sleeps—

De guards above,
De convicts underneath.

A stray nigger comes along
Wid de tale
Of a runaway nigger
He seen wid stripes on
Axen for bread.
De guards git hot for de trail,
An' de convicts is free again
For de time bein',
While de guards on de wrong trail
Is seekin' de life blood
Of sump'n dat's less
Dan a varmint—
Seekin' on de wrong trail.

Fooled by a ign'ant nigger
Wid de cunnin' of a fox—
Cunnin' bred
In de blood an' de bone
For de pertection
Er he race—
Cunnin' like dat
Of a beast
Dat run
At de sight of a man;
Wid a mind
Like dat of a bird
Or a horse or a dog
Dat knows
In de dark
Which way to go,
Which way is he home;
Pertection dat is bred
In de blood an' de bone.

Jes a fool nigger
Dat gees answer
Of ign'ance

To question—
Fool answer
Dat comes
Wid de sense
Er pertection;
Dat gees a longer life
Or a bigger chance
To one er he race.

Dis is Bannister Bridge,
De meetin' place,
De restin' place
Er convict an' guard;
Poorly on top
An' wusser beneath;
De place er help an' hurt,
Escape an' capture—
Maybe life,
Sometimes death.

Hard sleepin',
No sleepin',
Bloodhound cryin',
Flyin' foots,
Bullets singin';
Sometimes a grunt,
Sometimes a groan,
Gone or got you
At last.
God damn you,
Maybe last breath.

Bannister Bridge,
Meetin' place of convict an' guard,
Escape or capture,
Help or hurt.
Bannister Bridge,
An' maybe
We've got you,
God damn you.

Beautiful Bannister Bridge,
Our hope of escape,
Of food an' of help,
Our fear of capture,
Bannister Bridge.

NIGGER TO NIGGER

Big Annie

Tad: Tom even wid dat ole gal er he ownt now.

Voice: Wuh ole gal?

Tad: Annie. Ain't you know Big Annie, he wife?

Voice: How come? Wuh she do for him to git even 'bout?

Tad: You ain't know 'bout de time Tom tooken a ham over an' guin it to Bella? Somebody tooken de news to Big Annie, an' she git so mad she were b'ilin'. She git de news when she were takin' Tom' breakfast to him wey he been cuttin' cotton-stalks 'side a rail fence.

When she git to wey Tom been, he were settin' in he seat on de stalk-cutter. Annie come up, put de pot wid he breakfast in it on de ground an' look at Tom a minute, an' den reach over an' pull a rail off dat fence an' sweep Tom from de stalk-cutter on to de hind foots er one er he mule. Well, you know how a mule is. He ain't never loss a opportunity to use dem foots er he ownt. Dat mule lay he years flat back on he head an' neck an' squeal like a pig, an' lift Tom back over de stalk-cutter an' he drap 'gainst Annie.

Well, she look like she tooken dat for a personal insult. She git so mad she reach over an' grab dat pot wid Tom' breakfast in it an' poured hot hom'ny an' bacon grease all over Tom' head an' neck. Tom ack like she set him afire, an' I reckon she is. He ain' know ef he comin' or guine, but it ain't take him long to find out he guine. He twist 'round two or three time very actie, an' it look like he think two foots ain't 'nough to take him from dere. He went down dat road on all four foots for fifty yards, pacin' like a coon, 'fore he straighten out an' stretch he self. It look like hot hom'ny an' a rail teach dat nigger sump'n 'bout runnin' ain't nobody ever knowed afore.

He run in de house an' tored 'round it for a while, an' den he spy Annie comin' an' bu's' out de other side er de house an' kep' on guine. It been a good thing, too, kaze Annie look like she was jes gitten right to make her meanin' known to him. She run in de house an' broked up chairs, th'owed Tom's clothes out in de yard, took he mattress an' rip it open an' made a pile er de straw in it wid he clothes an' other thing an' set 'em afire.

She 'larm everything. A ole cat wha' been in de house sachayed out er dere an' 'round de yard like somebody been swingein' him. One er dem chillun goat th'owed he head an' little nub tail up in de air an' bl'ated two or three time an' leff dere bouncin' on dem stiff leg er he own like a rubber ball. An' dat ain't all. You oughter see Tom' cow. She curl she tail up an' bu's' out de barnyard bellowin'. Even a ole Plymouth Rock rooster stretch he neck an' whing an' leg, an' tooken to de creek wuss 'an he would er done in de big Sunday when de preacher guh take dinner dere.

Lord! Lord! it were a time.

Voice: She sho' is raise a rookus 'bout a little piece er meat.

Tad: She say it she meat.

Scip: Is you talkin' 'bout Tom or de ham?

Tad: Annie say she ooman 'nough for Tom. He ain' needs no other ooman. He ain' kin manage de one he got.

Scip: It look like Tom got poorly judgment.

Tad: It ain't so poorly all de time.

Scip: It do look like he gits ideas 'bout movin' sometimes.

Tad: Luh me tell you de end on it.

Tom heard Annie were sick, an' he say he were badly in need er labor in he field; so he tell he boss Annie were failin' fast. He reckon he guh loss her. An' he axe he boss which ooman he think de stoutest, Bella or Chainey.

Scip: Look like he oughter have a belly full er stout womens.

Tad: He tell he boss he mighty nigh fret he self to death 'bout lossen Annie, an' he got to have a ooman to work an' take care er he poor little motherless chillun.

When de news git to Annie, she crawled out er dat bed right now an' hoed a acre 'fore sundown.

Scip: I ain' change my mind 'bout Tom' judgment.

A Yellow Bastard

Tad: Who is you an' wuh is you? I ain' 'member to axe you 'fore dis. Who is you an' wuh is you an' wey you come from?

Yellow Jack: You axe me who I is an' wuh I is an' wey I come from. You axe a heap er question all in one, an' I guh axe you a question:

Who business is it who I is an' wuh I is an' wey I come from? Is you care 'bout me? Is you my friend? I ain' think so. Is you my enemy? I ain' think dat neither. Is you axe me jes for talk an' compersation? Maybe you axe me who I is for laugh an' game makin'. Well, it do not matter. It ain't make no diff'ence wuh you' reason. I guh tell you who I is an' wuh I is. It ain't matter ef you laugh or cry.

It ain't make no diff'ence, wuh I is I is. An' when dey puts me in de ground, I is wuh everybody is, or guh be is. You axe me wuh I is. Laugh, ef you has a mind to. I ain' care. Grin, ef you wants to. I ain't to fault, an' I ain' care.

I have thought an' dream, an' I dream beautiful dream, but it seem like I ain' kin tell my dream. I ain' seems rough enough. I ain' seems man enough to make my feelin's known. My dream ain' nothin' but for laughter for other folks, an' my dream is tear for me an' torment. But I dreams—dat's all dere is for me.

You axe who I is an' wuh I is an' wey I come from.

I come from wey de door is shet, an' I come to wey it still is closed. All I got is dreams, an' dey is drownded. I ain' kin make my feelin's known. Laughin' ain' make no diff'ence now. God has overlooked me. I is not strong enough. I ain' kin make my feelin's known.

You axe me wuh I is an' I guh tell you. I is wuh I is. I isn't wuh I mought er been. To my lonesome self I ain' nothin' but a yellow bastard—laugh, I ain' care—a yellow bastard wid no place—wid no place amongst de white folks an' a poorly place amongst de niggers.

De door is shet to me. Hemmed in on every side, I has nothin' but dreams. An' my thoughts is floatin' out, floatin' far above de tall tree tops, here an' dere, listenin' to de wind's soft tune above de tree tops an' de clouds. Across de stars dey wander for a lonely moment, an' den back again an' down, down, down into de mire. For de door is shet to me. Hemmed in, hemmed in on every side.

I ain' kin make my feelin's known, for I ain' nothin'—nothin' but a yellow bastard to white an' black alike. I is wuh I is—nothin' but a yellow bastard—an' I ain' kin make my feelin's known. Laugh, I ain' care.

Tad: I hear wuh you say. I ain' guh laugh an' I ain' guh cry. I ain' know wuh you is.

Scip: Le's we finish move dis fertilizer.

Joe

(A True Story)

Tad: Is you hear 'bout Joe? He back home. Look poor as a crane.

Voice: Wey he been?

Tad: Tell me he been to Washington.

Voice: How come he gone to Washington?

Tad: You know Joe' head been full er advancin' he self. He listen to a lot er talk by dese nigger dat leff here an' went off, an' to some er dem off niggers dat speak in de church an' at de society. Dey fill Joe' head full er all kind er notions 'bout de place he guh take in de world. He say he have ambition.

Joe ain' been nothin' but a common country nigger. Ain' never been no wey an' ain' have much schoolin', an' he ain' know nothin' but to work an' save he money an' have ambition. So him an' he wife come to Columbia an' went to a place dey call "Done Movin'" an' from all I hear 'bout de place, dat man ain' never mean to move, but he sho' had Joe an' everything 'round him movin' an' jumpin'. He ain' spare he self neither Joe when it come to work.

Well, Joe had one job workin' 'bout de place an' he wife were de cook. Joe save everything he make, an' him an' he wife live on wuh he wife make, till Joe save up four hundred dollars. Den he quit an' him an' he wife lit out for Washington. Dey was surprised when dey git dere. Dem niggers ain' gee him no consideration at all, an' dere ain' been no brass band to meet 'em.

Time Joe git dere he went to de White House to see de President. Thought he guh git a job right now 'tendin' to de garden an' feedin' hogs an' chickens an' lookin' after diff'ent little business for de President. He thought he were guh be de President's main 'pendence, but de guards run him off an' atter awhile dey talk 'bout puttin' him in jail ef he ain' stay from 'round de White House. He thought he guh have a job wid de President an' he wife were guh do de cookin'. He think all he got to do was to go dere an' axe de President for a job an' atter de guard convince him, he leff an' went to lookin' for another job.

He had a terrible time, but finally got his self a job workin' in a ice factory, an' he ain' make money 'nough to live on. Tooken mighty nigh all de money he have to warm up wid atter de ice-house cool him off. You know Joe been nuse to workin' in de hot sun wid de sweat rollin' off er him all day. A ice factory is a poorly place for a cornfield nigger. Joe say he ain' never work so hard, an' ef he is sweat he ain' know, but sometime he 'magine he could feel his self sweatin' on de inside. He work he self mighty nigh to death.

Things git to sech a pass till he wife tooken a job workin' for niggers, an' you know niggers is hard to work for. Dey has so much airs when dey gits up in de world. Dey is very partic'lar an' love to show dey servants off an' correct 'em when dey got vis'tors, an' dat ain' to de likin' er niggers. An' dere ain' nobody as discountin' as a big-doin' nigger when he is up in de world, an' he wife is disgustin'.

Dey tell me some on 'em has white servants—some er dese ole over-de-seas people wuh ain' know nothin' 'bout niggers. But white folks is sharp. It ain' matter wey dey come from, dey is white folks, an' ef dey works for a nigger, dat nigger pays. Every time de white folks bow an' scrape, it cost de nigger a dollar. Every time he white servant say, "Yes, sir," it natu'ally sickens me; tryin' so hard to make dey self notorious. High-class white folks laughs an' niggers knows niggers an' dey laughs, too. De only impress dey makes is game makin' by both white an' black. It is kind er funny, ainty?

Voice: Niggers does git 'side dey self ef you has to work for 'em. Dey sho' means to make you know you' place—dat's one thing dey doos—an' dat you ain' equal wid 'em. Ain' nobody, white or black, equal wid a big-doin' nigger.

Tad: Joe' wife say she ain' kin stand it no longer. Wey she come from a nigger is a nigger an' ain' nothin' but a nigger an' ain' guh be nothin' but a nigger dere an' no wey else. She say all niggers is niggers to her. An' when her an' Joe done spend all dey money but 'nough for a ticket, she make Joe buy a ticket home.

Scip: I see Joe. He look like one er ambition' wreck. God Er

Mighty ain' never intended Joe for nothin' but to view de hind part of a mule.

Tad: Joe' wife quit him 'fore she hit Columbia good. She say she ain' never means to live wid no nigger dat takes her off an' puts her to workin' for niggers.

Scip: Ain't no nigger guh blame her.

A Prison

Dat ole man look funny
Hobblin' 'long,
Lookin' every which er way
Kinder nervous like.
Make me laugh.
Wuh de matter ail him?
Why ain't he like people?
Is you know?

I is know:
Ten year in stripe,
Wey a man ain' kin talk
Onliest to answer a guard;
Ten year wey de whip fall
At de battin' of an eye,
Wey dey tie you' thumb,
Draws you up on a windlass,
Luh you hang for hours
Whilst dey sets down
Wid compersation an' laugh.

It's all a big joke,
It's fun for 'em to hear you groan,
An' when dey wants to punish
You some more,
Dey draws you up
Wid you' hand to hind you,
Dey says it hurts
A little wuss.

Dat ole man has been broked.
Ten year in de silence er death,
Mens an' womens all around
Ain' kin talk neither laugh.
Dey says don't pity de crimeal,

Ain' no nuse to say dat—
Dat agvice already is took.

In de cold cells in winter,
Hanged by you' wrist
Wid de north wind blowin',
You' foots jes techin' de ground—
Hanged by you' wrist
To de iron bars of you' cell,
All de long night through;
Tooked down in de mornin'
For bread an' cold water,
Wid a taste er de lash
An' a long day's work,
To be hung back again.
Work all day long,
Hung up at night
To broke you in good.
Don't laugh at dat ole man,
More better to weep.

Ten year wey de whip
Leave its mark on a ooman,
On a ooman stripped to de skin
For pickin' a flower.
Bear in mind wha' a mixtree:
A poor helpless ooman,
Tear an' a whip lash
An' a flower, dear God.

Broked—be dey mens or womens—
In de name er de law
An' de Lord.
Don't laugh. Don't laugh.
Jesus, my Jesus,
Wey is You' mercy now?

The Hawk and the Rooster

Tad: Bo Shoat an' Mensa run together today.

Voice: When de funeral guh be?

Tad: Wuh funeral?

Voice: Mensa'.

Tad: Why ain't you axe me when dey guh bury Bo Shoat? I ain' reckon you knows Mensa, is you?

Voice: I ain' knows Mensa, but I knows Bo Shoat. He wuh I calls a bad nigger.

Tad: He been a bad nigger, but he run into de tiger today.

Voice: Is he dead?

Tad: No, by de mercy er God, Allen come 'long an' him an' Jake an' several other niggers tooken Mensa loose.

Voice: Dey oughten to done it. Bo Shoat been beat up too much people. Look like every wey he go he spilin' for a fight.

Scip: He spilin' from one now.

Voice: How it happen?

Tad: Mensa been walkin' 'side dis here gal er 'Riah's an' lookin' down in her face talkin'. You know Mensa is a ooman's man. You know how science he walk. He walk like he own de world. He got a belly like a wasp an' su'ple as a snake. He carry he head wid he neck bowed like a studhorse, an' dere ain't no wildcat got more spring in he leg dan Mensa.

He was walkin' 'long wid he hat twist back an' he shirt open wid a red han'k'ch'ef tie 'round he neck. An' he was laughin' an' talkin' wid dat little gal an' every nigger 'round dere was cuttin' dey eye at 'em. An' one er dem niggers standin' 'side Bo Shoat say:

"Dere is a new rooster sidin' 'round de pullets today."

An' several on 'em kept on sayin' diff'ent little thing. Den Bo Shoat git 'side he self, but dem niggers kept eggin' him on. Ain' none on 'em got no nuse for Bo Shoat.

Atter while Bo Shoat swing his self off de store piazza an' walk up to Mensa an' says:

"Mr. Nigger, dey tells me you is a rooster, but I de big rooster 'round here."

An' Mensa look at him an' say:

"You does look like a rooster—a ole dunghill. Well, I ain't no rooster. I de hawk dat picks 'em."

When he say dat, Bo Shoat run into Mensa. You know Bo Shoat some man.

Scip: He been some man.

Tad: Well, dey was up an' down an' all over de road. An' atter a while things was gitten a little quieter. I seen dem long legs an' arms er Mensa' wroppin' dey self 'round Bo Shoat wuss 'an a king snake, an' I know de fight were mighty nigh finish. I see Mensa git Bo Shoat' head in he two hand an' start twistin', an' Bo Shoat' eye wall back an' dat was wey Allen an' dem other niggers runned in.

Voice: He ain' kill Bo Shoat, is he?

Tad: No, he ain' kill him. He say he jes tame him.

Mensa

Tad: Well, you axe me 'bout Mensa—wey he gone, wuh happen to him. I ain' know. All I kin say is, you know Mensa or is you know Mensa? I guh tell you wuh I know an' some er it wuh you know.

Mensa been a good man to look at. He talk kind an' he have a look dat satisfy you' eye, unless you jes natu'ally was a fool an' been huntin' for danger. You know Mensa ain' never known to meddle nobody, an' he talk soft an' kind to everybody, mens an' womens, old an' young. He ain' never change he friendly ways to nobody 'less dey been natu'ally tryin' to find trouble. Mensa was one er dese kind er niggers dat would cut you' th'oat ef you got him wrong, but he would bow down to de ground an' take he hat off 'fore he done it, but, my brother, ef you got him wrong, he were bad wrong an' he make everything look wrong 'bout him. Mensa would jes cut you' th'oat 'pologizin' for it.

He been de most polite, mannerable nigger I ever see. De white folks love him so till you mighty nigh thought he been one on 'em. Ole folks was crazy 'bout him, an' de chillun would follow him 'round like God sent him here. I ain' never know wuh kind er man Mensa.

He moest fault been womens, an' dey ain' say nothin' 'gainst him, none on 'em. An' dem mens wuh have diff'ence wid him ain' have full onderstandin', an' Mensa look like when he git tangle up wid er man he ain' never have sense enough to quit.

Wid all he good ways, he were sure God a dang'ous man. I ain' never see a bad man so much folk love, white an' black, an' I ain' never see such a kind, mannerable man so much people dread. He been diff'ent from other people.

Voice: Wey he?

Tad: I ain' know. Ain' nobody know. De last time I see Mensa, he wave he hand to we an' walk off. I kin see him now walkin' down de foot-path, walkin' like a tiger cat. He look back onct an' den swing his self away like a piece er music on de air, an' as I notice him, I see him walk away towards de sunset till he fade forever whilst we was gazin'. We ain' never see him since. He leff he reputation, he leff a memory er he walk, of de way he carry he self, he mannerableness. He jes connect up pleasant feelin's wid danger.

Mensa fade wid de settin' sun an' ain' never been heared er since. He pass out an' leff we wid out onderstandin'. He fade wid de sun.

Magic

Tad: When I been down on de coast, I sho' been interested. Dere was a nigger sleight-er-hand man down dere, an' he had a gang er niggers 'round him—a party—showin' 'em all kind er trick an' magic. He come out an' he say:

"Is dere any nigger here kin tie me so I ain' kin git loose?"

An' dere was one forward-lookin' nigger spoke up an' say:

"I reckon I kin tie you so you ain' kin do nothin'."

An' dat cunger nigger say:

"Here is a rope, brother."

An' dat nigger wrop him up wid rope. He tie him hog fashion, he say he tie him so Jesus His Self couldn't er git loose, an' look all 'round an' laugh like he done sump'n. An' den he turn 'round an' walk back to he seat—guine dere so he kin watch dat nigger struggle. 'Fore he set down, dat nigger say:

"Come here, brother."

An' de nigger walk back to wey de other nigger was. When he git dere, dat nigger were standin' up wid he hand 'hind he back, an' he say:

"Brother, dat was a good job you done. Wuh is you' name? Shake hands wid me."

An' dat nigger say:

"Ain' matter wha' my name is, I guh leff here."

An' he leff. He ain' notice dat cunger nigger's hand. He jes pull out er dere like he ain' had no load on him at all, an' he say he ain' never guh shake hand wid no nigger like dat, an' he ain' guh stay 'round him. He don't b'lieve in foolin' wid no magic.

Voice: Wuh is you think 'bout it, Tad?

Tad: I had a mind like dat nigger. I ain' blame him for leffen, an' he ain't de onliest one wuh leff.

Jazy

Tad: Jazy' boss axe me kin I git him a driver. I axe him wuh ail Jazy. He say Jazy in de bed sick.

I says:

"Is you got to have annudder nigger or is Jazy suit you?"

An' de boss say:

"Jazy suits me better 'an anybody I kin git." He say he has to broke in a new nigger. Den I says:

"Boss, I thinks I kin git Jazy. He don't look to me like he so terrible bad off."

Den de boss say:

"Tad, I'll gee you a dollar ef you puts Jazy back to work."

Voice: Wuh is you do, Tad?

Tad: I call Dummy to me an' I says:

"Dummy, is you wants to make a quarter?"

An' he says:

"Yes."

An' I says:

"Don't say nothin' to Jazy. Jes take dis here tape measure an' go in he room an' measure him."

Voice: Is Dummy measure Jazy?

Tad: Dummy went to Jazy' room an' start to measure him, an' Jazy git so excited he ain' could stand it; an' he leff he bed an' call Dummy all kind er sump'n. An' Dummy so feared he ain' guh git he quarter, when Jazy push him 'bout why he interest he self so much in he business, Dummy tell him Pinckney, de ondertaker, been so interested in he ailments till he promise Dummy a quarter to git Jazy' measurement. Dummy tell Jazy Pinckney think a heap er him, an' Jazy say he ain' want no ondertaker to think 'bout him when he in bed.

Scip: Dat sho' sound like ole Pinckney.

Tad: Dummy tell a lie on Pinckney, but he sho' had Pinckney' mind on de end er he tongue when he tell it.

Voice: Wuh Jazy do?

Tad: He went back to work.

Voice: He ain' been too sick, is he?

Tad: 'Twix' you an' me, he look like he were jes takin' a little rest.

Scip: Dere is a great diff'ence 'twix' sick niggers an' undertakers.

The Turkey Hunt

Tad: I been on a turkey hunt down to Vernon Lodge an' have some time listenin' to dem niggers tellin' lie.

Scip: An' havin' dem listen to you' lie.

Tad: Dey have de agvantage er me. Dey been too much on 'em 'gainst me one, an' dey all on 'em lie like dey was trained to it.

Scip: Dey must er been pretty good, ef dey make you forgit dat you is a professor.

Tad: I ain' lie all de time, but dem niggers down dere would tell a lie an' all de rest on 'em would swear it were de God's trute, an' dey have a respectable lookin' ole scoundrel wuh claim to be a deacon—or sump'n high up in de church—when he wan' de chief liar, he was de main witness.

Scip: You reckon he were any better at foolin' de white folks dan you is?

Tad: All I say is: dat ole scoundrel holds my respect.

Voice: You start to tell we 'bout a turkey hunt, an' you ain' do nothin' but talk 'bout dat ole nigger.

Tad: You all worry me an' I hasn't had time to git dat ole nigger out er my mind. Dat ole nigger tell me dat one tract er land is twenty-nine miles long de narrow way, an' a hundred miles de long way. I never said nothin'.

Voice: Wuh 'bout de turkey?

Tad: Dere's more turkey dere dan God saw, an' every other kind er game. Deers is so common you liable to git cripple from dey runnin' into you by accident, an' part'idge so common ain' nobody takes notice on 'em. Dey was so common till de air was 'luminate' wid 'em. But turkey, Jesus! dey 'larms de country wid dey gobblin'. Ain' nobody kin sleep for 'em atter sun-up. White folks kill a turn on 'em. Dey kill so much turkey, look like dey try to make a mule out er me totin' 'em.

Voice: Wuh sort er huntsman is de big boss?

Tad: He don't brag on he self, but he have acquire a reputation.

Voice: Is he shoot good?

Tad: He gits de game.

Voice: Is you see him shoot?

Tad: I seen a gobbler settin' in a tree an' de boss creep up on him an' aim' at him, an' when he fire dat turkey flewed a mile, an' dat nigger er he ownt say:

"Dat sho' God were a fine shot you make, Boss. You tored dat gobbler up. I ain' know why he ain' drap right wey you shoot him."

An' de boss say to dat nigger:

"It were not a bad shot. Go over to de woods wey he drap an' bring him to de house."

An' den he turn an' walk off like killin' turkey common to him. I ain' say nothin', but I watch to see ef dat nigger were comin' back wid dat gobbler, an' sho' 'nough he come back wid one swung 'cross he shoulder big as a whale. An' I axe dat ole nigger 'bout it, an' he tell me de boss is a noted turkey hunter. He say dat nigger is, too. He say whenever de boss shoot at a turkey an' he send dat nigger to find him, he always come back wid one. He say he best had.

An' I watch dem white folks make a great miration 'bout dat gobbler, an' I heared one er dem tell de little missus 'bout de marvelous gobbler—he call it—de boss kill, an' she smile an' say:

"Oh, is he have John" (or whatever dat nigger' name) "wid him?"

It sho' was a fine gobbler.

Old Lady Beck

Tad: I been over to Judge Jeems's court de other mornin' an' like to kill myself laughin' at ole lady Beck an' Lawyer Grease. She ruint him.

Voice: Wuh it all 'bout?

Tad: Dis here boy, Mose, er ole man Billy' have er argiment wid annudder nigger, an' dey went to fightin'. Ole Aunt Nancy try to part 'em. She run in 'twix' 'em wid a washpot an' kep' on rammin' 'em, but it ain' do no good. Dat nigger reach 'round dat pot an' he cut Mose every which er way, an' Lawyer Grease been tryin' to make out Mose cut he self. He make 'tend like dat nigger were de one suffer. He talk like all de niggers 'round dere oughter been prayin' to dat nigger. Sound like he tooken God's place.

He say he so sure dis nigger is innocent dat he want him free, but ef he guilty—ef dey prove him guilty—

"You' Honor, I wouldn't defend a guilty man. Ef he is guilty, you' Honor, I hope you give him de limit er de law. Give him life, you' Honor."

De nigger shake he head an' say, "Uh! uh!" He know wha' he do.

Well, sir, Lawyer Grease look like he guh eat dem niggers up. He axe 'em all kind er question an' try to tangle 'em up. He sho' worry an' swell his self up an' bellow like a bull. He out-talk four or five phonograph all workin' at one time.

An' den he git Aunt Beck on de stand, but Aunt Beck's a sharp ole ooman an' she ain' git excite an' fuss up. He axe her all kind er question, but she answer ain't satisfy him. Den he look at her an' he say:

"Look here, ole ooman, how come you know so much 'bout dis fight? You seems to know more 'bout it dan de mens dat was fightin'. I wish you would be so kind as to explain dat to de judge."

An' Aunt Beck say:

"A overseer always sees more wha's doin' dan de workman wha' doin' it."

Voice: Wuh Lawyer Grease say?
Tad: He say:
"You kin come down."
Voice: Wuh Judge Jeems say?
Tad: He ain' say much, but he tooken care er de nigger.

 **Red**

(A Ballad)

What did Red say?
Dey called him to de door:
"I ain't got but a thirty-two
An' Johnson's got a forty-four.
I guh take my chance,
Honey, like a man.

"Go an' git Mr. Heeny,
Ef he's dead asleep,
Tell him to come an' talk wid me,
I killed a man,
Honey, 'tain't no lie."

Red told Miss Sophie:
"Don't you weep an' moan,
Dr. Key an' Tom Wilson
Bound to bring me home,
'Tain't no lie,
Honey, 'tain't no lie."

What did Red say,
When de train made de station blow?
"I done some cryin'
I never done before,
I killed a man,
Honey, I killed a man."

Dr. Key an' Tom Wilson
Went out an' had a talk:
"Ef you clear McHenry, Tom,
You got to law."
'Tain't no lie,
Honey, 'tain't no lie.

Tom said: "I'm a lawyer,
An' everybody know
Ef I lose de McHenry case,
I ain't guh law no more."
'Tain't no lie,
Honey, 'tain't no lie.

Red told de jailer:
"Hand me down de key,
So my wife see de last of me,
I'm goin' home,
Honey, 'tain't no lie."

One foot on de step,
De other on de ground,
Told de conductor:
"I am homeward bound.
'Tain't no lie,
Honey, 'tain't no lie."

This ballad was composed and sung by an illiterate negro. I have purposely changed names and places.

Just One Time to Die

Nothin' to live for,
An' just one time to die,
An' that's you' job.
Dere ain't no nuse
To run an' dodge;
Just one time to die.
Ain't nobody
Can take you' place;
Dere ain't no nuse
To worry an' fret,
Ain't but one time to die,
Nobody can do it for you.
Go you' way, no matter
Ef it work or play;
You got just one time to die.
'Tain't matter what you is,
How great you be,
Rich or poor or lonely,
You got one time—
Just one time to die.

Becky

Tad: Is you know Becky?

Voice: Wuh 'bout Becky?

Tad: She been up to de white folks' yard wid she three chillun, an' when she leff, young Miss axe Alice, Becky' sister, how long Becky been marry. An' Alice say:

"Becky ain' never been marry."

An' young Miss say:

"O Alice, how come she have all er dem chillun an' she ain' got no husband?"

An' Alice say:

"Becky git she chillun de best way she kin. She say she ain' want no husband."

Scip: Dat's de surest way to git 'em.

The Savage

Tad: Ole man Peter is sho' a rough man.

Scip: He come by it right. Ole man Robin he daddy, an' dere ain' nobody rougher an' him.

Tad: He must er been mighty rough ef he wusser 'an ole man Peter.

Voice: Wuh you thinkin' 'bout?

Tad: I jes been thinkin' 'bout ole man Peter how he go to de judy house an' pray an' preach. He always take Tom wid him an' chain him in a cornder er de judy house an' talk 'bout de swine dat was on de steep hillside an' had de devil in 'em an' was run down in de sea.

Ole man Peter looks to me like he is a brutish ole man. Every day when he go to de sawmill, you see him comin' wid Tom walkin' 'long behind. He got a trace chain 'round Tom' neck an' he have him followin' him like he was a bear. When he git to he work, he chain Tom to a post an' he don't pay no more 'tention to him till twelve o'clock when he knock off for dinner, den he water him an' feed him.

You know Tom' mind ain' right. Ole man Peter say he is a black Roman an' Tom ain' nothin' but a beast, an' he know how to handle beast. He say Tom one er dem swine de devil in, an' he mighty nigh done beat de devil out, an' when he git in de meetin' house, he always p'int he hand at Tom an' say:

"Dat my son. I show you wha' de devil kin do."

Scip: Look to me like he do show de niggers wha' de devil kin do when he shows both he own self an' Tom. He ain' got no sense.

I ain't never forgit de time Riah have de smallpox an' ole Peter kep' up all dat talk 'bout he a black Roman, a great black Af'ican lion, an' he grab Riah up in he arm an' hug her an' kiss her. He say de black lion don't care for no little thing like de itch, an' he tooken de smallpox an' like to die.

Tad: I 'member dat. De ole doctor went to see him an' tell him:

"You ole savage, I oughter treat you like you done you' hog —pour kerosene on you an' set you afire to cure it."

An' ole Peter tell him he already afire.

Scip: He's jes ign'ant. Ain' no talk or nothin' but de grave guh straighten him. My brother, dere ain' no nuse to waste you' time on a fool.

Ruint

Tad: Is you hear de tale 'bout Ella?

Voice: Wuh Ella?

Tad: Ella up to de white folks' yard.

Voice: Wuh 'bout Ella?

Tad: You know Ella been raise up mighty proper. She ain' run 'round wid no mens. Ack like she ain' got no nuse for 'em.

Scip: I ain' never pay no 'tention to no lie like dat. She ooman, ain't she? Mens is mens, ain't dey?

Tad: Well, she ack dat er way.

Scip: She ack dat er way.

Voice: Wuh de tale?

Tad: It ain't no tale. Ella been a apple in de white folks' yard. Dey 'pend on her. An' atter she been dere God knows how long, she disappear an' ain' say a word an' ain' nobody know wey Ella.

Well, all dese niggers had a excursion an' went to Wilmington, an' Janey—you know old man Jube' gal Janey—say she went on de excursion an' been standin' on de street cornder waitin' for de street car. An' she say she see a ooman all dress up wid fine clothes an' high-heel shoes wid ribbon all over her, an' more paint an' talcum powder 'an you ever heared of. An' she look at her an' she say it look like somebody she know. An' Janey say she walk up a little closer an' take her time an' look good. An' she say she walk up to de ooman an' say:

"Ain't dis Ella?"

An' de gal say:

"Sho', dis Ella."

An' Janey say:

"In de name er God, wey you been? Everybody been axen 'bout you."

An' Ella say:

"Ain't you hear de news? I been ruint."

Edecation

Tad: I been listenin' to dat nigger speak on de agvantage of edecation for us race.

Voice: Wuh he say? I ain' fret myself too much 'bout dese slick niggers wid all dey scheme. Moest on 'em ain' got but one idea, an' dat's gitten out er work. Dey goes 'round here wid dey honey tongue geein' agvice. I listens to 'em, but I got my ownt ideas.

Scip: I never has seen a nigger wid edecation fitten for nothin'. Ef you send him off to school, he sho' God forgits how to plow, an' a axe or pick or a hoe looks like pizen to 'em. Dey is wuss feared on 'em dan dey is of a rattlesnake or a moccasin. Dat's one thing schoolin' does for 'em—it makes work a frightful thing. I always is notice 'em an' dey 'casions a heap er trouble. Don't luh dem hifalutin niggers make no fool er you. Dey done spile a heap er people' chillun wid all kind er notions dey puts in dey head.

Tad: Dat nigger is helt out heap er hope an' he talk mighty reasonable.

Scip: Ain't you got better sense dan dat? First thing you know, he'll be tryin' to have you settin' at de table wid white folks.

Tad: He ain' guh have me settin' at no table wid white folks. I respect my ownt feelin's, an' ef I was to set at a table wid white folks, I'd feel wusser 'bout it dan dey does. I ain' b'lieve everything dat nigger say. All I say is: he have got some good ideas of de nigger race improvin' dey self. I ain' think dat nigger all fool.

Scip: You better git to thinkin' he ain' nothin' but a fool. Is you ever see one er dem edecated niggers dat was fitten for anything but to be invited to you' house to eat, an' set up dere an' eat up more in ten minutes dan you could work for in ten days?

Tad: Well, he put me to thinkin'.

Scip: Dat wuh I says. Dey comes here wid all dey notions an' leffs us wid de calf to hold.

Tad: Scip, I 'clare to God you oughter git over you' disheartenin' ways.

Scip: I been here a good while.

Tad: By de help er God we mought better we condition ef we trys. Maybe de white folks will help we.

Scip: I'll tell you 'bout de white folks an' edecation: some on 'em wants it for everybody, but moest on 'em is aguin it. Some on 'em fights it not only for dey own chillun, but for everybody else, an' dey can't stand de thought of a nigger havin' it.

But I watch de world an' I never is see readin' an' writin' go 'long wid work. Ef you git a man nuse to holdin' a pen in he hand or readin' a book, he done forever wid work. De only thing he do den is to study scheme to work somebody else. It ain' make no diff'ence ef it a nigger or a cracker, it's all de same. A book an' a pen an' ink ain' nothin' but murderers er work.

Leff it to God Almighty—He put de pen in de hand dat best suited to handle it, an' He have made He own plan 'bout de best place for de plow. Luh God's work alone.

Darlay

Tad: Dey raise de debil wid Darlay last night.

Voice: I knowed dat was comin'.

Tad: I ain' know wuh make nigger ack dat er way.

Voice: Wuh dey do?

Tad: Dey beat dat poor gal unmerciful, tie her frock up an' wored her out an' call her all kind er hussy an' wench. An' she beg an' pray, but she ain' kin do nothin'.

Voice: Who beat her?

Tad: She ma an' Big Daughter.

Voice: Ain't she ma do de same thing, an' ain't Daughter got two chillun er she ownt? An' dey ain' neither one on 'em got husband.

Scip: Niggers is cu'ious. Beatin' ain' do no good. Ain' nothin' guh stop nature.

Voice: It ain' look right.

Tad: It de rule, but I ain' know why. Dat's niggers. Dey forgit all 'bout de punishment dey have. But atter dis it all end, Darlay is welcome to she man. He kin go an' come when he has a mind to, an' it ain' guh make no diff'ence. She guh forgit she troubles an' guh treat she sister or she chillun de same way.

Scip: I ain' onderstand it, but white folks is diff'ent an' wusser. 'Tain't nothin' but a beatin' an' hard words wid a nigger an' it's all over. White folks is diff'ent. Dey kills or turns 'em out in dey greatest trouble. It seem to me fool as niggers is, dey treatment is best.

Brass Ankles

Does you know 'em
Wid dey hungry dog look?
Calls dey self white.
Hates a nigger;
Calls he name
Wid a curl
Er dey lip.
Says "nigger" wid a snarl;
Puts a twis' on it;
Gits part er it
Through dey nose;
Twists an' turns it
An' put it on de air
As sump'n ain't fitten to hear.

Calls dey self white—
Brass ankles dey is—
White wid a little tech er yellow;
Niggers dat's passed on up,
Dey say,
Ain' have so far to go.
Better 'an a nigger,
Ain't nobody know it but dey;
Somebody tell 'em,
Find it out
When dey is grown.

Tryin' to prove it ever since
By insult an' murder—
Feared er dey standin'.
Some on 'em sets on de jury—
Turns dey kind loose;
Claims to be white—
Sets in judgment an' votes.

Bitter coffee drinkers,
Gall-berry eaters,
Brass ankles dat claims to be white.

A Peacemaker

Tad: Dey had ole Bung today.

Voice: How dey have him?

Tad: Had him 'fore de judge.

Voice: Wuh for?

Tad: For peacemakin', he say.

Voice: Wuh dey do wid him?

Tad: Fine him five dollars.

Voice: How come dey fine him five dollars for peacemakin'? Wuh kind er peacemakin' he been doin'?

Tad: Bung tell de judge he brother-in-law, Tom, an' annudder nigger git in a argiment an' mighty nigh fou't, an' he try to quiet 'em. An' de judge axe Bung wuh he do, an' Bung say he ain' do nothin' but try to pacify dat nigger. An' de judge axe him how he try to pacify him—wuh he do—an' Bung say he ain' do nothin'; say he merely slap dat nigger 'cross de face wid de back er he shovel—dat all he been atter, was peace an' quiet.

Voice: Is he git it?

Scip: Look like he calculation been good.

The Death of a Turkey Hunter

Tad: Is you all been to ole Bill' funeral? Dere sho' was moanin' an' weepin'.

Voice: Ain't dere always is moanin' an' weepin' at a funeral?

Tad: Dere was more on it at Bill' ownt; dere always is when a man is tooken dat er way.

Scip: Moanin' ain' guh bring nobody back.

Tad: Wuh happen were no more dan were expected. White folks owns dem swamp an' dey say nobody shall trespass, so Bill an' dem other niggers wuh been raise up in dere an' been huntin' an' fishin' dere ever since slavery time would er loss dey mind ef dey ain' kin go dere.

Scip: Bill loss he life.

Tad: Bill say ole Marster nuse to own dem swamp, an' dem swamp were he bread an' meat. He nuse to go dere wid ole Marster an' hunt turkey in slavery time.

Voice: Dat 'minds me er de time Bill tooken ole Marster' son, Miss Harry, down in de swamp. Miss Harry guin Bill enough liquor to drown a ordinary nigger, an' atter he drink it, he tell Miss Harry he guh call a turkey to him an' put it on de end er he gun. An' dat mornin' at de crack er day he had Miss Harry in dat swamp 'hind a blind, an' he ain' yelp but three or four time, when a big gobbler flewed out of a tree an' run up to wid in ten foot er Miss Harry, an' Miss Harry th'owed he gun to he shoulder an' fired. He 'larmed dat whole swamp. Dat turkey say, "Perk!" an' leff dere. Miss Harry ain' tech him. Bill look at Miss Harry an' say:

"Great God! Miss Harry, you done shame me. I put dat gobbler on de end er you' gun, an' you gone an' miss. I knows dat gobbler. Ole Marster shot at him in slavery time."

Miss Harry look at Bill an' say:

"Bill, here five dollars. Damn you' soul, don't you say nothin' 'bout dis."

An' Bill say:

"I ain' guh say nothin' 'bout it, but it guh be a mighty strain on me."

Miss Harry watch Bill all de time he been on dat hunt, tryin' to keep him 'way from de other white folks.

Tad: Is Bill say anything 'bout it?

Voice: You know Bill tell it. Dem white folks like to run Miss Harry crazy. Dey ain' never done tellin' it, an' dey grand-chillun tells it now.

Scip: Well, Bill never will tell no more tales. Him an' Miss Harry was all two on 'em sports, an' both on 'em is kivered up now.

Tad: We done wander off from wuh we been talkin' 'bout. Bill an' dem other niggers nuse to hunt in dat swamp an' gee sign to one annudder. When dey go in de swamp, dey ain' talk like no people. You could hear a owl holler 'way 'cross de swamp, an' you could hear owl gee answer; or you hear crow holler, an' dey make dey self known to one annudder dat er way an' makes wha' dey wants known. But dem kind er things can't last.

Scip: No, when mens has to take on de ways er animals, dey is mighty nigh helpless as animals an' guh be tooken agvantage of.

Tad: Bill manage to git home wid a bullet through he breast—went in he back an' come out he breast. Dey say he die er de fever.

Voice: Is dey know who done it?

Tad: De niggers knows who done it.

Scip: Wuh diff'ence dat? Bill is dead.

Lula

Tad: I 'clare to God. Lula tickled me today.

Voice: How come?

Tad: She been to de doctor. Say she been ailin' a good while, an' she tell de doctor she wants a zamination. An' de doctor put her on a table an' zamine her an' tell her she need to be operate on. An' Lula say:

"How much is you charge me for tellin' me dis?"

An' de doctor tell her two dollars. An' she say:

"Here's you' money. Good day, sir."

An' de doctor told her hold on, how 'bout de operation. An' Lula say:

"I ain' guh hab no operation."

An' de doctor say:

"It is very important. You has a serious trouble."

An' Lula say:

"I ain' guh hab no operation."

An' de doctor say:

"Ef you ain't operate on, you guh die."

An' Lula say:

"Good day, sir. I reckon I'll hab to go to my Jesus by myself."

Scip: Lula got more sense dan I gee her credit for.

Old Man Jim Kinkade

An ole man died
On a cold, cold night,
The trials of life he'd tried,
He died in the pale moonlight,
For he died on a cold, cold night.

The stars wid out love
Shone wid a cold, cold light
From the heavens above,
While he died in the pale moonlight,
For he died on a cold, cold night.

An ole man sleeps
In the cold, cold night,
While a black ooman weeps,
Kaze he died in the pale moonlight,
For he died on a cold, cold night.

An ole man froze
In the cold, cold night;
An' a black ooman knows
Why he died in the pale moonlight,
For he died on a cold, cold night.

An ole man feels
No pain in the cold, cold night,
While a black ooman kneels
Where he died in the pale moonlight,
For he died on a cold, cold night.

And the stars from above
Shone wid a cold, cold light
On a black ooman's love,
While he died in the pale moonlight,
For he died on a cold, cold night.

The Water Hole

Tad: Is you all hear 'bout dem Yows today? How is dey?

Bruser: Wha's de matter ail 'em?

Tad: Ain't you hear de news 'bout de fight wha' dey have to de water hole?

Bruser: I ain' hear. Wuh dey fight 'bout? Tell we.

Tad: Dey been back in de swamps seinin', an' dey bring dey fish down to de water hole on de creek, an' git in a argiment when dey 'vide 'em up. An' dey was terrible lookin'. Dey been back in one er dem guts, an' dey had on ole tored shirts an' dey breeches fasten up 'round dey waist wid a rope. Dey been barefooted an' half naked, an' dey been slimy wid yaller mud all over 'em—look like two ole alligators.

You know wuh kind er place de water hole—wid tall tree all 'round it an' mud an' slime, an' on de upper side it narrow wey de creek run in an' widen out an' dat wey dey got a crossin' log. All dem niggers goes down dere when dey's guine in de swamp an' comin' out, an' dat's wey dey have catfish stew an' fish-fry, an' wey dey guts dey fish.

An' when dey git in dis argiment, dey started to pushin' an' shovin' one annudder 'round like two ole boar hog. An' de talk dey hab at one annudder ain' nobody kin onderstand but dey self. Jes as well been two ole boar hog gruntin' at one annudder.

Atter while Peter run out on de crossin' log an' Crappo run at him, an' dey started fightin'. An' den dey slip off de log into de water hole, an' it were over ten foot deep. I ain' never see sech a fight. Part er de time dey was under de water, an' part er de time dey was risin' up wid dey head above it bobbin' all 'round. An' dey was growlin' an' gruntin', an' dat water was stirred up like a passel er alligators been in it. All two on 'em had dese here short fish knife wha' dey been guttin' fish wid. Dey cut one annudder all up, an' Crappo like to bit Peter's year off, an' blood been mess up all over de water hole.

We holler at 'em an' call 'em an' try to 'suade 'em, but dey ain' got no sense, dem's jes two wild niggers wid mind like two ole bull alligators, an' ef it ain' been for dis boy er ole Bill's, dey would er kilt one annudder. We call him an' tell him see can't he part 'em—talk ain' do no good. An' he grab up a pole an' run out on de log an' push 'em an' beat 'em apart.

An' den we drugged 'em out an' th'owed 'em in a wagon an' sont 'em home, an' I ain' hear no more 'bout 'em since.

Pick

Tad: Wuh is dey do 'bout Pick?

Scip: Bury him. Wha' else you reckon dey guh do?

Tad: I merely axe you a question.

Scip: You axe a fool question.

Voice: Wuh you mean when you axe wuh dey do 'bout Pick? Who Pick an' wuh he do? How come dey bury him?

Scip: De main reason dey bury him, he were dead.

Tad: Why ain't you gee de nigger a straight answer?

Scip: Gee him answer you' self.

Voice: Wuh it, Tad?

Tad: Pick were a business nigger. He live in a place wey dey make good craps, an' Pick buy cotton an' cottonseed an' make a pile er money. An' he lend money an' helt mortgage on white folks an' nigger. An' Pick make so much money till some er de white folks wants to get rid on him 'fore pay day come. But he ain' got no sense; he ain' pay no 'tention to 'em. He ain' scared.

Scip: An' he ain' livin' neither.

Voice: Wuh dey do wid him?

Tad: He were layin' down 'sleep one day when he were crep' up on an' kilt right wey he lay, wid out as much chance as a rat.

Voice: Is dey know who kilt him?

Tad: Dey say dey ain' know. I hear say it been whisper 'twix' niggers, but dat is nigger talk. Ain' nobody guh pay 'tention to dat, an' dey ain' guh say it out loud neither.

Scip: Some on 'em has got sense.

Tad: Well, a load er shot removed Pick. Wuh it matter ef a man gain de whole world an' loss he own life?

Voice: An' ain' nobody do nothin'.

Scip: Yes, dey is. Dey bury Pick.

Sweet Chile

Tad: Hank in a bad fix.

Voice: Is? Wha' ail him?

Tad: Him an' he wife, Sweet Chile, been back in de swamp pickin' berries, an' dey was comin' out through one er dem ole road in de night. Sweet Chile seen sump'n layin' 'cross de road an' say:

"Look er dere, Hank. Wha' is dat?"

An' Hank is dis kind er nigger: he always want er show off when he wid a ooman, it ain' make no diff'ence ef de ooman ain' nothin' but he own wife. He say:

"Ain' nothin'."

An' he haul off an' kick it. He think it was a rotten log, but dat log was a 'gator an' grab Hank by he foot an' th'owed him down, an' den de fun start. Hank have sense 'nough to reach in he pocket an' hand he wife he knife; an' she rode dat 'gator like he was a saddle horse, poppin' dat knife into him 'round he neck an' eye an' joogin' him under he arm an' callin' to de Lord. She tell de Lord don't luh dat 'gator bite Hank no wey else. She say ef he ain' loss nothin' but dat one foot, she reckon she kin make out wid it. An' when she finish wid dat 'gator, he was glad to turn Hank loose but it were too late for him; an' ef Hank ain' have a fightin' ooman, it would er been too late for Hank. An' Hank was sho' bit up bad, but dat ooman took him out er dat swamp.

Voice: Hank sho' is lucky to have a ooman like dat.

Scip: I reckon some mens mought think it luck.

Voice: Ain't she save him?

Scip: She is save him, but he know wha' kind er ooman he got now.

Tad: Ain'ts he better off for knowin' wha' he got?

Scip: It make thing look too certain.

Voice: Sweet Chile crazy 'bout Hank.

Scip: Dat make it wusser.

Tad: Wuh make you say dat?

Voice: Hank mighty love womens.

Scip: You has a idea.

Tad: I reckon he ain't so easy in he mind now.

Scip: You ain' never know wha' kind er notion a ooman guh take. I never is think too much er dese little wild womens wha' ready to fight so quick for dey mens.

Tad: Luh 'em fight.

Scip: Dat's all right 'bout luh 'em fight. Long as it somebody else, it ain't make too much diff'ence, but, brother, watch 'em. I knows so much 'bout womens I find out I ain't know nothin', but I larn dis: watch you' step wid 'em an' in watchin' it you best keep you' eye on you' own step, too.

Voice: You right, brother Scip. I sho' would hate to tangle up wid a ooman dat ain't hesitate to straddle a 'gator an' ride him through dem swamp, an' sharp enough to know wey to stick she knife. Jesus, no!

Tad: Here come Sweet Chile now. She is a fast lookin' little ooman.

Scip: She fast as she look.

Voice: Good mornin', sister.

Tad: How is you, honey?

Scip: God bless you, my sister.

Sweet Chile: Good day. Brother Tad, don't you "honey" me. I b'longs to Hank.

Tad: Sister, I was merely passin' de time er day. I ain' mean no harm.

Sweet Chile: I knows all 'bout de time er day. You wasn't "merely" nothin'. I know wuh you have in you' mind, but dis de ooman to put it out. You jes try to start wid me kaze Hank got he foot chew up an' you think he cripple an' ain' no 'count.

Tad: For God' sake, sister, you got me dead wrong.

Sweet Chile: I done read you' mind. Ef Hank was dead, I ain' never would have you for my man.

Tad: No, sister, Jesus knows dat. Great God, no!

Reverend Hickman: Be pacify, my sister. Tad have make full representation to you. The Bible say you must not hold animosity.

Sweet Chile: I guh drap it, Reverend. I ain' holdin' nothin' 'gainst Tad.

Voice: Is Hank holler when dat 'gator bite him?

Sweet Chile: No, he ain' holler. Is you tryin' to pick at me?

Reverend Hickman: Peace, my brother an' sister. Our sister is a little nervis today atter she experience. She is over-burden wid she trials.

Sweet Chile: I ain' guh say no more. Good day, brothers. I must be guine.

Scip: You is a noble ooman, sister. I likes to see a ooman like dat—stands up for she rights. Good day, sister. May God bless an' pertect you an' all dat b'longs to you.

Sweet Chile: Good day.

Tad: Looks like I got her wrong.

Voice: You is.

Scip: No, I don't want nothin' to do wid dem kind er womens.

Voice: Me either.

Tad: God have mercy on Hank' soul ef she ever gits wrong wid him. Ef I look much like er alligator as Hank is, I'd leff dat ooman time I could walk. You mark my word: ef she ever ketch Hank lookin' at a nudder ooman, she guh ride him wuss dan she done dat 'gator.

Voice: De trute.

Scip: Dey is too much ooman in de world for me to pick dem kind. I loves 'em peaceful.

Drug Up

Tad: Is you hear de argiment 'twix' ole Hark an' ole man Sam?

Voice: Wuh it is?

Tad: Dey git in a argiment 'bout how dey was raise—'bout which er dey fam'ly was de higher class. Ole man Sam claim all kind er thing for he fam'ly an' ole Hark put in all kind er claim, an' dey both been th'owin' off on one annudder' fam'ly. An' dey kep' it up till all two on 'em git hot. Ole man Hark have de agvantage, kaze all er ole man Hark' chillun boy chillun an' moest er ole man Sam' chillun gals.

Scip: It do look like ole man Hark have de agvantage. It's mighty hard to keep a good reputation in you' fam'ly ef you got a house full er gals.

Tad: Well, ole man Hark have de agvantage in chillun, but ole man Sam have de agvantage in tongue. Atter ole man Hark th'owed off on ole man Sam' chillun, he ain' satisfy wid dat, he start to makin' personally remarks 'bout ole man Sam. He tell ole man Sam he ain' blame he chillun for wha' dey is, as he has tooken into consideration de way ole man Sam was brung up.

An' ole man Sam say dere ain' no consideration to be tooken for nothin' in ole man Hark' fam'ly—dey ain' worthy er consideration, but he say:

"Hark, you talk 'bout de way I was brung up. You wasn't brung up, you was drug up."

Scip: I reckon dat was wey some trial justice put both er dey foots to de fire.

Tough

Tad: All er ole man Brown' folks is frettin' dey self sick.

Voice: How come?

Tad: Ole man Brown been ailin' a long time, an' de report git out he ain' guh live so long.

Voice: I ain' see wuh make 'em fret 'bout dat. He ain' never been nothin' but one er dem ole prayin' scoundrels wha' 'buke he chillun all de time, an' skin everybody he come in contact wid. He'll try to skin God Almighty out er a good place in heaven.

Scip: I reckon God Almighty already got him headed for hell.

Tad: I ain' know 'bout dat, not yet. I axe dat nigger wha' work for him how he is, an' he say people is frettin' 'bout him but he ain' think he gone yet. He say it would not be natu'al for him to pass out dat easy. Dat he life ain' never have nothin' in it but 'ceitfulness, an' he ain' see no reason wuh make dis guh be de exception.

Scip: I reckon dat de main reason dey have so much frettin'.

Tad: Dat nigger say annudder reason he think ole man Brown guh last a good while yet, he tough; he got de constitution er de Nunited States.

Thirteen Years

Tad: Is you hear 'bout dat nigger dey turn loose yesterday?

Voice: No, we ain' hear nothin' 'bout him. We hear dey turn a nigger loose. How come dey turn him loose?

Tad: He were innocent.

Scip: Wuh dat got to do wid it?

Tad: De ooman wuh scuse him say dat.

Scip: How long he serve 'fore she say dat?

Tad: De judge guin him thirty years an' he ain' serve but thirteen on 'em.

Scip: He ain' serve but thirteen on 'em. I wonder how come dat.

Tad: De ooman say he ain' guilty.

Voice: Wuh is he been scuse on?

Tad: He been scuse er rape an' have two trial 'fore dey convict him, but dey was in doubt, so de judge guin him de benefit er de doubt an' guin him thirty years. Dey say dat kep' 'em from lynchin' him. De real reason dey say was: dis nigger have land wuh he rent to dese white folks an' he want he land back for he ownt nuse, an' de white folks dey wants de land, so dey charge him wid rape, an' he loss he farm an' he spend thirteen long years in prison. Dey say he ain' have no friend an' he would write letter to de diff'ent governor an' plead wid 'em an' say:

"Please, Governor, help me. I am innocent."

An' de governor wouldn't pay no 'tention to him, an' he labor for thirteen long an' weary years—thirteen long years out er dis short time 'lowed a man in dis world.

Voice: Is he pray?

Tad: You know dat nigger pray, but good as prayer is, dere is times when it ain' no good—when you got to suffer for de sins er you' forefathers. Well, dat was dat nigger.

Reverend Hickman: You is wrong, brother. God is answer dat nigger' prayer. He jes leff him dere awhile to try he faith, an' 'sides dat, I reckon he done some wrong er some kind.

Voice: You ain' explain how dey 'cide dis nigger is innocent after he wear stripe an' chain for thirteen year.

Tad: Well, it were a white ooman wha' send him dere, an' she were mighty sick an' she knowed ef she ain' hurry up an' do sump'n, she were guh bu's' hell wide open. She know she done a innocent man wrong an' she time was comin'. She know when God Almighty hand you over to de devil, it ain' make no diff'ence wuh you' color—black or white or yallow, high or low—dat ole man don't fool wid you, dat one thing he don't do. You kin lay anything to de devil but dat—he don't never neglect he duty. When God hand a sinner over to de devil, He done satisfy in He mind dey ain' no 'count—dey ain' worth savin'—an' de devil don't waste no time puttin' de fire to 'em.

Well, dat ole ooman find out she guh leff dis world, an' she guine wey dey will burn a cracker wuss dan a cracker would burn a nigger in dis world. An' she say as she feel dat death is approachin', she would like to tell de trute for one time in she life, an' she own up dat dis nigger ain' never done nothin' to her an' she wants to acknowledge her wrong an' be saved.

Scip: De way I see it, she tryin' to save she self. She ain' care nothin' 'bout de nigger.

Voice: It looks dat er way.

Reverend Hickman: My brother, you mustn't have evil thought. Maybe she is repent in de name er de Lord an' is been thinkin' 'bout de nigger.

Scip: She must er been thinkin' 'bout de nigger.

Tad: Yes, she sho' was thinkin' 'bout de nigger.

Scip: I reckon she jes natu'ally couldn't been thinkin' 'bout bein' saved ef she had er leff dat nigger out her thought.

Voice: Le's we pray for she.

Reverend Hickman: It ain' guh do no harm.

Scip: Is you reckon it will do good?

Reverend Hickman: Prayer never is hurt nobody.

Scip: I reckon de Lord will see it all an' use He judgment.

Reverend Hickman: He ain' guh hold it 'gainst we.

Voice: I reckon it best we pray. It might help we sometime.

Reverend Hickman: Have faith.

Scip: Dat's 'bout all we got.

Reverend Hickman: Dat nigger had faith an' is free.

Scip: Him an' faith had a hard time for thirteen years.

Reverend Hickman: Well, de judge guin him thirty, an' faith tooken dat down.

Scip: It look to me like faith on de part er dat nigger ain' had nothin' to do wid it.

Tad: He are free. Dey all on 'em kin say dat.

Scip: He free. How 'bout de ooman?

Reverend Hickman: I stick to wuh I say in de first place: have faith. De ooman have faith an' she still is free.

Tad: You reckon faith kep' her free?

Reverend Hickman: Faith—I always preaches faith.

Scip: Faith in what? Thirteen years er faith. Faith in law; faith in God; faith in de everlastin' punishment dat would come to dis ooman, ef dis man had er served he full time. Faith in de court; faith in de liar dat testify; faith in dis sneakin' hag dat is tryin' to escape hell fire. Don't tell me 'bout no faith.

Reverend Hickman: Repent an' you will be saved.

Voice: Amen!

Tad: I b'lieve in repentance.

Reverend Hickman: My brother.

Scip: Repent.

Reverend Hickman: Repentance is de easiest way.

Tad: Dat's wha' I say.

Voice: Wuh is you all say?

Scip: All you all niggers has too much to say.

Reverend Hickman: Luh 'em say wuh dey has a mind to say.

Scip: I ain' kin stop 'em.

Tad: We talkin' to we.

Scip: Is you all forgit how to laugh? Laugh an' I jine you.

The Telephone Call

Tad: Is you hear 'bout dat nigger wuh had all dat long compersation over de telephone?

Voice: Wuh it is? Tell we.

Tad: De white folks to Hopkins have a store, an' he went out to 'tend to some business an' leff dis here nigger wuh work for him to mind de store. Dere been a passel er niggers in de store settin' 'round on boxes an' on de counter talkin' an' tellin' lie, an' one nigger was tellin' de other niggers 'bout de fine sixteen-dollar suit er clothes he order from Sears Roebuck in Chicago. He say he order it two weeks ago, an' ain' heared nothin' from it yet.

An' he was braggin' 'bout he clothes an' say he guh write de manage-ment an' axe 'em wuh make dey ain' send he clothes. An' one er de niggers axe him wuh make he guh loss all dat time writin'—wuh de matter wid dat big telephone. He says Sears Roebuck more'n apt to have a 'phone er dey own; an' ef dey ain' got one, all he got to do is to axe long distance to send for de manager an' he'll have him on de 'phone in no time. Dat nigger say he ain' never thought er dat. Say he glad de other nigger 'mind him of it. Say he walk right on over to Mr. Cue' 'phone an' tell long distance he wants to speak to de manager er Sears, Roebuck and Company, Chicago, Illinois. He tell long distance he ain' wan' 'em to make no mistake. He wants to speak to de big boss, an' right now. He tell 'em ef dey ain' got no 'phone to Sears Roebuck, jes to send a messenger.

Atter while he gits Sears Roebuck on de 'phone, an' him an' de boss talked about dem clothes for God knows how long. You could hear dat nigger tellin' de boss good-by like dey were ole friends raise up together.

Dat nigger was settin' dere talkin' 'bout he clothes an' he say de boss in Chicago tell him he clothes was already on de way. While dey was settin' dere laughin' an' talkin' de white folks come in. He start to 'tendin' to he business an' de telephone ring an' say:

"De charges for dis call is one hundred an' sixty-seven dollars an' twenty-eight cents."

White folks look 'round an' say:

"What? Who in de hell talk all dat over my 'phone? I guh put some damn nigger on de gang."

Dat nigger jes look 'round dat store one time an' he reach up an' grab he hat an' dash out dat store, an' when he went 'cross de field he leg was movin' so fast you couldn't see 'em—look like he have wing. An' ain' nobody see dat nigger for two weeks. De white folks jes look at him an' faint, an' white folks' daddy was a doctor an' have to 'tend him, an' dey say he hover 'twix' life an' death, an' dat nigger ain' been heared of till he find out de white folks were guh live.

An' de nigger try to make peace wid de white folks. Sent word to him ef he ain' do nothin' to him, he guh gee him dat suit er clothes. An' de white folks tooken to he bed again an' like to work he pa to death, an' dey has talk 'bout havin' dat nigger 'rested for makin' a 'tempt on de white folks' life.

Voice: Wuh is dey do 'bout de bill?

Tad: De white folks pay it, but 'fore he done it dat nigger' pa had to mortgage he crop an' horse an' cow.

Things git to sech a pass ef you showed de white folks a Bible an' ain' explain it quick to him wuh it is, he would have a fit thinkin' it were a Sears Roebuck catalogue.

He says de nigger is been heared of, but ain' been seen since, an' de white folks never has got quite right. Dey say he is peculiar now.

A Damn Nigger

Tad: I been to a trial today. It been some er dem bootlegger for killin' Jake.

Voice: Who dey have?

Tad: Three on 'em.

Voice: I hear dere been four.

Tad: Dere been four, but dey ain' have but three on 'em up, an' dey ain' try none on 'em.

Voice: Why ain't dey try 'em? Ain't dey murder Jake?

Tad: Dere's more reason dan one.

Voice: Wuh reason?

Tad: Jake was a nigger. De judge were a kind judge—a good man—wuh ain' b'lieve in too severe punishment for white folks when a nigger is kilt, ain' matter wha' kind er white folks. An' de solicitor wha' prosecute an' see dat de criminal git he full jues is a merciful man. An' he got great ideas er bein' light in punishment of dem white mens who wored de uniform er dere country in war.

Voice: You say you been to de trial, an' den you say dere ain' no trial.

Tad: Well, I been to de court, an' dere been some argiment an' private compersation an' head noddin', an' dis reason an' dat reason. An' den dey 'gree to luh 'em plead guilty to manslaughter.

Voice: Ain' Jake been a great friend to dem white folks?

Tad: Raise up together. Sleep in de same bed. But dat ain' make no diff'ence. Dey been friend ever since dey been chillun. Jake wait on 'em an' follow 'em 'round like a dog.

Voice: An' dey kilt Jake?

Tad: Wuh de diff'ence? Jake ain' nothin' but a damn nigger. I hear 'em say dat.

Voice: How come dey kilt Jake?

Tad: Dey say he stole dey liquor. An' dey find Jake an' put him in a automobile an' tooken him wey dey had de liquor, an' dey guin him all kind er punishment. An' dey say 'fore dey kilt him dey fix him so he ain' neither man nor ooman. Ef he'd er lived, he wouldn't been nothin'.

Den dey took him an' lead him out in de woods an' beat he brain out, an' dey had hole in he head wey he brain was ooze out. Den dey leff him, an' dey come back an' git him an' th'owed him in a automobile an' tooken him back in de swamp an' th'owed him in a ditch. An' later on somebody find him an' de news git out who kilt him. Several niggers seen it, but dey was feared to tell it till some white folks started to pushin' 'em.

Voice: Why ain't dey 'rest all on 'em?

Tad: In de first place, a nigger was kilt. An' de next place, dey says one on 'em had friend on de police force, an' ain' nobody do nothin' 'bout it. It were jes a damn nigger.

Voice: An' dey luh 'em plead guilty to manslaughter?

Tad: Dey say dere were some white mens wid a conscience, an' dey was feared of de jury.

Scip: Somebody were a fool to luh 'em plead guilty, an' de solicitor must er sho' God been atter 'em an' wants 'em punish, or else dere would er been a great cry 'bout. "Dese men must feel de hand of justice. Ef dey has taken human life—de life of a poor helpless nigger"—an' a heap er talk like dat, an' den dey would er been free.

Voice: Dey plead guilty to manslaughter. Wuh is dey do wid 'em?

Tad: 'Fore de judge pass on 'em, dere been so much tender feelin' in de court, dat de judge were axe:

"May it please you' Honor, owin' to de fine war record of dese mens who serve dey country in time er 'stress, I guh do de onusual thing an' axe you' Honor to be lenient wid dese mens accordin' to dey merits."

Scip: An' I reckon de judge do de usual thing an' were lenient, an' a nigger was kilt.

Tad: It were a merciful solicitor an' a feelin' judge.

Voice: Is de court been lenient?

Scip: Fools like you is one reason it ain' make no diff'ence ef a nigger is kilt. I'll axe you a question: Who been kilt an' who de court?

Voice: A nigger were kilt an' white folks de court.

Scip: You done answer you' ownt question.

Hatchet: I been settin' here an' listen to wuh you all say. I listen to all dis round about talk an' ain' no talk guh git you an' me no wey. From de way I looks at it, a nigger hab white friend he raise up wid. He work for him. He live wid him. He follow him. He do he biddin'. An' den de nigger git de white man's justice. He were kilt like a beast, an' dat were de end er de nigger. An' justice jes look up an' laugh an' grin.

Dey go in de court an' dere's a great to do about dis sad an' unfortunate affair—'bout dese poor white boys wha' serve dey country bein' in great trouble an' dey must be hoped. An' atter dey go through a little form wid dey own lawyer pleadin' for 'em, an' wid de aid of a merciful prosecutin' attorney, de law is satisfy. A nigger is dead.

Dere ain' no nuse. De courts er dis land is not for niggers. Ain' nothin' for 'em but a gun an' a knife in a white man's hand, an' den de grave, an' sorrow an' tear for he people. De Bible say, "De Lord watcheth de fall of every sparrow," an' I says: Why ain't He take He eye off sparrow an' luh 'em rest some time on bigger game?

It seems to me when it come to trouble, de law an' a nigger is de white man's sport, an' justice is a stranger in them precincts, an' mercy is unknown. An' de Bible say we must pray for we enemy. Drap on you' knee, brothers, an' pray to God for all de crackers an' de judges an' de courts an' solicitors, sheriffs an' police in de land, for we must er been all er we livin' in sin. We stands in fear of de avengin' angel, for he's here an' we is surrounded. Drap on you' knee, brother, drap on you' knee, jes a nigger—a damn nigger—was kilt.

The Lynchers
(A Ballad)

What did de lynchers say?
Bertha bleated like a goat
When dey shot her down.
What did Bertha say?
I ain't done no wrong at all,
Just tried to 'fend my little home;
I can only weep and moan,
White folks got my body,
Oh, Lord! Have mercy on my soul,
Have mercy, have mercy on my soul.

What did de big boss say?
He say I is hog tie
And on able to do my duty.
What did de Lowmans say?
I ain't done no wrong at all,
Just tried to 'fend my little home;
I can only weep and moan,
White folks got my body,
Dear Lord! Have mercy on my soul,
Have mercy, have mercy on my soul.

What did de government do?
Dey say dere was no evidence,
And dey feared de murder crew.
What did Demon say?
I ain't done no wrong at all,
Just tried to 'fend my little home;
I can only weep and moan,
White folks got my body,
Oh, Lord! Have mercy on my soul,
Have mercy, have mercy on my soul.

What did old man Lowman do?
For liquor dey did claim to find,
Dey guin him two years on de gang.
What did de poor nigger say?
I ain't done no wrong at all,
Just tried to 'fend my little home;
I can only weep and moan,
White folks got my body,
  Oh, Lord! Have mercy on my soul,
  Have mercy, have mercy on my soul.

What did de lynchers do?
Put a bullet in my mother,
Kilt a babe unborn.
What did de Lowmans say?
I ain't done no wrong at all,
Just tried to 'fend my poorly home;
I can only weep and moan,
White folks got my body,
  Oh, Lord! Have mercy on my soul,
  Have mercy, have mercy on my soul.

What did de murderers do?
Open up de jail door;
Dragged de helpless from dere cell.
What did de weeping woman say?
I ain't done no wrong at all,
Just tried to 'fend my little home;
I can only weep and moan,
White folks got my body,
  Oh, Lord! Have mercy on my soul,
  Have mercy, have mercy on my soul.

What did de noble heroes do?
Dey butchered helpless niggers,
Kaze dey had a mind for murder.
What did de screaming woman say?
I ain't done no wrong at all,
Just tried to 'fend my little home;

I can only weep and moan,
White folks got my body,
Oh, Lord! Have mercy on my soul,
Have mercy, have mercy on my soul.

What did de lynchers do?
Dey shot a helpless woman
In de back begging mercy.
What did de weeping woman say?
I ain't done no wrong at all.
Just tried to 'fend my little home;
I can only weep and moan,
White folks got my body,
Oh, Lord! Have mercy on my soul,
Have mercy, have mercy on my soul.

What did de lynchers say?
We shot a bunch of niggers,
And we'll kill some white folks, too.
What did de bruised and weeping woman say?
I ain't done no wrong at all,
Just tried to 'fend my little home;
I can only weep and moan,
White folks got my body,
Oh, Lord! Have mercy on my soul,
Have mercy, have mercy on my soul.

A Bottle of Liquor

Julius: I 'clare to God! I done laugh till my belly hurt.

Willie: Wuh make you hurt you' belly laughin'?

Julius: I ain' been able to help myself.

Willie: Wuh you laugh 'bout?

Julius: I jes laugh 'bout de scand'lous way Tad treat de white folks.

Willie: Wuh he do?

Julius: You know how sharp Tad is, an' how he love liquor.

Willie: Wha' it is all 'bout?

Julius: White folks come down here dis mornin' an' give Tad a quart er liquor an' say:

"Tad, keep dis here liquor till tonight, an' don't drink none on it. I got some friend comin' down here to take supper wid me tonight."

An' Tad tooken de liquor an' went off wid it.

Willie: Do Jesus! White folks sho' is trust he liquor. Tad ain' hardly got dat much faith in he self.

Voice: Wuh Tad do wid de liquor?

Julius: I ain' know. De onliest thing I know when de white folks come back, he call Tad an' say:

"Tad, git my liquor."

An' Tad brung him de bottle an' half on it been gone.

Willie: I could er told de white folks dat.

Voice: Wha' de white folks say?

Julius: White folks look at Tad an' he say:

"Tad, wha' in de hell you drink up my liquor for? Ain't I tell you I guh hab people here for supper? An' now you done drink up half er my liquor."

Willie: Wha' Tad say?

Julius: Tad look at de white folks an' say:

"I 'clare to God I ain't teched dat liquor. When you guin it to me, I hand it to you' brother an' he lock it up an' put de key in he pocket, an' I ain' see dat liquor since."

An' de white folks brother been standin' dere, an' he look at de white folks an' he say:

"Wuh you kickin' up all dis fuss about? Ain't nobody trouble you' liquor."

An' Tad look at him an' say:

"Boss, you too funny. You 'mind me er de time de animals had a party. One er de animals spoke up an' say, 'De ugliest man got to go git a bucket er water.' Time he say it de monkey jump up an' say, 'I know I ain' guh git it.' "

Voice: Wuh de white folks' brother say?

Julius: He turn red an' look at Tad an' say:

"Go to hell."

An' den he leff.

Old Mammy

Tad: I been to some meetin'. A nigger tickles me wid he fool ideas. Ef he ever gits up in de world, his breeches starts to bu'stin' right now. Dere ain' never been a pair er pants big enough to hold a nigger, ef he ever rises up; he gits 'side he self right now. Notions runs all 'round inside he head an' has a wuss time 'an a bug crawlin' 'round on de outside. He head kinky inside an' out. It's wusser inside.

Scip: Tad, wuh you have on you' mind?

Tad: I jes been thinkin' 'bout all dat big-doin's, fancy-talkin' nigger say.

Voice: Wuh he say?

Tad: He been talkin' 'bout de advancement of de nigger race, an' he read all kind er things 'bout niggers writ by white folks, an' talked 'bout de great onderstandin' de author—he call 'em—have of the negro. He read a heap in a book 'bout ole mammy.

Voice: Wuh is a ole mammy?

Scip: Ole mammy ain' nothin' but a ole ooman wid a han'-k'ch'ef tied 'round she head. Dere's all kind er ole 'ceitful niggers gittin' dey self called ole mammy—more'n you can shake a stick at. Dere's all kind er white folks runnin' 'round lookin' for ole mammys wuh been in dey fam'ly an' tooken care on 'em ever since dey was born—an' afore. An' Lord! some on 'em carries on at sech a rate 'bout "my ole mammy" till it jes natu'ally makes a respectable nigger sick on he stomach.

Tad: Dat nigger say a ole mammy is a respected, lousy ole ooman dat knows her place.

Scip: All dese white folks dat got ole mammys from 'way down south! Oh, Jesus!

Tad: Scip, you oughter hush you' mout'. Them de white folks—the ole istockacy from 'way down south. Oh, Lord!

Scip: Cash money is de istockacy. It gees de right to a ole mammy. Let a cracker git a little money an' he edecate he chillun, an' dey always has ole mammys, ef dey git far enough from home.

Tad: Ain' us white folks have ole mammy?

Scip: Is we talkin' 'bout us white folks?

Voice: Wuh else is dat nigger talk about? Is ole mammy hold all he compersation?

Tad: No, he have a heap to say 'bout edecation an' 'gainst white folks. He read from books an' papers 'bout white folks, an' all on 'em is dog to him. Dat nigger's mind jes natu'ally stinks.

Scip: Luh him go 'long. All I hates 'bout dem kind er niggers is ef dey ever starts to stretchin' dey necks, dey is liable to git mient stretched 'long wid dey ownt.

Tad: Dat nigger read all kind er thing wha' he call literature 'bout womens an' frettin' 'bout dey havin' chillun, an' 'bout dey been tooken agvantage of in dey ign'ance.

An' he say it depick de humble condition of a depressed people. An' ef you listen to dat nigger, you'd think dat every lousy, slew-footed ole nigger 'round here oughter be President of de Nunited States. Sound like God forgit 'em, an' when He find 'em, He guh prove dey's better dan white folks.

Scip: Luh dat nigger go on wid he edecation talk. Look like everybody frettin' 'bout niggers' private business wusser dan de nigger, cepen dem edecated, trouble-makin' niggers. I jine him wid he ideas 'bout ole mammys, but I ain't think too much 'bout de rest er wha' he say.

Tad: Dat nigger say us race ain't kin accomplish nothin' wid out edecation. Edecation is power.

Scip: Dem edecated niggers losses dey manners, an' goes 'round reared back wid dey thumbs stuck behind dey galluses wid seegar cocked up in dey mout' like it guh scorch de rim er dey hat, makin' dey self disgustin' an' stirrin' up trouble an' leffen when de fire gits good an' hot. An' den de white folks starts holdin' us foots to de fire.

Edecation is power, an' when dey gits too powerful, dey sometimes gits on de gang, an' a edecated nigger on de gang is a power, sho' 'nough; an' when some er dem white folks gits to rompin' on 'em, dey swings a pick like dey loves it, an' dey's always tested out to see ef dey hide is natu'al, or ef dey got alligator hide.

Voice: De moest on 'em hates dey self.

Scip: No, he ain't.

Voice: Ole Cuffy is still feelin' 'round in de dark. Gee him a chance. He'll see de light bumbye.

Scip: Ef he ain' careful 'bout how he feels 'round white folks, he'll see de light—it guh be a mighty dim light, an' it guh flicker out.

Le's we talk 'bout sump'n interestin'.

A Good Looking Man

Scip: Is you hear wha' Tad tell he boss?

Voice: Wha' he tell him?

Scip: De boss come out all dress up an' shave, for God' sake. An' Tad look at him an' say:

"Boss, you sho' God is a good lookin' man. You de best lookin' man I ever see."

An' de boss look at him an' say:

"You think so, Tad?"

An' Tad say:

"You sho' is. I reckon the reason wuh make I think so is you moest generally looks so wuss."

Voice: Wuh de boss say?

Scip: He ain' say nothin', but he look like somebody guin him a dose er physic.

Three Doctors

Tad: I 'clare to God ef dese doctors ain' rough, I ain' know.

Voice: Wuh you have in mind?

Tad: I jes been thinkin' 'bout time dat storm blowed down ole man Josey' house an' a j'ist broken Millie' leg an' ole Dr. McCrea been call, an' he look at it an' he say it ain't but one way for he to save it. An' he guin Millie sump'n to put her to sleep an' took out a knife about a foot long, an' he ring it 'round Millie' leg an' he grabbed up a saw an' sawed de bone off up above she knee. An' he tooken de leg an' lean it up 'side de fireplace an' say he ain' got time to stay dere, he got a white man sick down de road; he'll be back.

An' when he git back, Millie been prop up on pillow lookin' at she leg an' hollerin' an' moanin'. An' dat ole man look at her an' tell her to hush she damn fuss, dat she is a lucky nigger; she kin live to see she own funeral. All she got to do is to save dat leg, an' when she git better she kin have she own time wid it. Ain' none er dese niggers would miss de funeral.

An' when he leff, he was grinnin' an' Millie was still hollerin'.

Si: He is been kind er rough. One night I been to he house an' a nigger come dere an' knock on de door. An' he axe him wuh in de hell he want. An' de nigger say another nigger done split Sam' head open wid a axe. An' de ole doctor say:

"Ain't you know better dan to come here an' wake me up dis time er night? Ef dat nigger is livin' in de mornin', you kin bring him here atter breakfast."

An' he turn right over an' went back to sleep an' went to snorin' jes as peaceful as ef he been doin' God's work.

Frank: I 'member de time another doctor been comin' down de road, an' Easter been standin' on de roadside waitin' for de doctor. An' she sign him down wid her apron. She say:

"Doctor, Tom got ringworrum an' sore on de back er he neck. I wants you to look at him."

An' de doctor say:

"I ain' got time. You take dis here little vial an' pour a few drops on de back er Tom' neck an' rub it in good wid a corn-cob."

An' he guin Easter a little vial er carbolic acid an' she tooken it home an' poured it on Tom' neck an' start to rubbin'. An' he grunt two or three time an' jump up an' bu's' out dat house an' tored down three or four panels er garden palin' an' went 'cross dem cotton-patches an' cornfield wuss 'an a mad dog, an' he bellow same as a bull. It tooken all de niggers in Pine Bluff to ketch him an' bring him back. An' dey had to hold him down till de furore wored off.

Tad: Well, dem's white doctors we been talkin' 'bout. Dey sho' is rough, but dey is good mens.

But I wants to tell you 'bout another doctor—a ooman, a nigger—one er we ownt race, an' I tell you she got a heart.

One night a nigger come in she office wid he head split open from a razor cut from de back er he head to he forehead; de skin done drawed down on both side er he head. It leff a wound wide as you' hand an' I look right at his skull. Well, sir, dat doctor wash he head off an' sew it up like she was sewin' up a mattress. When she finish, she wrop it all up. An' he say:

"I ain' got no money here. I got to go back 'cross de river to git some money. I'll be back atter while."

An' she say:

"Hold on a minute. Sump'n I forgot. Luh me look at you' wound again."

An' she tooken off dem bandage an' tooken her scissors an' run it right down de wound an' cut every one er dem stitches. An' she say:

"Now, you go home an' git you' money, an' when you bring it, I'll sew you up again."

A Fisherman

Tad: I got a tale you all ain' hear.

Voice: Wuh it?

Tad: I been to de white folks' house, an' while I dere, de white folks come in wid a five-pound trout an' th'owed him down in de kitchen sink like he nuse to ketchin' dem kind er fish. He treat dat fish jes as common as he would er done ef he been a catfish. He talk 'bout fish ain' bitin' much, an' den tooken four or five drinks an' walk over to de sink an' look at dat fish an' say:

"Dem's two nice little ones, ain'ts dey?"

Voice: Wuh you say?

Tad: I ain' say nothin' but look at dat lone fish an' make a great miration over it.

Voice: Wuh you say?

Tad: I pick dat fish up an' say I ain' never see two finer trout.

Voice: Wuh de white folks say?

Tad: He tell me take one on 'em to one er he friend an' one to annudder friend an' to cook de other one for breakfast.

Dat's wey him an' me part comp'ny. He ain' have 'nough fish to feed no multitude. He more'n apt would er had 'em ef I had er gee him time. I ain' feel like guine to jail. Dem fish was increasin' too fast, an' I ain' know wuh guh happen when dey all done guin away, so I leff.

Land Rent

Tad: Some people sho' has got a heart.

Voice: Wuh you talkin' 'bout?

Tad: I been thinkin' 'bout how cold it is an' de time Miss Henry take ole man Jim Kay an' put him out er doors 'bout he land rent.

Voice: Wuh 'bout it? It seems to me I 'member but I ain' sho'.

Tad: Ain't you 'member dat winter it been so cold an' everything freeze up an' been kiver wid snow an' ice, Un' Jim Kay ain' kin pay he rent, an' Miss Henry cuss him out an' tell him he guh pay or git off he place? I 'member it well. I been dere an' I see ole man Jim Kay come in de little house wuh Potee stay in an' say he ain' kin make it furder, he feel so wuss, an' he ain' kin walk no more. Axe me tell Miss Henry please, sir, come here. An' I went in de big house an' call Miss Henry an' he come out to Potee' house an' I never is hear a man so rough. I stand one side an' look an' listen.

Ole man Jim Kay been a ole time slavery nigger. When Miss Henry come in, he been settin' by de fire leanin' over—look like some ole prophet. I ain' never will forgit him wid he white beards an' shaggy hair. He say:

"Good day, Boss. How's my young Marster?"

An' Miss Henry say:

"Jim, you got my money?"

An' Jim say:

"Young Marster, I got all I got in my hand."

An' he lean over an' rest on he stick wid one hand, settin' dere by de fire, an' wid de other he held up a shot bag an' say:

"Here is all I got."

An' Miss Henry say:

"How much?"

An' Jim Kay say:

"My rent is one hundred an' twenty-five dollars, an' one er my chillun been sick an' I ain' got it all. I have to pay de doctor. I ain' got but ninety dollars."

An' Miss Henry say:

"Hand it here. Wuh de hell you spend my money payin' you' damn doctor for you' damn chillun? I ain' care nothin' 'bout you' damn chillun."

An' he take de money an' he say:

"Move. You can't stay on my place."

An' Un' Jim Kay say:

"Young Marster, for ole Marster' sake please for God' sake have mercy."

An' Miss Henry say:

I ain' wan' none er you' damn weedlin' talk to me."

An' Un' Jim Kay bu's' out cryin' an' hobble off through de snow.

An' I say Mars' Henry sho' got a heart.

Voice: Wuh ole man Jim Kay do?

Tad: He went back to he house an' next mornin' move out. I ain' never forgit it kaze it been one er de wuss freeze we ever is had.

Un' Jim Kay have he wife an' chillun—dey been five or six little chillun scusin' a sucklin' baby an' several on 'em half growed up. Dey move into de middle er de branch field an' git some plank an' put 'em up end on end an' sleep under dem, an' dey stay dere till God an' some er de white folks tooken pity on 'em an' guin 'em a little house.

Loyalty

Tad: Dey tell me Guy in a mighty bad fix.

Voice: Wuh ail him?

Tad: Dey say he ain' never been satisfy since de ole doctor die. You know he been de ole doctor' servant ever since he were chillun an' when de ole doctor die Guy ack like he were lost, he ain' never quit frettin'; an' now he done git to wey he won't eat nothin'. He wife an' all de niggers try to 'suade him to eat sump'n, but he say he time come. He ain' wan' to eat nothin'.

He say de other night de ole doctor 'peared to him an' dey have a long talk. He say he wife were in de next room an' hear everything wuh he say.

Den dem niggers went to Miss Frank an' tell him he better see atter Guy, an' he axe 'em wuh ail Guy. An' dey tell him Guy guh die. Dere don't seems to be nothin' de matter wid him cepen he won't eat. But Miss Frank say he ain' got time to go look Guy up. He tell he driver an' Wash to take he car an' go over dere an' git Guy an' bring him wey he is. He guh have a talk wid him. An' when Guy come, Miss Frank say:

"Guy, wuh is de matter ail you?"

An' Guy look at him kinder hollow-eye like an' he say:

"De ole doctor 'peared to me de other night. It make de second time. De first time he come, he jes showed he self to me, an' de next time he come was 'way in de night. He come in my room an' make me git out er my bed an' light de lamp. An' he set dere an' talk to me 'bout all kind er thing. An' den he tell me he needs me, an' I got to go."

Miss Frank say:

"Guy, is de ole doctor say wey he is?"

An' Guy say:

"No, sir. He ain' zackly say wey he is, but he don't seems so well satisfy. Dat's one er de thing wuh frets me so, kaze it seems to me he is in great trouble an' he needs me. I got to go."

Miss Frank say:

"Guy, you' attitude in dis affair is very commendable, but you must try to live an' be of some service in dis world, an' maybe you is mistaken 'bout wey de ole doctor is."

Guy say he know dat one thing he ain' make no mistake 'bout.

But Miss Frank cheer up Guy' mind an' send him on back home, an' he tell he friend 'bout Guy an' say he never is seen sech a demonstration of loyalty.

Scip: Dat ain' no loyalty Guy got. Sump'n de matter ail Guy, an' he frettin' kaze he tryin' to think er some plan to escape guine wey he sho' is guine.

They Oughter Had a Sign on It

Tad: Dey sentence Brayden today.

Voice: For makin' liquor?

Tad: No, not for makin' liquor. De court say he worked at a still wuh oughter had a sign on it sayin', "DIS IS A STILL."

Voice: Who else dey sentence?

Tad: Ain' nobody.

Voice: Is it been Brayden' still?

Tad: You know it ain' none er Brayden' still. You know Brayden ain' nothin' to have no still. He ain' got sense enough.

Voice: Tell we 'bout it.

Tad: Brayden been haulin' sugar a mile from de still, when five or six mens jumped out er de bushes an' fire dey gun in de air, an' Brayden jump off he wagon an' run, but dey shot him down like a dog an' shoot him again whilst he layin' on de ground. Dey ain' kill him, but dey 'rest him an' put him in jail, an' dey try him today.

Voice: Who still it been?

Tad: White folks, dey say, but dey ain' make it convenient to ketch none er dem, an' Brayden were try an' sentence. When dey shoot Brayden, dey cut de harness off he mule an' built a fire under he wagon an' burn it up.

De judge say it been sech a big still he guh sentence Brayden wid out a fine. He say he know Brayden ain' own de still an' dat de white folks wuh own it guh pay he fine ef he fine him, an' he say he guh make a example er Brayden. He got to git out er de liquor business. He guh uphold de law.

Voice: Who testify?

Tad: White folks. Dey claim Brayden drawed a knife on 'em.

Voice: How he kin draw a knife on 'em when he been runnin'?

Tad: He ain' draw no knife on nobody. Dat was de evidence, an' de judge an' de jury were satisfy wid it.

Voice: Wuh kind er white folks testify?

Tad: My brother, I ain' got nothin' to say 'bout wuh kind er white folks testify. I lives in dis place, an' dere ain' no sense in you' axe me dat question. You know wuh kind er job dey have. You know wuh dey is. De jury an' de judge know who dey is an' wuh dey is, but dey is white folks an' dey principles ain' got no bearin's on de case. Dey is white, de court is white an' Brayden is a nigger. I reckon you right. Dere ain' nothin' we kin do.

Scip: Dere ain' nothin' to do. Dey kills niggers in de name er prohibition, in de name er de law, in de name er de Lord an' Christianity.

Tad: De law an' de Lord an' all on 'em sho' is jine up wid de devil an' he servants.

Scip: De law say, "Dere shall be no liquor."

Tad: How 'bout puttin' sign up sayin', "DIS IS A STILL." It 'gainst de law to know anything 'bout a still wid out dat sign.

Scip: Dey don't need no sign.

Tad: But dat's de law.

Scip: I see heap er sign.

How to Kill an Owl

Tad: I 'clare, Jazy oughter be 'shame er he self foolin' all dem white folks' chillun.

Voice: Wuh he do?

Tad: He been tell 'em lie 'bout how to kill owl.

Voice: Wuh he say?

Tad: He tell a passel er lie an' got dem chillun guine all over de country lookin' for owl. He tell 'em de best way to kill a owl is to find him when he settin' on a tree an' start walkin' in a circle 'round de tree, an' ef dey walks 'round him long enough, de owl will wring he own neck off an' drap on de ground. A owl ain' never got sense 'nough to unwind he neck. He tell dem chillun a owl will set on a limb an' won't move he body, but he twis' he head right on 'round an' wring it off, ef dey follows he agvice.

Scip: Dat's good for dem chillun. It's good to tell 'em lie an' create s'picion in dey mind, kaze dey guh listen to lie all dey life an' dey better be prepared. Dis world ain' much more 'an one big lie anyway. Luh him learn dese chillun while dey young.

The Ventriloquist

Tad: Is you hear de tale 'bout de white man an' de nigger an' de mule?

Voice: I hear a heap er tales 'bout white folks an' niggers an' mules. Wuh you have in mind?

Tad: One time dere was a white man an' he runned a big farm, an' he notice one er he mule was gitten mighty poor, so he got to watchin'. He s'picion dat de nigger wuh was workin' de mule was stealin' he feed. Dis white man was one er dem people wha' kin pitch dey voice any wey dey wants. He could throw he voice into a cow or dog or any kind er animal an' have 'em talkin'—make 'em carry on reg'lar compersation.

Voice: I has heared dem kind er people.

Tad: Well, he git to de crack er de stable an' he seed de nigger wid a bag reach in de mule' trough an' take out some corn an' put it in de bag. When de nigger do dat, de white man pitched he voice right into de mule' mout' an' make de mule say:

"Nigger, don't take my little bit er feed."

When he say dat, de nigger walk off an' look at de mule for awhile an' de mule ain' say nothin' more. Den he walk back an' dip in de trough again an' start takin' de mule' corn, an' de white folks make de mule say again:

"Nigger, please don't take my feed."

An' again de nigger walk off an' look at de mule.

Voice: Ain' no mule ever would er spoke but one time to me.

Tad: Dis here nigger ain' have good sense, an' he went back de third time an' dive into dat corn. An' dis time de mule turn he head an' look at him, an' de white folks th'owed he voice into de mule' mout' one more time an' make de mule say:

"Nigger, ain' I axe you please for God' sake quit takin' my feed. You mighty nigh done perish me to de't'."

When he say dat, de nigger drap he bag an' bu's' out er dat stable, an' de next mornin' he went to he boss an' say:

"Boss, I guh quit."

An' he boss say:

"John, I ain' want you to quit me. I satisfy wid you."

An' de nigger say:

"Well, Boss, I ain' zackly satisfy. You mought as well gee me my time, kaze I done quit."

Scip: Dere ain' no nigger ever would er been zackly satisfy atter he heared a mule talkin'.

Voice: It was quittin' time.

Tad: Dat ain' all. De white folks paid de nigger he wages an' de nigger walk off a piece down de road an' turn 'round an' walk back to de white folks an' say:

"Boss, I done quit. Dere ain' no nuse for nobody to say nothin' to me. I done quit an' I is guine, but 'fore I goes I got one thing to say to you."

An' de white folks look at him jes as kind an' say:

"Wha' it is, John?"

An' de nigger say:

"Boss, I done quit sho' 'nough, but 'fore I goes I wants to tell you one thing. Anything dat mule say to you is a damn lie."

An' den he leff.

Scip: I knowed in de first place dat de white folks done loss a nigger.

The Courts

Tad: I was to de court all day an' listenin' to dem lawyers rearin' an' pitchin'. Dey set niggers afire.

Scip: De court's a good place to build up a reputation. All a prosecutin' attorney got to do is to rear an' snort when he gits a poor helpless nigger 'fore him. Some on 'em bellows like a bull—jes natu'ally paws up de earth. Dey look like dey thinks dey has been personally insulted an' wronged. Dey will double up dey fist an' shake it at de nigger an' call him a black brute an' a dirty nigger, an' clap dey hand together an' point dey finger at de beast. Dey know de nigger is helpless. An' de judge will set dere in all his honor an' 'low it, an' send de nigger up for a long term an' come out er de court room rubbin' he Christian hands together an' talkin' 'bout wha' a fatiguin' day he hab.

I has a mind 'bout dese things. So much nigger comes up for trial wha' ain't got no money an' ain' kin git no lawyer, an' de judge picks out some little no 'count lawyer wha' ain' have no experience an' tell him to 'fend de nigger, an' den de nigger ain' got no chance at all. 'Sides dat, he most generally gits punish for every mistake he lawyer make.

Dey say courts is for justice. I ain' b'lieve it. Ef you gits justice, you has to buy it. Dere ain' no judge looks like to me he sets out to do justice. It seems to me like de courts oughter have two lawyers—one jes as good as de other—one to prosecute an' one to 'fend de helpless. It is very seldom a prosecutin' attorney got justice in he mind. It is mostly a name for he self. Wuh he care 'bout justice? Wuh he care 'bout sufferin'? De sound er chains is music to him. It helps him to rest well. Luh it be a bank president, it is all diff'ent.

An' de prosecutin' attorney will axe a long question an' say, "Answer it yes or no," an' dere ain' nobody kin answer it right ef dey answer it yes or no. Dat kind er question ain' meant for justice. Ef justice were wha' de court were after, dey would mighty soon sqush dat kind er question an' answer. But judges sets dere like dey think dey self God Almighty an' unjustice rules de court.

Tad: Dere is a heap er sense in wuh you say, Scip, but you best keep it to you' self. You ain' know wuh time dis here compersation ain' guh be in de minds er de court ef dey hears it.

Scip: I knows all er dat, but I guh say dis: dere is a heap er diff'ence in robbin' a bank an' stealin' a chicken.

Ain't Never Own Niggers

Tad: We been down de river huntin'.

Voice: Who?

Tad: Me an' Preb an' de boss an' annudder white folks, an' we sho' had a big time ketchin' fish an' turkle, an' had more liquor dan we could drink.

Voice: Is dey gee you anything?

Tad: Dey was mighty good to we. De other white folks gee me an' Preb each on us five dollars.

Voice: Wuh kind er people were de other white folks?

Tad: Mighty good. Free wid he money an' all er dat.

Voice: You ain' zackly gee me straight answer.

Tad: I ain' know wuh kind er answer you wants.

Scip: Tad, wuh make you ain' gee dat nigger a straight answer? You so 'ceitful. I guh gee him answer for you. I see dat white folks. You know ain' none er he people ever own niggers.

Fundamentals

Tad: Wuh is all dis I hear 'bout Sam bein' kilt an' dey ain' even try de man wuh kill him?

Voice: It must er been a white man.

Tad: Dat ain' oughter make no diff'ence. I ain't expect nothin' to be done wid 'em for killin' niggers, but dey oughter try 'em.

Voice: Well, dey ain' done it.

Tad: Wuh is dey do?

Voice: De judge say he ain' guh try 'em an' order de jury to bring in a verdict of not guilty.

Tad: Who de judge?

Voice: I ain' know dat, an' ef I is know I guh keep it to myself.

Scip: I has a mind 'bout dat judge. He don't count no nigger killin', but ef you was to have a pint er liquor in you' pocket, three years wouldn't be too much. I reckon somebody whisper in he year dat dem was liquor-drinkin' niggers an' dat dey had been known to take de name er de Lord in vain, an' dat settle it.

Voice: I ain' kin b'lieve all er dis.

Scip: It ain' make no diff'ence ef you b'lieve it or no.

Tad: Wuh you reckon in de mind er a judge when he ack dat er way—use he own judgment an' set free murderers wid out knowin' nothin' 'bout 'em?

Scip: Dere ain' nothin' in dey mind. Dey mind done shet up. Dere ain' never been nothin' in dey mind, an' dere ain' never guh be nothin' in dey mind. Dere is very little room in dey mind, an' I listen to wuh one er us white folks say.

Tad: Wuh he say?

Scip: He say he ain' kin hand de mentality er de bench er dese parts no bouquet er flowers, an' he talk 'bout one er dem judges. I ain' know exactly wuh he mean, but it sound kind er scand'lous to me. He say whenever you hears a judge talkin' 'bout he b'lief in de fundamentals—dem is de things to live by—you better try to escape he court.

Tad: Ef you escape he court, wuh is you guh do?

Scip: Dat is a hard question, but I has heared dere is one or two judges dat has got some sense, but I ain' think dey is often seen an' dey must be a accident.

Voice: I has heared on 'em.

Tad: It is hard, an' much as I b'lieve in Christianity I feel mighty doubtful when one er them thing, I ain' kin call it, sets in judgment.

Scip: You mean one er dem fundamentals?

Tad: Yes, one er dem fundamentals.

Voice: I heared one er de white folks say dey ain' pay 'em nothin', dat's wuh make we ain' got nothin'.

Scip: I has my mind 'bout dat. It sho' do me good to see 'em swell up an' spread dey self when dem lawyers git up an' say, "May it please you' Honor." It seem to me every time a lawyer say dat, he have to strain he self to keep from laughin'.

Tad: Fundamentals ain' de onliest judge we got, is he?

Scip: No, dere is several on 'em.

Voice: I know dere is one on 'em sets in judgment an' ain' fail to gee long sentence to anybody come up 'fore him for liquor, an' send right down stairs an' git dat same man's liquor an' drink it. I know dat, kaze me an' de porter is close friend. He send mens up for two an' three years for violation er de prohibition law, an' sets right dere in de back room er de courthouse an' drinks dey liquor.

Scip: You tellin' dat like it were news. Dey is known, an' some on 'em doos things dat dey sends mens to de gang for years for doin', an' dey do it right in de temple er justice.

Tad: You kin say wha' you has a mind to, but I knows some has distinguished dey self in de conduct er some er de bank cases. I heared a white folks say dat.

Scip: I done.

Tomper's Song

She told her lover, "Come to my home,
Captain Lord Welton's on a long journey gone."
That night he come to de arms of he lover,
"Take you' time for you can hear de winding of his horn,
Captain Lord Welton is a long way from home."

Don't you hear what de sparrow say?
"Captain Lord Welton is one hundred miles from home."
Don't you hear what de footspeed say?
"Captain Lord Welton ain't but ninety-five miles from home."

"Take you' time," de ooman say,
"Ain't you hear what de sparrow say?
Captain Lord Welton is ninety miles from home."
Oh, listen to what de footspeed say,
"I can hear de soundin' of the horn,
Captain Lord Welton is only eighty-five miles from home."

"Oh, stay! oh, stay!" de ooman say,
"Captain Lord Welton is a long way from home."
Ain't you hear what de sparrow say?
"Captain Lord Welton is eighty mile from home."
Oh, listen to what de footspeed say,
"Captain Lord Welton ain't but seventy-five mile from home."

"Oh, stay!" de sparrow say,
"Captain Lord Welton is seventy mile from home."
Oh, ain't you hear what de footspeed say?
"I can hear de blowin' of he horn,
Captain Lord Welton ain't but sixty-five mile from home."

"Hush you' mout'," de sparrow say,
"Captain Lord Welton is sixty mile from home."
"Listen! listen!" de footspeed say,

"I can hear de soundin' of he horn,
Captain Lord Welton ain't but fifty-five mile from home."

"Oh, listen!" de lover say,
"I must be guine,
I can hear de windin' of he horn,
Captain Lord Welton ain't but fifty mile from home."

"Take you' time; oh, take you' time,"
De sparrow say,
"Captain Lord Welton is forty-five mile from home."
Don't you hear what de footspeed say?
"I can hear de soundin' of he horn,
Captain Lord Welton ain't but forty mile from home."

Oh, listen to what de sparrow say,
"Captain Lord Welton is thirty-five mile from home."
"Oh, don't you listen to what de sparrow say,
Captain Lord Welton is ridin' hard for home.
Ain't you hear de soundin' of he horn?
He ain't but thirty mile from home."

Oh, listen to what de sparrow say,
"Captain Lord Welton is twenty-five mile from home."
"You will not listen," de footspeed say,
"I can hear de windin' of the horn,
Captain Lord Welton ain't but twenty mile from home."

"Have no fear," de sparrow say,
"Captain Lord Welton is fifteen mile from home."
"Make haste! make haste!" de footspeed say,
"I can hear de soundin' of he horn,
Captain Lord Welton ain't but ten mile from home."

"Take you' time; oh, take you' time,"
De sparrow say,
"Captain Lord Welton is five mile from home."
Oh, ain't you hear what de footspeed say?
"I hear de soundin' of he horn,
Captain Lord Welton is arrive at home."

"Too late, too late," de footspeed say,
"I hear de slashin' of he sword,
Captain Lord Welton already home."

GHOSTS AND ANGELS

Old Moccasin's Ghost

Tad: Ole Moccasin 'peared to me de other night.

Voice: Is you have talk wid him?

Tad: Is I had talk wid him? I ain' had nothin' but talk, an' some on it been mighty frightenin'. He tell me a heap er inter-restin' thing 'bout hell an' de devil. He say it would surprise you to know de diff'ent kind er people de devil got in hell. He say he see a heap er people he know. He say hell got all kind er diff'ent place in it. He say it got a reg'lar pasture wey he puts dese Congaree people in. Say every mornin' de devil has some er he chillun runnin' dese people out er de pit an' puttin' 'em in de pasture. Put 'em out dere to luh 'em cool off a little bit.

Scip: Ole Moccasin been dead a good while.

Tad: I know he is, an' he say dere is many folks in hell he was well acquainted wid in dis world. When he come, I been layin' on my bed restin' an' de moon was shinin' through de window mighty nigh bright as day, an' I say:

"Who dat?"

An' I heared a voice say:

"I sho' is glad to be here one more time."

He seemed to be heap gladder dan I was. It ain' matter how well I knows a man—how close a friend he been to me—when he dead, I wants him to stay dead; I ain' want his sperrit come hangin' 'round my house brokin' my night's rest an' tellin' me all kind er tales 'bout hell an' de devil, an' diff'ent dead people I nused to know.

But I listen to him an' one inter-restin' thing he tell me were a compersation he have wid de devil. He say de devil tell him he nused to all kinds er people—mens an' womens, niggers an' white folks. He say hell jam full on 'em. Moccasin say de devil tell him dat de people in dis world wuh has hopes er keepin' out er hell has to be very partic'lar, an' he say whenever any-body see a man walkin' down de road in de big Sunday wid a high hat an' a long tail coat on, wid a ambrella in one hand an' a prayer-book under he arm an' lookin' sanctified, he say dey is dang'ous. He say one thing he sho' hand God: He know wuh

He been talkin' 'bout when He warn He disciples to beware of wolf in sheep's clothin'. He say great God! dey sho' is got teet' an' moest on 'em got claws, too. He say every time dey commit a crime, dey does it wid a prayer. He say every time he see one er dem ole scoundrels try to start up a prayer in hell, he puts a little more fire to 'em. An' he tell me dat dere is several on 'em right around here—he call dey name—dat he is prepared for. An' when he leff, he mighty nigh make me feel like dat dere ain' no nuse to struggle no more, dat most everybody dat die goes to hell an' dat heaven ain' nothin' but a great wilderness.

Scip: I ain't sure, but I has a feelin' dat Moccasin leff you wid de right impression.

The Ghost of White Hall

Tad: Is you all hear de tale 'bout Gabe?

Voice: Wuh is de tale?

Tad: It ain' so much of a tale neither—I heared it for de trute.

Scip: I heared heap er tale for de trute. Wuh is de tale, Tad?

Voice: Tell it, Bur Tad.

Second Voice: Who Gabe been?

Scip: Luh Tad tell de tale.

Tad: Gabe was a nigger—a slavery time nigger—wha' lived in dese parts. I ain' know wey he come from. He come here; an' he disappear; an' he come back. Ain' nobody know too much 'bout him. He have friend, but he ain' have no partic'lar friend. He have onrestless ways an' make people oneasy, but people git sort er nuse to him. An' den Gabe disappear for so long till he were mighty nigh forgit.

Now, I guh tell you de frightenin' part er dis tale.

All you all 'member ole man Long Jim. He tell me Gabe leff here for a long time, an' come back. He meet Gabe comin' out er de wood one evenin' late. He say it been so cold he was mighty nigh froze. An' him an' Gabe pass over Tom's Creek, an' went into de ole White Hall house. All de white folks been gone off, an' dere ain' nobody on de place. Ain' nobody been livin' dere for God knows how long.

He say dey git wood an' made a fire in de chimney place. An' when he look 'round dat house, it look like some er dem sinful ole white folks was guh slip out er every cornder. Every time de wind would whistle a chune 'round de cornders er dat house, he shiver an' 'magine sump'n terrible was guh happen.

Voice: Great God! He trust he self.

Tad: Jim say dat ole house tremble an' crack an' groan an' cry; an' he say he been chuned up to do everything dat ole house been doin', an' more. He say any time he cast he eye 'round, he think er some er them ole time slavery niggers he nused to know.

He say dere was one little knotty-head wild nigger he nused

to know. It look like he seen him several time peerin' thoo de window; an' every time he zern he face, dem shutters would rumble an' roll, an' de sweat was poppin' off him like it were hot summer time.

Another Voice: Have mercy! My Jesus!

Tad: An' Long Jim say he try to make compersation wid Gabe, but it don't look like nothin' kin cure him of de way he feel. An' Gabe look like he ain' no partic'lar good comp'ny, an' he say he jes set down.

An' den he heared a voice out in de wind—'way out in de night—call Gabe. An' de voice riz up an' scream, "Gabe, Gabe!" An' den it moan an' wail, "Gabe, Gabe, Gabe!" An' Jim say he look at Gabe, an' Gabe laugh. He say he ain' exactly laugh, he cackle; look like he was tryin' to agevate de voice dat was callin'.

Voice: Dat's when I would er leff.

Tad: Jim say dat was in he mind, but he was wuss scared to leff dan to stay.

An' den de voice got closer an' wusser an' more dreadful, an' den Jim say, "Thank God." Gabe got up an' stretch he self like he was tired, an' walk out.

An' Jim say his mind tell him to move 'way from dat fire; an' he staggered over to a cornder of de room, an' set on a box in a place wey dere ain' been too much light. An' time he set down, de door opened an' a tall man walk into de room right in front er de fire—right wey Jim been settin'—an' th'owed a crocus sack full er sump'n on de floor, an' bend over an' ketch it by de bottom end an' shook a lot er bones out on de floor. He say dere was arms an' hands an' backbones an' foots an' a man's head.

An' den de tall nigger start pickin' them bones up an' jinein' 'em together, till he had de full skeleton of a man jine up; an' he look down at de skeleton an' laugh an' grab him by de hand an' liff him up.

Den he put one arm 'round he waist an' started dancin'. Dey done every kind er dance; dey was steppin' on dey toes an' on dey heels, an' jumpin' an' cuttin' de wing an' de buzzard lope.

An' Jim say he look, an' he ain' been able to do nothin' else, an' while he look, he see dat de dead man was Gabe.

An' Jim say dat 'casion he white head.

Scip: De Bible warns you 'gainst de weak vessels an' strange womens, an' you is better off ef you luh all strange things alone—an' dat ain' scusin' mens.

The Angel of Cow Pen Lake

Tad: I has larn a heap 'bout angels I ain' know, but I hear a tale 'bout a angel dat mighty nigh kept me from sleepin'. It sho' broked my night's rest.

Ole man Leck tell me one night he been comin' out de swamp. He say de moon was shinin' bright as day 'twix' de trees, but dem canebrakes was dark an' everything was still 'cep now an' den he could hear a snake draggin' his self off. An' he could smell some er dem ole moccasins so stink till he was feared to put he foots down. He say every now an' den a ole owl would laugh till it make he flesh crawl; an' when dem big frogs would jump, it sound like a log drappin' in de water.

He say much nuse as he is to de swamp, he nerves was frettin', an' on top er all dis when he gits by Cow Pen Lake, he zern sump'n on de edge er de lake movin' 'round, an' he stop an' look at de wuss sight he ever see. He say a angel quit wuh he been doin'. He look like he been scratchin'. All de ground been tored up.

Well, dat angel quit an' walk 'long slow to a ole cypress dat was layin' dere, an' jumped up on it an' rumple he feather an' flutter an' shake his self an' look all 'round him. Leck say he been standin' on dat log, an' he ain' been ten steps from him, an' he look at him good. He didn't think dere was nothin' in de world so wuss lookin'.

He say he was bald on de top er he head, an' it look like dere was some kind er red scales on he head. An' he had a fringe 'round he head, he reckon de angel would er call it hair. He say he ain' have hand an' foots like people, but he have claw like a hawk, an' dey was two foots wide. He ain' have no years, but sump'n look like a rat hole he listen wid. An' he say he was a big-bellied ole scoundrel ten foots high. An' he say he whings was fasten on by regular ole gate hinges. An' he feather was all mess up wey he been ilen 'em. He say he whing an' tail been feather, but he breast an' belly were cover wid bristles. He say he nose look like it were made out er sump'n like a cow horn, an' he mout' were full er tushes. An' he was rank as a boar hog.

Voice: Do my Lord!

Second Voice: Have mercy, Jesus!

Tad: An' Leck say he was so scared till he heart rose up in he mout' an' liked to choked him. He say he have to push it back down he th'oat wid he finger.

He say atter while dat ole angel spied him, an' reach out one er dem big claw er he ownt, an' wrop it 'round him an' liff him up an' put him on de log 'side him an' axe him wuh he doin' on Cow Pen Lake dat time er night. An' he tell Leck he b'lieve he been messin' in he business, an' Leck say he have a terrible time tryin' to explain dat he been back in de swamp lookin' atter he cow an' hog; an' he say he plead so frightful till atter a while de angel look like he were pacify an' start talkin' to him.

He say it much as he kin do to bre'th. Dat angel were so rank till it liked to stifle him. He say he been gittin' 'long as well as a man in sech a fright could git along, till de angel look at he watch an' say:

"The night is lated, an' I still has duties to perform."

An' Leck say he thought he would try to be friendly. He tell dat angel he hates to part wid him, an' de angel say he ain' guh part wid him. He tell Leck he like him so well he guh carry him back to he nest wid him for he chillun to play wid. An' Leck say he ain' want no angel chillun playin' wid him, an' 'fore he knowed it he say:

"No, my God!"

An' he say dat angel got furious an' reach over an' grab him an' riz up wid him. An' Leck say when he started passin' over dat big cypress wid him, dat wey he die. He ain' know no more till dey find him next day all tored up on de edge of a briar patch.

The Smokehouse Angel

Tad: I heared annudder tale 'bout angels. Ole man Willis tell it to me.

He say one time he been makin' sausage an' puddin' an' fixin' up meat for Mr. Kamler; an' he went back in Mr. Kamler' yard to look after diff'ent little things he say he might forgit, an' he never is see sech strange doin's. He say he ain' say nothin' to Mr. Kamler 'bout it, kaze he know jes how Mr. Kamler would look. He say he wouldn't er been rough or nothin', but he would er been discountin'. He say he know he would er say:

"Willis, you oughter be shame er you'self to drink so much liquor, much confidence as I puts in you. Go on an' quit you' lyin'."

So he say he ain' say a word to Mr. Kamler, as him an' Mr. Kamler all two one, same as brothers. He say dey got ways alike, an' ef dey skin was de same, dere wouldn't be no dif-f'ence 'twix' 'em. Dey got a full onderstandin' of one nudder. He say dey is a little diff'ent, too. He say he is expert makin' sausage, an' Mr. Kamler is expert at eatin' 'em.

Scip: Dey mought put a white face on ole man Willis, but dey wouldn't fool no nigger. Whenever I see nigger hangin' 'round Willis huntin' rations, den I know dey is de same.

Voice: Some niggers is mighty fool.

Scip: Dey is, but dey ain' dat fool.

Tad: Willis say dat night he cross de yard, he see sump'n white come out de smokehouse wid a turn er meat an' sausage. He say he spoke. He thought it was Mr. Harry. An' de thing jes look at him an' walk out an' cut de buck all 'round de yard. An' he see he got whing, an' den he riz up an' lit on top er Mr. Kamler' house, an' he knowed it was a angel.

Voice: Jesus! Ole man Willis must er been drunk ef he tooken Mr. Kamler for a angel.

Second Voice: Yes, my God!

Third Voice: Wuh angel guh do wid meat?

Scip: Willis better pray an' luh liquor 'lone. Dat ole man too ole to be guine 'round messin' in Mr. Kamler' meat house, an' talkin' 'bout him an' Mr. Kamler one, an' den mixin' Mr. Kamler up wid angels. Next thing he do, he'll be guine 'round here provin' everything he say by ole Tom Fox. An' ef ole Fox had er been livin' when God writ de Bible, he never would had no nuse for Ananias.

Tad: Ananias wouldn't been no more dan chillun 'side ole Fox in a lie.

Scip: My brother, you braggin' on ole Fox an' Ananias. It look like you done forgit Willis.

Reverend Hickman: I guh pray an' axe God to help dat sinful man to repent.

Voice: Dey scuse God er doin' heap er forgivin', but is you reckon he ever guh soften He heart to a nigger wuh mix up one er He angels wid robbin' a smokehouse?

Scip: Is dat all he do? Ain' he mix up one er He angels wid Mr. Kamler?

Tad: Mr. Kamler are a good man, but I ain' never thought to connect him up wid no angel.

Voice: I heared a heap 'bout angel, but dis de first I ever heared of a meat-stealin' angel.

Reverend Hickman: It mought er been one er de devil's angels, an' dey got heap er place to cook meat.

Scip: Yes, an' de devil cooks a heap er meat from Gadsden. I reckon he got a br'ilin' iron somewhere for Willis.

Voice: You reckon Willis an' Mr. Kamler guh stick together when dey leff dis world?

Scip: Willis say dey all two one. I ain' say nothin'.

Tad: Dat ain' all. Dat tale on Willis git to Mr. Kamler' wife an' tear come in she eye, she so glad to git she husband' name call 'long wid a angel. It ain' make no diff'ence wuh kind er angel—she jes want it call wid a angel.

Voice: Some women sho' has a heap er hope.

Scip: Some on 'em needs it.

Tad: Dat ain' all. Mr. Kamler' wife luh she chillun hear she talkin' 'bout angels an' dey pa, an' dey all bu's' out cryin'. Time dey hear dey pa' name call 'long wid a angel, dey thought dey pa had meet wid a accident, an' dey ain' have but one place in dey mind.

Scip: Chillun onderstands more'n moest people thinks.

Tyu's Angel

Tad: Wuh dat tale I hear 'bout you walkin' down de big road in de dead er night an' angels litten all 'round you?

Tyu: Dat ain' no tale. Dat's de God's trute.

Voice: Is you feel cu'ious?

Tyu: No, I ain' feel cu'ious; I been dat scared till I 'magine I been walkin' down one er de lonely roads in de sperrit world. You know angels ain' no common things to have litten 'round you, an' it look like them kind er things happens when dere ain' nobody 'round—when you alone wid your conscience.

Tad: Go on wid your tale.

Tyu: Ain't I tell you it de trute?

Scip: Luh him tell dat lie wid out so much argiment.

Tyu: It ain' no lie. 'Fore God it de trute.

I been walkin' down de road from Pine Bluff. It been 'fore day in de mornin' an' de moon was shinin'. It was bright so you could see, yet dere were a dead look 'bout de world. It were dat kind er night when it look like sump'n were guh happen—like dere been sump'n hangin' over de world.

I was walkin' 'long by my lone self when I heared a sound up in de sky. I look, an' seems to me like I see shapes floatin' an' flyin' 'round an' doin' all kind er thing 'way up dere in de sky; I hear dey whing myself, an' I walk an' ain' look up no more.

An' atter a while I heared a whirrin' sound, 'way up dere at first, but it was gittin' nearer an' nearer, "V-o-o-o, v-o-o-o, v-o-o-o, v-o-o-o." Den sump'n wid its whings spread out jes like a goose lit down in de road near me, an' stop an' spread he whings two or three time, an' stretch he neck out an' work it back an' forth. Den it drawed its whings up close to he side an' walk up to me jes like people. My Jesus!

Voice: Do God!

Second Voice: Why ain't you run?

Third Voice: I would er flewed wid out whings.

Tyu: I ain' been able to run ef I wants to; I have a bad time walkin', an' dere ain' no nuse to run from sump'n dat's got foots jes like mient, an' hands jes like mient an' a pair er whings wid feather in 'em a yard long. Jesus, no! An' I ain' been able to bear de idea of layin' down wid dat angel standin' over me.

Voice: Did he have a flamin' sword?

Tyu: No, he ain' have no sword. He ain' need no sword.

Voice: I ain' blame you for not layin' down. Great God! I couldn't stand de idea er layin' down wid a angel standin' over me. I couldn't rest in my bed ef I knewed dere was one settin' on top er my house wey I couldn't see him.

Tad: I heared ole man July say dere was a house back by de ole mill dey nuse to lit all over in de night. He say you could hear 'em walkin' over de roof, an' one night dey was cuttin' up so, dey tored some er de shingles off. He say it git so ain't nobody would stay in it, dey couldn't git no rest. An' some tooken to dey bed an' die ravin'.

Voice: Wey dat house?

Scip: You all quit interruptin'. Luh dat nigger tell he tale.

Tyu: Well, dat angel walk up to me an' I try to act kind er careless like, an' walk right 'long. An' de angel say:

"Well, brother, you out late. Which way is you walkin'?"

An' I say:

"I ain' partic'lar 'bout which way I walk."

An' he say:

"It do not matter. I'll walk 'long wid you."

Den he say:

"Brother, is you prepared?"

An' 'fore I could gee him answer, I heared footsteps comin' towards me, an' I look an' I see de wuss lookin' angel walkin' towards me. An' I say:

"Jesus!"

An' de angel wuh been wid me say:

"It guh be him an' me."

An' I knowed dem angels ain' been no friend; an' I thank God, kaze I was feared dey was guh double team me, an' one on 'em was wuss enough.

Dat angel dat met we was spotted all over an' he face look like some kind er bill. An' he had spurs on he leg like a rooster, an' dey was long as a walkin' stick.

Well, sir, when dey meet, dey make all kind er cu'ious sound an' started to sachayin' 'round one nudder, an' lookin' like dey was tryin' to git a openin' at one nudder. Dey was fightin' wid dey whings wuss dan a pair er ole ganders. An' while I watch 'em, angels of every description started litten in dat road, an' dey make all kind er cu'ious sound. One on 'em flewed at annudder angel an' missed him an' knocked me down, an' dat's wey I come to my senses. Dey was so busy fightin', dey ain' see me slip off.

Scip: It was a good idea you had—to slip off. Ef you ain' slip off, we wouldn't er heared dis tale.

BUR RABBIT

Bur Rabbit in Red Hill Churchyard

I pass 'long one night by Red Hill churchyard an' I hear all kind er chune. I stop an' look an' my eye like to jump out er my head at wha' I see. De ground was kiver all over wid snow, an' de palin's on de graveyard fence was cracklin', it been so cold. De moon was shinin' bright—mighty nigh like day. De only diff'ence been it ain' look as natu'al. An' I look an' listen —an' ain' nothin' been de matter wid my eye an' ain' nothin' been wrong wid my hearin'—an' I seen a rabbit settin' on top of a grave playin' a fiddle, for God's sake. All kind er little beasts been runnin' 'round, dancin' an' callin' numbers. An' dere was wood rats an' squirrels cuttin' capers wid dey fancy self, an' diff'ent kind er birds an' owl. Even dem ole owl was sachayin' 'round—look like dey was enjoyin' dey self. An' dat ole rabbit was puttin' on more airs dan a poor buckra wid a jug er liquor an' a new suit er clothes on.

Well, sir, I jes stood der wid my heart in my mout' an' my eyes bu'stin' out my head. I been natu'ally paralyze, I been so scared. An' while I were lookin', Bur Rabbit stop playin', put he fiddle under he arm an' step off de grave. He walk off a little piece an' guin some sort er sign to de little birds an' beasts, an' dey form dey self into a circle 'round de grave. An' dat was when I knowed sump'n strange was guh happen.

You know a rabbit is cunnin'. He got more sense dan people. He sharp. My brother, he ain' trust no mistake.

Well, I watch an' I see Bur Rabbit take he fiddle from under he arm an' start to fiddlin' some more, an' he were doin' some fiddlin' out dere in dat snow. An' Bur Mockin' Bird jine him an' whistle a chune dat would er made de angels weep. Even dem ole owl had tear drappin' from dey eye. Dat mockin' bird an' dat rabbit—Lord, dey had chunes floatin' all 'round on de night air. Dey could stand a chune on end, grab it up an' throw it away an' ketch it an' bring it back an' hold it; an' make dem chunes sound like dey was strugglin' to git away one minute, an' de next dey sound like sump'n gittin' up close an' whisperin'.

An' as I watch, I see Bur Rabbit lower he fiddle, wipe he face an' stick he han'k'ch'ef in he pocket, an' take off he hat an' bow mighty nigh to de ground. Bur Mockin' Bird stop he chune an' all de little beasts an' birds an' dem ole owl bow down.

An' wuh you reckon? While I been watch all dese strange guines on, I see de snow on de grave crack an' rise up, an' de grave open an' I see Simon rise up out er dat grave. I see him an' he look jest as natu'al as he done 'fore dey bury him. An' he look satisfy, an' he look like he taken a great interest in Bur Rabbit an' de little beasts an' birds. An' he set down on de top er he own grave, an' carry on a long compersation wid all dem animals. An' dem owl look like dey never was guh git through. You know dem ole owl—de ole folks always is say dey is dead folks.

But dat ain' all. Atter dey done wored dey self out wid compersation, I see Bur Rabbit take he fiddle an' put it under he chin an' start to playin'. An' while I watch, I see Bur Rabbit step back on de grave an' Simon were gone.

Bur Jonas' Goat

Tad: You know one time Bur Jonas had a goat an' somebody stole Bur Jonas' goat, an' Bur Jonas look every which er way for he goat an' he ain' kin find who stole him, an' Bur Rabbit were tryin' to clear he self. Bur Rabbit were friend wid Bur Jonas, but Bur Rabbit were sech a scoundrel he ain' kin help stealin' an' he got sech low ways. He would steal from anybody, it ain' make no diff'ence ef dey was he friend or no. He stole Bur Jonas' goat an' Bur Jonas were makin' so much inquiry 'bout it till Bur Rabbit git oneasy.

Bur Rabbit is been mighty close friend wid Bur Wolf, but dat ain' make no diff'ence, he been like lots er people we knows. Wuh he care ef he send Bur Wolf to de pen'tentiary? He would jes laugh an' make game at Bur Wolf for bein' sech a fool. You know Bur Rabbit is a sport an' ain' care nothin' 'bout nothin' cep playin' he fiddle an' frolicin' wid de gals. He love to go to dance an' play dat fiddle er he own. Ef you was to take dat fiddle 'way from him, he would perish 'way an' die.

Well, Bur Rabbit ain' got no conscience an' he mind jes fill up wid all kind er sport an' devilment, an' he go to Bur Jonas an' say:

"Look er here, Jonas, der guine be a dance 'cross de creek tonight, an' I wants you to be dere an' I guh prove to you who stole you' goat. All you got to do is to stand one side an' I guh show you wuh a good ole church member done."

Voice: Bur Rabbit sho' is 'ceitful. He talkin' 'bout Bur Wolf.

Scip: Look like he got church member size up.

Tad: You know Bur Wolf was a shaggy ole fellow wuh love to go to dance an' frolic, an' try to 'pear young an' cut up wid de gals an' do fool thing like a heap er ole mens wuh try to be smart an' 'tract 'tention to he self, an' make de gals think he so young an' sech a sport. An' de gals would jes dance wid him to show some kinds er respect for he years. He ain' got no sense. Bur Rabbit fool he eye out. Bur Rabbit tell Bur Wolf he guh fiddle an' sing at de dance an' he had a little song he'd sing while he fiddlin', an' he axe Bur Wolf to jine. Bur Rabbit tell Bur Wolf, he say:

"Wolf, I guh fiddle an' sing:
'Who stole Bur Jonas' goat?
Who stole Bur Jonas' goat?'
"An' you must gee answer an' say
'I stole Bur Jonas' goat.
I, by God, I stole Bur Jonas' goat."

Dat night sho' 'nough Bur Rabbit start up he little song an' Bur Wolf gee answer:

"I stole Bur Jonas' goat.
I, I stole Bur Jonas' goat.
I, I, by God, I stole Bur Jonas' goat."

An' den Bur Jonas had him 'rested an' Bur Wolf call on Bur Rabbit to help him prove it were jes a song. But Bur Rabbit laugh at Bur Jonas an' tell him to put Bur Wolf in jail.

"Ain't you hear Bur Wolf own up he stole you' goat? Ain't you hear him brag 'bout it 'fore all de gals?"

An' Bur Jonas had Bur Wolf put in jail.

The Rat

Tad: I heared dat ole red nigger tell some lie 'bout a rat.

He say he been back on Lykes's plantation in de ole field by de river. He say he was walkin' 'long 'tendin' to he business when he see sump'n crawl out from under a pile er straw. He say he stand up an' look at it, an' he ain' know ef he see sump'n or no, or whether he eye jes gone wrong. He say at first sight it look like a rat totin' another rat on he back, but when he look good he see it been two rat, back to back, growed together. All two on 'em been full rat. Each on 'em had he own head an' he own leg an' he own tail.

An' dat nigger say he make up he mind he guh try to ketch 'em for he boss. He say he know ain' nobody see no sech rat as dat. An' he say when he make for him, dat rat start 'cross de field—an' him an' dat rat. He say he ain' never been so outdone. He say when he think he mighty nigh ketch him, lo an' behold! dat rat lay down an' roll over an' de other rat start to runnin'.

An' he say dat wey he quit.

The Dance of the Little Animals

I ain' never mess up 'round graveyard at night, kaze I know ef I is I guh see thing I ain' wan' see. But one night—it was duenst de Christmas—I was guine home an' all de earth was kivered wid snow, an' I knows my own self dat Bur Rabbit is a fiddler.

I been passin' down de road by dem big trees on de ole mill place in de dead er night, an' de moon was shinin' an' every star in de element was geein light. An' as I walk 'long, sump'n tell me to stop an' look; an' Lord, I sho' is seen a cu'ious sight. I see Bur Rabbit walkin' on he hind legs wid a fiddle in he hand. An' while I watch him, he th'owed dat fiddle up under he chin an' started playin' reels. He whirl he self 'round an' dance an' cut every kind er caper. An' it look like he call all kind er animal to him—all kind er little animal. An' dey all went to dancin'. It look like in de Christmas ef de moon is shinin' an' dere's snow on de ground, dat is de time when you sees all kind er sights.

Bur Rabbit is got a heap er sense an' heap er scheme, an' he love to sport 'round an' enjoy he self. An' I ain' know why he go 'round graveyard, kaze he look like he love life. He a sportin' man. He ain' no Christian. An' he got more stucked up ways.

Well, sir, all dem little animal was jumpin' an' dancin' an' cuttin' capers for he amusement. But I ain' got but one fault wid Bur Rabbit. He so stucked up. He done fool so much people, till 'tain' nothin' for him to have he fun out er de other little animal. He always is been make a fool out er Bur Fox.

Well, sir, while I been watchin' all dese guines on, I see Bur Rabbit gee a sign to de other little animal, an' dey scatter every which er way an' run in hole. An' I see Bur Rabbit put he fiddle under he arm an' lope off, jes as careless as ef he ain' care for nothin'. An' I ain' know wuh happen till I see Bur Fox come runnin' up under de tree wid he tongue hang out an' he teet' shinin'. Den he run all 'round wey Bur Rabbit was fiddlin', smellin' every little hole; an' den he struck Bur Rabbit' trail an' lit out.

But Bur Rabbit sharp. He done lay he plan. Bur Fox follow him an' Bur Rabbit lead him right on 'cross de country. An' he tooked him to ole man Fed' place, an' he stop a minute an' tech dat fiddle er he ownt, an' lit out again. He jes tech it enough to wake dem hound up. He got sense. He know hound ain' guh run no rabbit when he got a chance at a fox. When Bur Fox pass 'long runnin' Bur Rabbit, den dem hound started to singin' an' cryin'. Dey sound like a choir. An' atter while dey struck Bur Fox' trail, an' Bur Rabbit jes step one side an' like to kilt his self laughin'.

De las' I hear on it, Bur Rabbit was settin' on a stump playin' he fiddle, an' dem hound had Bur Fox stretched like a string runnin' a race wid death.

The Spider and the Rabbit

Hatchet: You know Bur Spider an' Bur Rabbit use' to run together an' both on 'em had low ways. One night dey been guine to a dance 'cross de river. Bur Rabbit was a great fiddler, an' he always have a good time. De gals always crazy 'bout him—he dress up so fine an' so lively an' sech a sport.

Well, him an' Bur Spider got to de river an' dere wa'n't no place to cross. So Bur Spider tell Bur Rabbit he will spin he web 'cross de river an' Bur Rabbit kin walk 'cross on dat. Bur Spider ack so nice Bur Rabbit trus' him—sump'n he ain' never done before—an' when he git mighty nigh to de other bank, Bur Spider cut he web loose an' drap Bur Rabbit in de river an' sp'iled all Bur Rabbit' clothes.

Well, Bur Rabbit an' Bur Spider went on to de dance together an' Bur Rabbit look so wuss till all de gals was makin' game at him an' makin' great miration over Bur Spider. An' dey had all kind er compersation 'bout Bur Spider' beautiful web an' axe Bur Spider to teach 'em how to spin.

But you can't outdo Bur Rabbit for long. He too sharp an' cunnin'. He grab up he fiddle an' tored off several little chunes an' sing a song 'bout Bur Spider an' how he spin he web an' all 'bout it. An' when he done, he make all de gals 'shame' an' dey turn dey back on Bur Spider an' wouldn't have nothin' to do wid him.

A Roost on the Rim of the Moon

I seen a owl settin'
On de rim er de moon.
He draw in he neck
An' rumple he feather,
An' look below at de world.

He shook de horn on he head,
Wall he big eye
An' laugh at de things
Above an' below
From he roost
On de rim er de moon.

He woke de fowls
In de barnyard,
An' de dead stirred
In dey grave,
When he laugh
From he roost
On de rim er de moon.

An' de ole folks say
He were a dead man;
Dat evil did float
Wid de sound er he voice,
When he laugh
From he roost
On de rim er de moon.

An' de dead
In de graveyard
Raise up dey voice an' moan;
Dey laugh an' dey cry
At de sound er de owl,

When he laugh
From he roost
On de rim er de moon.

He stir up de fever an' chill
Wid he shadow,
When de sound er he voice
Pass over de swamp,
When he laugh
From he roost
On de rim er de moon.

The Frog and the Snake

Tad: You know 'Poleon oughter quit lyin'.

Ishmael: I'll quit work any time to hear 'Poleon lie. He done lie so much till he b'lieve it his self.

Voice: I done listen to 'Poleon, an' he tell a lie so natu'al till I ain' know ef it de trute or a lie. I heared him 'scribe thing till dey jes look like a natu'al picture somebody drawed.

Ishmael: I has laughed 'bout 'Poleon till my belly was drawed up in a knot an' hurt me for a week. He make game at everything an' everybody.

Tad: De last lie 'Poleon tell been on a snake an' a frog.

'Poleon say he been settin' down on de edge er de creek fishnin when he heared a frog whistlin'. An' den he see a snake poke he head up 'twix' two log an' rise up straight like a man, lickin' he tongue out an' lookin' all 'round. Den he see de frog jump an' heared him whistle, an' dat snake git down an' cut all kind er capers through de bulrushes an' 'round de bulrushes—him an' dat frog. Every time de frog jump, he would whistle, an' he done a heap on it. An' dat frog had a sound in dat whistle like a death sentence been pass on him.

Voice: I reckon he is.

Tad: 'Round dem bush dat frog an' dat snake had it. 'Poleon say de end was certain. He say he watch good, an' dat snake ketch dat frog by he hind part an' de frog drugged him a piece; but de snake wrop his self 'round de frog an' look like he unjint he jaw an' started swallowin' de frog; he was takin' he good time.

He say atter while de frog quit scramblin' an' he look like chillun. He say de frog' eye fill up wid tear, an' he cry like a baby. 'Poleon say he was facin' him an' he helt out both he arm an' started hollerin':

"Save me, save me, save me!"

'Poleon say he look jes like a chile, an' he say he took a stick an' tapped de snake an' de snake spit de frog out. He say time de frog git loose, he hopped off a piece an' turn 'round an' spit in de snake' face. Time he do dat, de snake curl up an' die.

Voice: Why ain't de frog spit in de snake' face at first startin'?

Tad: He ain' been able to. De snake know any time a frog spit in anything' face, it guh die, so he make it he business to keep behind de frog. A snake kin turn 'round faster 'an a frog.

Scip: Ain't you reckon 'Poleon kill dat snake?

The Monkey and the Elephant

Tad: Is you hear de tale 'bout de monkey an' de elephant?

One day de monkey meet up wid de elephant an' dey hab compersation. An' de elephant say to de monkey:

"Monkey, I is in great distress. I been in torment all day, an' I wants you to help me."

An' de monkey say:

"Wuh de matter ail you, Elephant?"

An' de elephant say:

"I been messin' 'round in de field throwin' grass an' dirt all over myself, an' dey been a heap er cuckle burr in dat field. An' I grab up a whole lot er grass an' cuckle burr an' throw 'em up in de air, an' one er dem cuckle burr drap in my year an' I ain' kin git it out. An', Monkey, I wants to axe you to do me a little favor. I wants you to climb up on my year an' reach in dere an' pull dat cuckle burr out, an' any time, Monkey, I kin do you a favor, I'll be glad to do it."

An' de monkey say:

"Elephant, I ain' think too much er climbin' up 'round you' year."

An' de elephant say:

"Please for God' sake help me out dis time, for I sho' will do you a favor any time you axe me."

An' de monkey say:

"Well, all right, Elephant."

An' he run up on de elephant an' reach 'round an' run he hand down in de elephant' year an' pull dat cuckle burr out an' th'owed it on de ground. An' den he jumped back on de ground, an' de elephant say:

"I'm much obliged to you, Monkey. Good day. I must be guine."

An' de monkey say:

"Hold on, Elephant. Don't be in sech a hurry. You tell me any time you kin do me a little favor, you'll be glad to do it. An' so I wants you to ride me a piece."

An' de elephant say:

"All right, Monkey. Git up."

An' de monkey jumped up on de elephant's back an' dey went for a long distance through de forest. An' de elephant stopped to rest a little while under de shade of a cocoanut tree, an' a cocoanut drap an' hit de elephant on de head. An' de elephant grunt an' say, "Uh!" An' de monkey say:

"Elephant, I ain't too heavy for you, is I?"

Voice: A monkey sho' thinks his self sump'n.

'Gators and Snakes

Tad: A alligator is sho' a vigus thing. I been talkin' 'bout 'em de other day, an' dere was a white folks come down here tellin' we dey is not dang'ous an' 'bout ef you trace out all dese tales 'bout 'gators killin' people, you will find out dey ain' nothin' to it but a passel er lie. I listen to him good, but I knows wuh I knows. Ain' no nuse for nobody to write book an' all kind er foolishness 'bout alligators. Dey kin tell people all kind er inter-restin' thing, but I knows dis here swamp an' I knows alligators.

No, dey ain' harm nothin' or nobody, ef dey keeps out er dey way. I was up to de ole mill one day an' heared a great squealin', an' we runned down dere to de side er de pond an' a 'gator had a four hundred pound boar hog in he mout'. It were terrible. Dat boar hog was pullin' toward de land, an' dat 'gator was pullin' towards de water an' he was gainin' on de hog, pullin' him down inch by inch, an' dat hog was hollerin', for God's sake. But dat 'gator had he eye shet jes like he had gone to sleep on dat hog, an' de only thing dat save de hog was: one er de niggers slipped up on him an' sunk a axe in de 'gator' head up to de eye an' pull him out.

Den one time in one er dem ole mill pond a 'gator grab old Joe' boat in he mout' an' like to bit it in half. It like to scared Joe to death. It guin him heart disease an' he died a short time afterwards.

Den dere was dat nigger down to de fork church walkin' 'long in de big road at night an' stumble over a 'gator layin' in de road. Dat 'gator bit one er he arm off an' he manage to drag his self to a low rail fence 'side de road an' fall over de other side. An' dey find him from dat 'gator bellowin', an' he was bled mighty nigh to death. De 'gator crawl up to de fence an' couldn't git through, an' he 'larmed de country.

An' I knows many tales, an' dey ain't no tales neither.

Reverend Hickman: It 'minds me er dese white folks dat comes 'round tellin' people don't hurt no snakes, dat dey doos good. I luh 'em talk. I got my own mind 'bout snakes. De Bible tell you to crush dey head under you' heel, an' I b'lieves de Bible. Course, I don't take no chances wid my heel on no snake' head, but I brokes 'em up wid a stick.

Scip: Dere is a heap er agvice I don't pay no 'tention to.

The Bell-Ringing Rat

Tad: White folks is sharp an' got all kind er scheme an' trick, but sometimes dey over-doos dey self.

Voice: Dey sho' is got scheme an' heap er sense.

Tad: Yes, dey is; but sometimes dey scheme runs 'way wid 'em, but I has to laugh at wuh ole man Cap'n Bob tell me, an' he say it ain' no tale but de God's trute.

Voice: Wuh he tell you?

Tad: He tell me dat 'way back in slavery time he marster' place been overrun wid rat, an' one er dem niggers tell him ef he gits a big rat an' put a bell on him an' swinge him good an' turn him loose, he never will be trouble wid no more rat. An' Cap'n Bob say he young marster got him a big rat an' put a little bell on him an' fasten it 'round he neck wid wire an' turn him loose. An' he say it lucky for de niggers he young marster ain' swinge de rat or else he wouldn't had no excuse to make. Dat rat create all kind er trouble.

Voice: How de rat create trouble?

Tad: Cap'n Bob say he ring dat bell all hours er de night. He say ain' no body kin sleep. Time anybody would drap off to sleep, dat rat would start ringin' dat bell an' broke dey night's rest. Over dey head in de ceilin' an' floor an' 'twix' de walls, dat bell were ringin'; an' more'n dat, ain' nobody ever could see dat rat no more.

Voice: Is he run de other rats off?

Tad: He ain' run nothin' off cep people, an dey says it look like dat rat raised a drove er bell-ringin' rats. De white folks git so miserable 'bout dat rat till dey had to move out, an' dat rat move everybody else out dat ever move in dat house; an' he ain' been satisfy wid dat, he visit de nigger houses, an' it ain' been long 'fore niggers was runnin' away, an' atter slavery time dey leff for good.

Voice: You know ain' no nigger guh stay in a house wey sump'n dey ain' kin see is ringin' bells all time er night.

Tad: Dat rat ain' onliest make niggers leff, dey had white folks makin' one kind er excuse or annudder an' leffen wid all dey airs 'bout ain' scared.

Voice: Wuh you reckon happen to dat rat?

Tad: I ain' know but one thing: dey put dat bell on him in slavery time an' dey tell me he still ringin' it.

Voice: You reckon dat de same rat?

Tad: I ain' know 'bout dat. De bell were put on him in slavery time, an' any time ef you goes 'bout dat ole place in de night, you kin still hear it ringin'. It might be a sperrit. Ef you wants to hear it, go up to de ole house in de dead er night, or sometime 'twix' midnight an' dawn, an' you will hear it for you' self.

Voice: I ain' wants to hear it.

Cootas

Tad: I been down to de coast talkin' to dem ole Gullahs. Dey sho' is talk bad. Moest er dey talk been 'bout fish an' swimp an' oyster an' coota an' toide. Dey don't seems to know nothin' else. Dey bog up all 'bout in de ma'sh ketchin' coota. Dey tell me a heap 'bout 'em. Dey say de little bull coota ain' fittin for nothin', but dey says ef you wants sump'n good, git you a fat hen coota. Dey is fine. I never is hear so much talk 'bout coota. Dey call 'em bull coota an' hen coota an' cow coota. Dem niggers is de biggest fool. Jes kaze a coota lay eggs dey calls him a hen. I axe 'em is dey cackle, an' dey jes look at me. When dey call 'em cow, I axe 'em is dey gee milk, an' den dey thought I was a crazy nigger.

Carry on a heap er dat ole island talk. I ain' know wuh dey say, but I know dey ain't see no p'int to wuh I say, so I had a mind to axe 'em wuh make dey ain' have a rooster coota 'round dem ma'shes crowin' to match dem hens, but I ain' axe 'em. Dere was several little things I wants to say to dem niggers, but I thought it were best to pacify 'em more ruther dan agivate 'em. Dere was so many on 'em.

A Jay Bird Thief

"T-a-y me, t-a-y me, t-a-y me."
In de name er God,
How come you say,
"T-a-y me, t-a-y me, t-a-y me?"
You needn't look
Dat er way.
You ain't fool me
Wid you' lyin' self,
"T-a-y me, t-a-y me, t-a-y me,"
Ain't I ketch you
In my cornfield?
Ain't you de rogue
Wid you' bill
In my roasen-year,
Wid you' lyin' tongue
Hollerin' an' peckin?
"T-a-y me, t-a-y me, t-a-y me."

How come you say,
"T-a-y me, t-a-y me, t-a-y me?"
You de t'ief—
I done cotch you
In my cornfield,
'Larmin' de neighborhood
Wid you' lie 'bout
"T-a-y me, t-a-y me, t-a-y me."

"T-a-y me, t-a-y me, t-a-y me."
Shet you' lyin' mout',
You say tay you;
Ef it tay you,
I guh hold you
Till you fetch
De right man;
Ef you ain't fetch 'em,

I guh wring you' lyin' neck.
"T-a-y me, t-a-y me, t-a-y me."
I reckon it "T-a-y me, t-a-y me."

Every wey I gone
I see 'struction
In my cornfield;
An' hear you hollerin' an' lyin',
"T-a-y me, t-a-y me, t-a-y me."
You mought fool ole Marster
An' you mought fool ole Miss,
But you ain't fool me
Wid you' lyin' mout' 'bout
"T-a-y me, t-a-y me, t-a-y me,"
I got you.
Dey ain' guh see you.
"T-a-y me, t-a-y me, t-a-y me."
Dey ain' guh hear you.
"T-a-y me, t-a-y me, t-a-y me."

All t'ief holler
When dey ketch 'em
"T-a-y me, t-a-y me, t-a-y me."
Shet you' lyin' mout',
"T-a-y me, t-a-y me, t-a-y me."
I know it ain' you,
An' tay me. Who it is
Ef it tay you? Tay me.

Ain' no nuse
For you to flutter
An' look dat er way.
I got you.
"T-a-y me." No, I know
It "T-a-y me."
I like to know
Wuh make it ain' you.
"T-a-y me, t-a-y me, t-a-y me."
You mought as well own up,
But dat ain' guh save you,

You done lie too much
'Bout it "T-a-y me, t-a-y me."
You done steal my corn.
I might ain' kin change 'em,
But I guh stop you' chune 'bout
"T-a-y me, t-a-y me, t-a-y me."

PREACHERS

Allen's Idea of Preachers

Allen: I gits mighty sick er all dis preachin' to womens 'bout live in de ways er de Lord an' don't have nothin' to do wid no mens. Dese preacher keep on hollerin', an' dey is de biggest rascals on 'em all. You kin hear dey mout' a mile—like God can't hear ef dey whisper. But I kin mighty nigh see de ole devil poke up he fire an' lick he tongue out at dey goin's on. Listen to 'em an' dey make you think dey been right up in heaven walkin' 'round arm in arm wid God Almighty wid angels followin' 'em 'round wid milk an' honey.

Ef de angels know wha' I know, dey would know dey ain't none on 'em would think heaven fitten wid out a jug er liquor wey dey could git a drink every time dey turn 'round, but ef I is any judge, moest er dem big-mout', big-bellied ole bastards is guh bu's' hell wide open.

Dey holler, "God, Jesus" an' "Lord," an' talk 'bout heaven an' Sunday atter dey done preach, an' you better pray or you'll burn in hell, den dey will eat up all de grub you kin put on you' table, set down an' go to pickin' dey teet' an' lookin' at you' baby gal.

Don't tell me 'bout no preachers.

A Bit of Correspondence

Congaree, South Carolina.

Dear Reverend Johnson:—

De niggers is havin' a baby show same as de white folks. I knows you always is been inter-rested in babies an' we is axen you to use you' great influence in helpin' us. We has a four-months-old baby an' I know you knows as much about dis child as I does, an' I feel we kin 'pend on you to assist us.

Us baby's name is Lillie Sara an' we has entered her in de baby show. We is special anxious for her to win de first prize which is guin to de baby what gits de most votes. Dese votes has to be paid for an' dey sells for twenty-five cents a ticket an' de tickets counts twenty-five votes, an' you has a right to buy as much votes as you wishes to. You kin buy dese votes from us or from baby headquarters, an' I understands dat you knows all about dat. Ef you gits 'em at de headquarters, you got to be sho' to pick out de baby you wants voted for.

We don't want Lillie Sara to loss out, but we has to have all de co-operation you kin gee us, an' we knows we has had you' co-operation in de past, an' we is dependent on us friends an' relations to make little Lillie Sara a winner.

Axe all de brothers an' sisters to help us. We would highly appreciate all de votes you could git for us baby.

Yours truly,
Mary Etta Jones.

Hopkins, South Carolina.

Dear Miss Jones:

I take my pen in hand to answer you' letter. I ain't know wuh makes you wants to enter you' baby in dis here show. It always is a resk on account er diff'ent kind er diseases dat is floatin' 'bout. To my mind it ain't no place for babies. Course, ef you enters it, I will do wuh I kin to 'sist you.

Now, Sister Jones, I speak to you as a member of my flock. I hasn't de knowledge of you' child you seems to s'picion I has, an' I ain't never been in no way connect up wid no baby headquarters; an', my sister, I would ruther you don't mention them kind er things. You know I is a man er God an' has to be careful.

Now, I wishes little Lillie Sara all de success in de world, but I ain' wan' people to think I knows much 'bout her as you 'tends to think I does.

Now, God bless you, my sister. I ain't never lost intrust in you as a member of my flock.

Yours in de name er de Lord.

May God bless you an' you' husband an' you all' chillun.

Yours truly in de name er de Lord,
Reverend Marcus Johnson.

Congaree, South Carolina.

Dear Reverend Johnson:—

I isn't tooken you' agvice 'bout de baby show, an' us baby win an' ain't seems in no wise injured.

Is you went to de show? Is you look at Lillie Sara an' see who she favor? Everybody say she is a fine chile an' ain't none on 'em zackly say who she favor. Ef Lillie Sara had er been a boy chile, I would er name her atter you.

You' letter were receive an' I jes want to say dis: don't never let you' mind git angle up 'bout me havin' s'picions. I don't have no s'picions 'bout nothin'. When I talks I knows wha' I talks 'bout, but I ain't said nothin'. When you knows me longer, you will find out I ain't never suffer from no s'picions.

Ain't you proud us baby win?

Yours truly,
Mary Etta Jones.

Hopkins, South Carolina.

Dear Miss Jones:—

I has you' letter and sure is proud you' baby win.

Yes, Sister, I glimpse de show over an' I seen you' baby, an' I ain't kin see wuh call you has to think er namin' you' chile atter me ef it been a boy. It is best never to do dat in de church. Course, I know de faith you has in you' pastor an' 'preciates it, but for you' sake, my sister, as a member er my flock, I agvise you 'gainst dem notions.

In de name er de Lord, my sister, I is visitin' you soon. I has been so busy.

Yours in de name er de Lord,
Reverend Marcus Johnson.

Congaree, South Carolina.

Dear Reverend Johnson:—

I receive you' letter an' is expectin' you. You was busy before. You has a heap to say, 'bout me as a member er you' flock an' in de name er de Lord. You know who dat chile look like. I wish it was a boy chile. All us friend looks at dis chile an axe how you is.

I is expectin' you.

Yours truly,
Mary Etta Jones.

Congaree, South Carolina.

Dear Reverend Johnson:

Dis is a word to luh you know I is comin' to see you on a very important matter, an' I is geein' you dis notice in time wid de idea dat you won't make no mistake an' be out when I comes.

It is very important. My wife an' her baby is comin' wid me.

Yours truly,
Jesse Jones.

Hopkins, South Carolina.

Dear Mr. Jones:

It is a great disappointment to me to luh you know dat I is onable to be home when you comes.

I has had a sudden an' onexpected call an' is leffen home right now, an' God His Self ain't know when I guh return.

In de name er de Lord, you' truly friend,

Reverend Marcus Johnson.

Two Prayers

Hatchet: When ole man Shiger come to die, Ole Miss were so worry up 'bout de condition er he soul till she send for all de niggers to hold a prayer-meetin' over him. You know ole man Shiger been a wicked ole man. He have a heap er niggers an' he been a sportin' man. He love to fight game chickens an' play cards an' race horses an' gamble, an' he have hound dog an' run fox, an' dat wha' he mind run on—dat an' livin'.

When all dem niggers git dere, he had he niggers bring him out in a big armchair an' set him down wey he could look at 'em an' listen to dey prayer in he behalf. An' he pick out two ole niggers to lead in prayer. De fust one been ole man July, an' he say:

"Lord, dey ain't nothin' to all dis talk 'bout Ole Marster guh die. He guh be here. Luh him live, Lord, for de peace er dy servants. Luh him live to breed dat mare an' raise one more colt like de one he done raise, for he got de greatest race horse in all de land. Listen to my voice, Lord, an' luh him live to take he game chickens an' keep on whippin' all de other chickens like he been doin'.

"Luh him live, my Lord, so dat dis community kin keep de best hound. Ole Marster's hound kin outrun all de hound er all de other white folks in de world. Lord, you know dey ain't no nuse for you to worry an' debil Ole Marster 'bout dyin' now. He nothin' but a youth."

You know ole man July was a hundred an' fifteen year ole an' Ole Marster ain't been but eighty.

"Lord, hear my prayer. Put Ole Marster's mind at ease. Don't debil him no more. Put he mind at ease, Lord. Dey ain't nothin' de matter wid he body."

Ole Marster love to hear dat. He git 'side he self he so please.

"Lord, I done axe you—"
An' de sisters was hollerin':
"Hear him, Lord! Hear him! Amen!"

An' den Ole Miss call ole man Noae an' ole man Noae git up an' say:

"Lord, listen to my prayer. I ain't botherin' 'bout Ole Marster' body. I guh axe you 'bout he soul. Help him, Lord. Take him up an' turn him 'round in de palm er you' hand an' luh him git a glimpse into de life he been leadin'. Luh him see he self as all dese lyin' niggers sees him. Save he soul, Lord. Save he soul.

"Take him up, Lord, an' hold him over hell an' swinge he hind-part good. Make tenst like you guh drap him in. Lord, bring him to he senses. Lord, it ain't matter 'bout he body. Save he soul, Lord."

An' den all dem niggers got to hollerin' an' geein' answer:

"Save he soul, Lord! Save he soul! Swinge he hind-part, Lord! Swinge he hind-part good!"

An' Ole Marster call he overseer an' tell him to gee ole man July a quart er liquor an' a plug er tobacco, an' to take ole man Noae into de stable an' gee him twenty lashes.

An' he die next day.

God

I vision God standing
On the heights of heaven,
Throwing the devil like
A burning torch
Over the gulf
Into the valleys of hell.
His eye the lightning's flash,
His voice the thunder's roll.
Wid one hand He snatched
The sun from its socket,
And the other He clapped across the moon.

I vision God wringing
A storm from the heavens;
Rocking the world
Like an earthquake;
Blazing the sea
Wid a trail er fire.
His eye the lightning's flash,
His voice the thunder's roll.
Wid one hand He snatched
The sun from its socket,
And the other He clapped across the moon.

I vision God standing
On a mountain
Of burnished gold,
Blowing His breath
Of silver clouds
Over the world.
His eye the lightning's flash,
His voice the thunder's roll.
Wid one hand He snatched
The sun from its socket,
And the other He clapped across the moon.

Virgins

(Fragment of a Sermon)

I take my tex' from de five wise an' de five foolish virgins. I ain' guh make no great miration tonight, but I guh speak to you in a onderstandin' way. I guh try to make it so you'll onderstand wuh I mean.

You know when dese virgins set out to de weddin', it was dark an' de Lord tell 'em to fill up dey lamp; an' de five wise ones fill up dey ownt, an' de five foolish ones ain' put no oil in dey ownt. I ain' know ef dey do it a purpose or ef dey jes been triflin', but ef dey is been triflin' dey make a great mistake an' 'casion dey self to be shet out from a great feast. Dey mought er had some kind er cunnin' notion 'bout wha' dey kin do slippin' 'round in de dark. I ain' know, but I s'picion 'em.

Now, my brothers an' sisters, 'fore I go any furder wid dis here sermon, to all er you all wha' ain' know wuh a virgin is, I guh tell you. God Almighty in He great wisdom have made all dese little nigger gals virgins. Dey born dat er way an' He keeps 'em dat er way till dey is about twelve years old, an' atter dat dey ain' no virgins.

Now, ef you all ain' know wuh a virgin is, I guh tell you. Ef you go out in dat woods an' find a tree an' it got a scar on it—ef it's mark any wey—dat ain' a virgin tree. An' ef you walk 'round dat woods an' keep you' eye open, you'll find dere's very few er dem trees dat ain' got mark on 'em, even right down to de little saplin's. Ain' matter how pretty de leaf an' how clean de bark grow on 'em, ef you look at 'em close enough, you'll find moest on 'em got scar some wey. But ef you come to a tall beautiful tree wid glossy leaf on it an' look at it close an' ain' find no scratch or mark or scar on it no wey, dat's a virgin tree—dat's wha' God Almighty talkin' 'bout when He mention dem virgins.

An' at all dat great weddin' feast it ain' seem like dey been but ten on 'em, an' five er dem luh dey light go out an' fell by de wayside for de lack er oil. It look like dey was jes as skace in dem times as dey is now.

Now, guine back to dat virgin tree you find out in de woods, luh a nigger come along and spile it wid a axe, it's ruint. It ain't no virgin no more. An' dat's de way wid dem virgins. De oil dey talks about was de sperrit. De sperrit ain' been strong enough in 'em to keep 'em guine, an' dey fell by de wayside an' de door to de weddin' feast was closed to them. I ain't no great mourner an' ain't frettin so much 'bout wuh is past, but take de agvice er God as I gee it to you an' keep you' lights burnin', keep de oil in you' lamp or you'll fall by de wayside an' de doors of a heavenly home will always be shet to you.

Old Brother Tries to Enter Heaven

Ole Brother have had he time in dis world. He have never done nothin' to ease de mind er a human, an' when he time come, he leff dis world wid a mighty cry an' struggle for de heavenly heights, an' wid he sly ways he manage to git to de top er de long hill. He hung 'round de gates er heaven for days, an' ole Peter recognize him an' run him off, but he kep' on comin' back.

He seed de Lord pass de gates one day an' stop Him an' plead wid Him, but it is mighty hard to fool de Lord an' de Lord 'fuse him an' tell him He feared to 'low him in, he record down below been so bad. He tell de Lord he have truly repent, an' de Lord tell him He know he is, but he ain' done it till too late. He tell him dey ain't no nuse to come wid all dis repentance ole as he is; dat he ain' start it till he were lookin' right through de bars, an' he must be ain' like wuh he see in hell. He tell him He know he ain't repent for no love er Him, but kaze he wants to do he devilment wid pleasure an' ease; dat He b'lieve he jes tryin' to git into heaven kaze he think hell fire will be too distractin' an' he will be too busy payin' 'tention to de fire an' scorchin' to properly make other people miserable.

But de ole God have too much experience an' tell Ole Brother He wants him to git away from de gate. Ef he keep on hangin' 'round dere, it will gee heaven a bad reputation. An' de Lord went back into heaven an' call He servants an' tell 'em He want 'em to run Ole Brother 'way from de gate. He tell 'em He done gee him notice, but dey must gee him a little time, an' atter dat dey must call all de dogs together an' put 'em outside de gate an' run Ole Brother spang into hell. He tell 'em don't trust no mistake. Ef dey go to de gate an' ain' see Ole Brother, put de dogs out anyhow an' see can't dey strike he trail, as he more'n apt to be dodgin' 'round under some er de bush. You see God is sharp an' is mighty hard to change He mind.

But Ole Brother ain' guin up hope. He dodge 'round till he

see Jesus. He know you kin do more wid chillun workin' on dey feelin's, an' he start workin' on Jesus. Axe Him to intercede wid He Pa for him. Well, he git hold er Jesus jes as de Lord's servants come out wid dem dog, an' Jesus, wid He lovin' kindness, was 'bout to let him go into heaven, but He Pa s'picion wuh were 'bout to happen—He been watchin'—so He come to de aid er He servants an' tell He Son not to interfere wid He commands, an' call Gab'el an' tell him to blow he horn an' git all de dogs together. He were so inter-rested in gitten Ole Brother 'way from dere, dat He stood out on de hill wid He hand over He eye shadin' it from de glare er de sun. He git so inter-rested till He climb up on a stump an' started whoopin' up dem dogs He Self. You could hear He voice ringin' all over de hill, an' I reckon it sound mighty nigh to hell. An' den de race commence.

De Lord is a sport when He has a mind to be. He gee dat Ole Brother a good start, but he were like a fox. Dey run him all over heaven hill. He struck out in a bee line for a cornder er heaven wey he heared dere were a hole in de fence, but de Lord done had dat crack stop up. He done have every hole repaired in He fence, but dat Ole Brother was hard to git shet er. He slip all 'round heaven—him an' dem dogs—an' angels was every wey whoopin' to de dogs. He run every wey—under brush an' through briar. He try every scheme known to a fox. He went over ditch an' through thicket, but dem dogs ain' never took dey nose off er he scent. You know Ole Brother got a scent, dat's one thing he can't git rid er.

Atter dey run around for over a hour, dey got him straighten out an' dem dogs was so hot to hind him, dat he leff de narrow path an' thicket an' tooken to de broad road wey dere ain' no obstruction an' headed he self for hell, den he done some runnin'. He runned like dere ain' no place but hell dat he wants to go to. He was guine at sech a rate till he was jes techin' de road in spots, an' dem dogs was stretched like a string an' cryin' for God' sake sho' 'nough. But dat nigger done got all idea out er he head but one, an' dat was makin' hell 'fore dem dogs make him. He know he done wrong, dat de Lord done make up He mind an' ain' guh fool wid him now since He find out he try to corrupt He son.

De devil knowed wha' was guine on an' he had de gates er

hell closed, an' as dat nigger approach he sorter shy off a little bit as he seen de flames lickin' through de gates, but he look back an' see dem dogs an' seen a man on a pale white horse, an' he knowed everlastin' death was on he trail. Den he look at de gates one more time an' ain' pay no 'tention to de flame an' discount de groans he heared. He ain' hesitate no more, but went over de top an' enter de flames like a varmint guine to he den, an' de Lord like to kill He Self laughin'.

He say He ain' never waste much time on sports, but He has to take He mind off He regular business sometimes. He say He hound never has run better, an' it gee Him so much pleasure to think er how He outdone de devil. He say it ain' no nuse for de devil to be closin' he gates an' settin' he self up 'gainst Him. He say whenever He starts a sinner for hell, He moest generally puts him dere.

The Harps of God

(Fragment of a Sermon)

For de harps er God is ringin',

Voice in congregation:
For de harps er God is ringin',
Ringin', ringin',
For de harps er God is ringin'.

Ringin' de chunes er Jesus,
Wid de angels singin'.
Come, brother, ain't you hear de harp,
De harp wid de golden strings?

Angels' hands helt out

Voice of a sister:
Hands, hands, hands helt out.

For God's poor chillun,
Singin' wid de harps er Jesus,
Music ringin' through de air;
God's voice above it all.
Come, my brother, ain't you hear de harp,
De harp wid de golden strings?

Voice:
Golden strings, golden strings,
De harp, de harp wid de golden strings.

For de voice er Jesus
Is callin' you to come,
An' listen to de angels singin',
Singin' wid de harp.
For, my brother an' my sister,

Dere is peace an' rest
Wid de distant music,
For Jesus leads de far off choir,
An' God is superintendent.

One voice with several joining in:
For Jesus, Jesus leads de far off choir,
An' God is superintendent.

An' de harps is playin',
An' every sound is sayin',
"Come, my brother, father, mother, sister,
For dere's peace an' love an' kindness
Where de harps er God is playin'."

Several voices:
For dere's peace
Where de harps er God is playin'.
De harps, de harps,
De harps wid de golden strings.

For de harps er God is playin' for His chillun
In dis sinful world below.
Come, my brother, come an' listen,
Listen to de harps of heaven;
For dey are playin' 'round de snowy throne,
For de harps er God is playin',
Is playin' for His helpless chillun here below.

Whole congregation:
For de harps er God is playin'.
Playin' for His helpless chillun.
De harps, de harps,
De harps wid de golden strings.

Converted

Tad: Is you hear 'bout de time Long Jim jined de church?

Voice: Tell it to we.

Tad: You know he been mighty sinful wid dancin' an' gamblin', an' he done all kind er outdacious things; an' he talk ain' been fitten for hogs to listen to, much less people.

One day, right in de big Sunday, him an' a passel er niggers been settin' under dat big oak tree by ole man Alex' sidin' playin' cards. Them niggers win everything he hab but he shirt an' he hat, an' Jim was talkin' mighty blasphemous. He th'owed he hat down an' say he will gamble dat off an' ef he ain' win, he hope to God de lightnin' will bu's' him an' all de other niggers into hell. An' he ain' got to pitchin' dem cards good 'fore a flash er lightnin' come, an' a thunder bolt tored dem cards out er he hand—tored 'em up an' scattered dem niggers all over de ground.

Dey all on 'em leff, an' Jim run four miles in he shirt tail. An' when he git home, he crawl under de bed an' he wife ain' been able to git him out till next day; an' a strange nigger wha' been gamblin' wid Jim ain' never been seen no more, an' ain' never been heared of. I reckon he is runnin' yet.

Atter dey git Jim out from under de bed, he been a pure Christian an' was baptized.

Voice: Is he stay a Christian?

Tad: He walk 'round for 'bout a month an' any time anybody axe him a question, de onliest thing he hab sense 'nough to say is, "Blessed is de lamb." An' he ain' never blasphemed or put he hands on cards since.

Scip: Some on 'em gits religion natu'ally, an' some on 'em has it knocked into 'em.

Tad: King Jesus picked Jim out to do He work.

Scip: It 'pears dat er way, but Jesus picks out some cu'ious people for He business.

Tad: De ways of de Lord pass all onderstandin'.

Scip: Me an' you is together on dat, brother.

The Bear Fight

Deacon Jones an' he gal live in a section of de country wey dere been a heap er bears. An' one night he been guine to an experience meetin', an' dere been two roads, an' he gal say:

"Papa, le's we don't go through de woods road, kaze I seen a bear dere today."

An' de deacon say:

"I ain' care notin' 'bout no bear. I a Christian an' loves God an' God loves me, an' I puts my trust in Him. I loves God. God is good. I'm guine through dem woods."

An' de gal say:

"Papa, le's we don't make no mistakes. Le's we go 'round."

An' de deacon say:

"I'm guine through dem woods. I trust God. I puts my faith in God. God is good an' will pertec' me."

An' de gal say:

"I ain' trustin' all dat. I'm guine 'round."

An' de deacon say:

"Well, I'm guine through de woods. God is my pertecter."

An' he went through de woods, an' de gal went 'round.

An' when de deacon git half way through de woods, a bear jumped on him an' he had a terrible time fightin' wid dat bear. De bear tored mighty nigh all he clothes off, an' bit him up an' mighty nigh ruint him. But when he git loose, he made he way to de experience meetin'. An' when he git dere, dem niggers been tellin' 'bout dey experience wid God an' Jesus an' de devil an' wid angels—an' a passel er lies.

An' den dey spied Deacon Jones in de back er de congregation, an' dey call on him for his experience an' he say he ain' got nothin' to say. An' all dem brother an' all dem sister keep on hollerin' for him. An' atter while de deacon git up an' say:

"My brothers an' sisters, all I kin say is: God is good. God is good. I loves God. I sho' loves Him, an' I puts my faith in Him. God is good an' He'll help you in a lot er little things, but, my brothers an' sisters, good as God is, He ain' worth a damn in a bear fight."

Gullah Joe

(The Story of an African Slave)

Tad: Joe, 'fore you come here wey did you originate—wey was you' home?

Joe: I come from Af'ica.

Tad: How come you come here?

Joe: When I been a boy, a big vessel come nigh to my home. An' it had white folks on it an' dey hab all kind er bead an' calico an' red flannel, an' all kind er fancy thing. An' dem white folks gee a heap er thing to de people er my tribe an' entice 'em on de boat. An' dey treat 'em so good for two or three days, till atter while de people ain' been scared. At first start off, ain' but a few on 'em git on de boat when dey were invite; but atter de other people see 'em git on an' git off an' come back wid all kind er present, dey git so dey ain' been scared.

An' one day dey hab de boat crowd wid mens an' womens an' chillun, an' when dey find dey self, de boat was 'way out to sea. An' some er dem niggers jump off an' dey was drowned. But dem white folks overpowered dem what was on de boat, an' th'owed 'em down in de bottom er de ship. An' dey put chain on 'em an' make 'em lay down moest of de time.

Dey been pack in dere wuss dan hog in a car when dey shippin' 'em. An' every day dem white folks would come in dere an' ef a nigger jest twist his self or move, dey'd cut de hide off him wid a rawhide whip. An' niggers died in de bottom er dat ship wuss dan hogs wid cholera. Dem white folks ain' hab no mercy. Look like dey ain' know wha' mercy mean. Dey drag dem dead niggers out an' throw 'em overboard. An' dat ain' all. Dey th'owed a heap er live ones wha' dey thought ain' guh live into de sea.

An' it look like we been two or three month in de bottom er dat ship. An' dey brung us to dis country an' dey sell us, an' a slave trader brung me here an' sold me to ole Marster.

Tad: Is you satisfy?

Joe: It seems to me I would be satisfy ef I jes could see my tribe one more time. Den I would be willin' to come back here. I is a ole man now an' de folks here been good to me. Anything good atter dat vessel.

Tad: You reckon ef you was to go back to Af'ica you'd know any er dem people?

Joe: Ef dey would jes take me an' set me down on Af'ica shore, I could walk right to my tribe, for I know everybody. My daddy was a chief an' I got aunt an' heap er kin folk an' friend, an' I know dey'd be glad to see me.

I is a ole man now, but I has a longin' to walk in de feenda. I wants to see it one more time. I has a wife an' chillun here, but when I thinks er my tribe an' my friend an' my daddy an' my mammy an' de great feenda, a feelin' rises up in my th'oat an' my eye well up wid tear.

A Slave

Cap: Has you ever hear 'bout ole man Rebor an' he slave?

Voice: I is hear a heap 'bout ole man Rebor. He been a great friend to de niggers, dey tell me. Went 'gainst de white folks an' tooken up for de niggers in slavery time.

Cap: Dat's de trute an' I reckon some er de things he done were for de best, it matter not he intentions, but I has my own thoughts 'bout he reasons.

Voice: Wuh is de tale 'bout de slave?

Cap: 'Fore de war a fine gentleman from up North were visitin' ole man Rebor—us white folks ain' enter he house an' wouldn't 'low him in dey own—an' he see walkin' in de hall er ole man Rebor' house a nigger, a white nigger, you ain' kin tell him from a white man, an' de gentleman say:

"Who is dat man?"

An' ole man Rebor say:

"He is a nigger. One er my slave."

An' de gentleman say:

"I can't b'lieve it. He is a wonderful lookin' man. He looks so distinguish."

An' ole man Rebor say:

"He is a slave, a loyal an' humble slave."

An' he wiggle he finger to de nigger an' say:

"Come here."

An' when de nigger come, ole man Rebor say:

"Open you' mout'."

An' when de nigger open he mout', ole man Rebor step up close to him an' spit down he th'oat an' say:

"I told you he were my humble slave."

Voice: Wuh de gentleman say?

Cap: He ain' say nothin'. He turn he back an' walk out er ole man Rebor' house.

Old Man Hildebrand

Ole man Hildebran' was a bad ole man,
He live in slavery time.
He heart been iron an' he head been stone,
An' he pleasure been a nigger's groan.
He eye been yallow, an' he soul been dead,
An' he live in slavery time.
  Ole man Hildebran'! Ole man
    Hildebran'! Ole man Hildebran'!

A rawhide whip he hold in de hand,
For he love a chain an' he love a whip;
An' he been a bad ole man,
An' he live in slavery time.
  Ole man Hildebran'! Ole man
    Hildebran'! Ole man Hildebran'!

He nose been split an' he face been cut,
An' he neck been short;
Wid teet' like a hog, an' a mind like a dog,
He smile been a frown, an' voice a growl.
He been a bad ole man,
An' he live in slavery time.
  Ole man Hildebran'! Ole man
    Hildebran'! Ole man Hildebran'!

An' he ooman was a nigger wench
Wid ways crooked as de trail of a black snake;
An' she'd grin at we trouble an' laugh at we pain,
An' she live in slavery time.
  Ole man Hildebran'! Ole man
    Hildebran'! Ole man Hildebran'!

Ole man Hildebran' was a bad ole man,
An' he live in slavery time.
He's equal wid de niggers now;

De worrums crawls through de holes in he head.
He was a bad ole man,
An' he live in slavery time.
  Ole man Hildebran'! Ole man
    Hildebran'! Ole man Hildebran'!

The Slave Barn

See dis barn here
Wid its iron window,
Its walls er brick?

Here wey de wail an' moan
Of Af'ica sound
Wuss dan de cry
Of Af'ica chillun
When dey bone been crack
By de lion' jaw.

Here wey ooman sleep
Wid her babe on her breast,
To wake wid de mornin' sun
For de partin'.

Here wey de last
Er de slave-trader
Sing a song er misery
To a nigger in pain.

Here wey man an' he ooman
Is parted forever,
An' a prayer was answered
Wid de song of a whip.

Here wey de brain
Of a baby wid fever
Stain de walls,
Kaze a ooman for sale
Shed tears an' fought
For de chile dat she love.

Here, right here, is de spot
De yoke of de ox

Was wored by de humans—
Mens an' womens alike—
Chained to de walls
In misery an' pain;
Sold in de daytime
Wid laughter an' joke
Like hogs in a pen.

An' de trader live
To die in honor,
Forgiven by de church,
Prayed for, helt up,
He sins forgotten,
He name guin to a school—
To de young as a sample
Of virtue an' trute.

For here's a slave barn
Wid memories of sorrow;
An' de name
Of a brute
Handed down wid a lie
Of love.

A little gold to de church,
A prayer in he name;
An' a dog wid out honor
Die wid a name
Equal to a follower of Christ.

De names of a thousand
Poor devils is forgit;
Dey is nothin' to pain,
Dey sufferin' a joke.

A dollar to a school
An' a dollar to a church
Would hang de poor nigger
Dat told dat tale.

But God's my witness,
An' de tale's no tale
But de trute.

The Wild River Shore

Down on the wild river shore,
Wey de lion fou't
Wid de wild tangleroo;
Wey de serpents crawl
In dat far distant land,
Down on de wild river shore.

Down on de wild river shore,
Wey de lion fou't
Wid de wild tangleroo;
Down on de wild river shore,
Wey de elephants roam,
An' vines on de tall trees grow,
Down on de wild river shore.

Down on de wild river shore,
Wey de lion met de wild tangleroo;
Down on de wild river shore,
Wey de nights are dark
An' de tigers roam;
Down on de wild river shore,
Wey de lion killed de wild tangleroo,
Down on de wild river shore.

FUNERALS

Silas

(Fragment of a Sermon)

De body of Silas
Stiff on de coolin'-board lies.
De battle of life is done;
His soul has passed
To his far-off home—
Passed through de pearly gates.
He passed in de night,
His soul's gone forward,
But his body is left
For de weepers and mourners,
For de singers of songs
And de prayer of prayers.
His soul's gone onward
To de golden throne.
He has no regrets,
His labors was hard
And he passed in de night,
In a heavenly flight,
By a holy light.
He's gone to his home—
His far-off home—
To de golden throne.

Ain't No Corn-Bread There

My brothers an' sisters, we is here today to pray, to weep an' to moan over de earthly remains of our beloved brother. His life has been full of trouble an' hardship an' he last days was spent in pain an' sorrow an' great sufferin', an' he's gone, gone at last to a restful place; done wid de people of dis world; done wid de doctors an' medicine an' pain an' pizen. De Great Master is his doctor now.

On dis earth his trial was great, his labors hard an' his misery many. He live on bacon an' corn-bread an' cabbage, but wey he's gone he picks he food from de tree er life; he drinks of Jordan's holy waters; he feeds on heavenly manna, for dey ain't no corn-bread dere. No, my brother, dey ain't no corn-bread dere. Dey don't eat no bacon and dey ain't eat no cabbage. Dat's de feed dey gee to hogs. Down here in dis world you see people buildin' fence 'round dey cabbage patch, sickin' dog on de hog when dey tryin' to bu's'in de garden, but in heaven you see our Heavenly Father directin' He angels to tear down de fence an' drive de hogs into de cabbage patch. Dey don't eat no cabbage. Dem angel wouldn't dare to set de dog on a hog in a cabbage patch in heaven, not when de hog' Master was lookin' on.

Yes, our brother is gone, gone to de Lord. He days er corn-bread an' cabbage is done.

Sister Lucy

(Fragment of a Sermon)

I seen our sister in life,
An' she done her duty,
She served her God
An' done her earthly labor
As best she knowed how,
An' listened for the blowin' of the trumpet.
Death had no fears for her,
For the blowin' of the trumpet,
The Master's trumpet,
Was the music that she loved;
The blowin', the blowin' of the trumpet,
The Master's trumpet.

At the mornin' sunrise,
She was on her row,
An' when the sun had set,
Her daily task was done;
An' when the night was come
She knelt in prayer beside her bed
An' listened for the blowin' of the trumpet,
The Master's trumpet,
The music that she loved,
The blowin', the blowin' of the trumpet,
The Master's trumpet.

She had met the world
Wid strength an' grace;
Although her life was trailed by hardship,
Love was in her heart for man
An' in her soul for God.
An' she listened for the blowin' of the trumpet,
The Master's trumpet,
The music that she loved,

The blowin', the blowin' of the trumpet,
The Master's trumpet.

Wid a frosty life behind her,
Wid misery savage
As a hungry hound
Ever wid her,
She never lost her faith in God,
An' she listened for the blowin' of the trumpet,
The Master's trumpet,
The music that she loved,
The blowin', the blowin' of the trumpet,
The Master's trumpet.

Rejoice Ye at Dey Goin' Out

Willie: Is you hear de argiment 'twix' Tad an' de white folks?

Preb: Wuh dey say?

Willie: De white folks been raisin' de debil wid Tad 'bout leffen he work an' guine to a funeral. He tell Tad he ain' know wuh make he sech a damn fool 'bout funeral. An' Tad tell him everybody should pay proper respect to de dead. An' de white folks say:

"Tad, how you talk dat er way? You tell me dat was a low down ole nigger. Ain' nobody guh miss him when he dead. He ain' never been no friend er you ownt."

But Tad out talk de white folks.

Voice: Wuh Tad say?

Willie: Tad tell him de Bible say, "Rejoice ye at dey goin' out," an' de white folks say he ain' got annudder dam thing to say.

Fragment of a Funeral Sermon

For God looked down
And spoke to His son,
Wid a smile so kind:
Take care of my own dear chile
Who has served me so well
On de kingdom of earth
Wid its trials and tears.
For God looked down, looked down and spoke to His son.

Flowers was placed on her grave,
And tears was shed at her name.
Her sorrow now is over,
In life she was not for herself.
For God looked down, looked down and spoke to His son.

Her home is de freedom of heaven
Wid de friendship of angels.
She rides in de sky,
Rides on a pale white horse.
For God looked down, looked down and spoke to His son.

He spoke of de world below
And de heavens above;
His face lit up and His voice rang out,
And He pointed His hand to glory.
For God looked down, looked down and spoke to His son.

His face was radiant wid smiles,
As He held out His arms
And welcomed her home.
For God looked down, looked down and spoke to
His son.

Elizabeth Coleman

Out in de graveyard
In silence she sleeps.
Our heavenly sister is free
From de world and its sins;
Her soul in the quiet of night
Stole away to its Maker,
While out in de graveyard
In silence she sleeps.

Her life on dis earth
Was spent on de good she could do;
And now her reward's a rest
In the arms of her Maker.
And her love and her kindness
Is never forgot on earth or above,
Though her soul's in heaven,
Out in de graveyard
In silence she sleeps.

And de friends of dis earth
Will always remember our sister,
Elizabeth Coleman. Dey will wrop
In memory tender and gentle
Her name, and reverence de place
Wey her body finds rest
'Neath the blossoms of spring;
And her soul's at rest
Midst de glories of heaven,
While out in de graveyard
In silence she sleeps.

She's at Rest

(Fragment of a Sermon)

She's at rest, asleep and free;
Her soul from sorrow is lifted
Far above the trials
Of this world
With its joys and its tears.
Born a child of freedom,
Yet a slave;
Full of pride and grief,
With a heart of love,
Yet a slave
In a land of freedom—
Freedom to the slave that was;
Free when freedom was not.
A slave to love and friendship,
Guided by her conscience,
Loved by those she loved.
True to every trust, she's dead.
She sleeps as she lived—
Above the lowly things of earth.
She's at rest where the angels
Sweetly sing, and Christ
Has kissed the clouds away,
And her spirit rests
Far above the mists.

Funeral of a Brother

(Fragment of a Sermon)

Our brother is dead and gone,
Gone to the heavens above,
Gone where the angels guard him,
Free of the world below.

He lives in a land of joy,
At rest in the arms of glory,
At peace with all mankind,
Free of the world below.

He labors in the love of God,
He listens to the song of angels,
He breathes the air of Jesus,
Free of the world below.

Asleep in the old churchyard,
The green grass grows on he grave,
And above him the mocking birds sing,
Free of the world below.

In heaven he looks wid pity
Upon the grief of he friends,
And smiles at the wonders awaiting,
Free of the world below.

She Sleeps on a Hillside

(Fragment of a Sermon)

She sleeps on a hillside
Wey de peach blossoms bloom,
An' de wild birds sing
To de soul dat is flown
From de cotton fields of earth
To de mansions on high.

De arms of her Savior
In welcome are open
To receive her proud soul;
An' de white robes of Jesus
Are held out at last,
An' de black face of life
To de white face of glory
Is de triumph of heaven,
De reward of her virtue
In de land of her labor.

On Jordan's chilly flares,
In tempest and storm,
Her boat sailed safely
In de harbors of heaven;
An' she rests in de arms
Of her Maker,
In de love of her God;
Her sins are forgiven,
Paid in repentance full jue.

Her home is a heavenly mansion,
Her guard an angel of rest,
For she sleeps on a hillside
Wey de peach blossoms bloom,
An' de wild birds sing,
Sing to de soul dat is flown.

The Galloping Hosts of Heaven

Sister Martha was on her knee,
When de gallopin' hosts er heaven
Passed out er de clouds
Callin', "Come, come,
Come, my sister," de angel voices said,
"God is callin' you. Come, oh, come!"

Sister Martha was waitin' for them,
Her life 'most over,
An' wid her fleetin' breath
She said, "I am weary, Lord, I am comin',
My journey on earth is end."
An' the angel voice cried, "Come, oh come!"

Sister Martha stepped in de chariot
Wid golden wheels so bright an' shinin',
An' angel set beside her,
An' driv her 'cross de stars
To wey that voice was callin', "Come, oh come!"

For de gallopin' hosts of God
Was callin', "Come, my sister, come."
An' Sister Martha mounted de chariot
Wid a smilin' face. She say, "Farewell,"
An' wave her hand to her earthly friends
As she mounted above de cloud.

For she was ridin' wid de gallopin'
Hosts of heaven.
Angels circled all around,
An' her chariot was drawed by snow-white horses
As she mounted above de cloud,
As she answer de voice dat was callin',
"Come, oh come!"

Sister Martha passed through de gates of heaven.
She was dressed in robes of snowy white,
She stepped from her beautiful chariot;
God tooked her by the hand
An' led her to He throne
An' said, "Come, my sister, come."
An' she set by God on He throne in glory.

Her face was snowy white,
An' her eyes had a holy light,
When she gazed on de pearly gates,
When she looked in de eyes of God.
For de chariot wheels was rollin',
An' de gallopin' hosts of heaven
Was whirlin' to go
Wid de snow-white horses,
For God's servants on de earth below
An' heavenly voices was callin',
"Come, come, oh come!"

Sister Martha sets by the throne of God,
Her arms is folded in peace,
An' she watch wid pleasure
The gallopin' hosts, an' she
Listen wid joy to de voices
Callin' to her friends below,
"Come, come, oh come!"

GLOSSARY

This is a compilation of all the words in E. C. L. Adams's original glossaries to *Congaree Sketches* and *Nigger to Nigger*. The editor's additions are clearly marked.

a: have, as in "must a wrop he arm" for "must have wrapped his arm." Often a slurring sound of indefinite or no independent meaning.
ack: act.
actie: active.
agevate: aggravate.
agvantage: advantage.
agvice: advice.
agvise: advise.
aige: edge.
ain' or *ain't*: am not, are not, did not, do not, is not, etc.
ain' kin: cannot.
aints: is not.
ainty: isn't it.
ambiere: tobacco juice or spittle from a pipe.
an': and.
'an: than.
angle up: mixed up, confused.
angled up: mixed up, confused.
annudder: another.
apple (in de white folks' yard): highly thought of.
argiment: argument.
atter: after.
axe: ask, ax.
axen: asking.
big-doin': pompous, bullying, showing off.
b'ilin': boiling.
brass ankles: white trash (or light-skinned Negroes, ed.).
bre'th: breathe.
br'ilin': broiling.
brung: brought.

buckra: white, white man, or white men. Used without qualification it means upper-class white men, but "poor buckra" are crackers, poor white trash, the lowest kind of white men. This word is of African origin and is used by Negroes of the African coast and the West Indies. In the language of the Calabar Coast *buckra* means "demon, a powerful and superior being."

'buke: rebuke. (First syllables are often dropped.)

bum-bye: bye and bye.

Bullace: the wild muscadine grape vine.

Bur: Brother.

bu's: burst.

bus': break, hit.

call: call, cause.

'casion: occasion; occasioned or caused.

'ceitful: deceitful.

cep, cepen: except, except that.

chune: tune.

clam (sometimes clumb): climbed.

coase: of course.

compersation: conversation.

Congaree: The Congaree swamps lie on both sides of the Congaree River a few miles from Columbia, South Carolina. They vary in width from seven to twelve miles, and extend along the river about forty miles. A series of other swamps continue below them for a hundred miles or so toward the sea. There is also a community called Congaree. This is possibly the last surviving word of a lost language, the speech of the vanished Congaree Indians who once inhabited the region. There are no more Congaree Indians living, but many of the Negroes of this district plainly have Indian blood in them.

conscious: conscience.

coolin-board: the wooden board on which a corpse lies during the wake or "settin up."

coota: terrapin or freshwater turtle. ("In the neighborhood of Timbuctoo [the American 'coota's'] near relative is called a *Kuta*." From Lydia Parrish, *Slave Songs of the Georgia Sea Islands* [New York: Creative Age Press, 1942], p. 227n, ed.)

cornder: corner.

cote: court.
cotch: caught.
cracker: a poor white man. According to the traditional origin of this word, the country people used to drive their ox teams to town wielding long whips or "crackers."
craps: crops.
crimeal: criminal.
crocus sack: coarse sacking, as gunny or burlap (ed.).
cuckle burr: cockle burr.
Cuffy: Negro.
cu'ious: curious.
cunjer: conjure.
dan: than. ("Th" at the beginning of a word is often replaced by "d.")
dassent: dared not.
dat: that, that is. Copulative and auxiliary verbs are often omitted. For example, "Dat wey I ben," for "That (is) where I (have) been."
de: the.
dem: them, those.
den: then.
depick: depict.
dere: there, their.
de't: death.
det' owl: death owl. There are many owls in the Congaree.
dey: they, there, their.
diff'unt: different.
discountin': belittling, contemptuous.
dis here: this.
do Bubber, do Jesus, etc.: A common exclamation. In this use *do* has no independent meaning.
doos: do, does.
drap: drop.
dreen: drain.
driv: drove.
drug, drugged: dragged.
duenst: during.
dy: thy.
eber: ever. (The letter "v" is often pronounced "b," as in *heben* for "heaven.")

ef: if. The same Negro will often use the regular form, "if." This is true of many dialect forms.
egg 'um on: urge them on, incite them.
'em: them.
en: and.
er: of; an indefinite slurring sound used at will for many verb forms, especially "have," "was," "were," "is"; often means "a" and sometimes does duty for "is a"; in some phrases a syllable without independent meaning, as in *dis er way*, meaning "this way."
every which er way: in every direction, everywhere.
feared: afraid.
feenda: an African word for "forest."
fice dogs: mongrel dogs of mixed breed and poor quality.
fine: find. The story "Fine my chile" has been told around Gadsden, South Carolina, for a hundred years to the certain knowledge of the author. The little old woman with the keys is still seen frequently near Gadsden, though the author has never had that good fortune. According to legend she was a housekeeper for the "white folks," and her only child was burned to death.
fitten: fit.
footspeed: an imaginary creature appearing in "Tomper's Song." The author never heard it elsewhere.
fou't: fought.
free issue: the son of a white mother and a Negro father. By law, in slavery time, no child of a white woman could be a slave; he was a free issue. Some of these same darkies are still living and the term is still used. They often have gray or yellow eyes; hence the term "goose-eye yaller nigger."
fren': friend.
f'um: from.
furder: further.
'fuse: refuse.
fuss up: excited, confused.
fust: first.
game makin': ridiculing, joking. (See *make game*.)
gee: giver. (See *guin*.)
geein: giving.
gittin: getting.

go down below: the author does not know what this expression means. He uses it just as he heard it.
'gree: agree.
grub: food.
guh, gur (often *huh*): going, is going to, are going to. Never used in the sense of going to a place, but as an auxiliary as in "gur git hurt," "he guh do wha' he guh do."
guin: give, gave. (The pronunciation of this word varies and is difficult to indicate. It is often more like "geeun," "gean," or merely "gee.")
guine: going, is going.
guines on: goin's on, happenings.
gut: a natural drain in the swamps, during the rainy season full of water. Every gut has a name, often known only to the Negroes.
gwyne: going, is going.
hab: have.
han'k'ch'ef: handkerchief.
ha'nts: ghosts.
he: he (regular), his, him. Often used with self, as in *he'self*.
heap of a: many, much.
helt: held. (Final "d" and "ed" are often changed to "t.")
'hind: behind.
hisn, his'n: his.
hog fashion: four feet tied together.
hom'ny: hominy.
hoped: helped (ed.).
hoppergrass: grasshopper.
how come: why.
ign'ance: ignorance.
ign'ant: ignorant.
ile: oil.
ilen: oiling.
'im: him.
impress: impression.
inter-restin': interesting.
intrust: entrust.
is: used variably for *is, are, has*, etc., plural or singular, and often for *have*.
istockacy: aristocracy.

jes: just, just now. (Also pronounced *jist*.)
jine: join.
j'ist: joist.
joogin': jabbing.
jue, jue-drop: due, dew, dew drop.
juty: duty.
kaze: because.
ketch: catch.
kilt: killed.
kin: can, kin.
kiner: "kind of," rather, somewhat.
kiver: cover.
'larm: alarm.
larn: learn.
'lated: late, feeble health.
leff: left, leave.
leffen: leaving.
less: let, unless.
le's: let us.
light out: to rush away or start running. (In past tense, *lit out*.)
litten: alighting.
'low: allow, allows.
luh: let.
l'um: let them.
'luminate: illuminate.
'magine: imagine.
make game: ridicule, joke. (See *game makin'*.)
make tenst like: pretend.
mash: marsh.
Mensa: The origin of this name is unknown. Mensa is dead, but when he was alive he was the pride and terror of a wide district—feared, loved, and respected. The author has never seen a finer human body. A regular Casanova.
mient: mine.
miration: a complimentary fuss over.
Miss: sometimes an abbreviation for "Mister" (ed.).
mixtree: mixture.
moest: most.
more'n: more than.

mought: might.
moultin': shedding feathers or hair (ed.).
mout': mouth.
nervis: nervous.
nothen: nothing. (Also pronounced *nuttin'* and *nothin'*.)
'nough: enough.
nudder: another.
nuse: use. (Either noun or verb.)
nusin': using.
ole: old.
ole field is a fire and de hawk is here: When an old field or a patch of woods is burning, the hawks gather and watch for refugee rabbits.
on: on (regular), of.
onct: once.
onliest: only.
onrestless: restless.
'oman, 'ooman: woman, women.
oughten: ought not.
oughter: ought to.
outdacious: outlandish, outrageous (audacious, ed.).
pamelia: familiar, friendly.
pass de time: to greet.
passel: several.
perfanity: profanity. ("Pro-" and "pre-" are often changed to "per-.")
pertec': protect.
persizely: precisely.
pizen: poison.
pizer: piazza, front porch.
purtty or *pritty*: pretty. The story of the "purtty little folks" was told the author by an old Negro mammy who was half Indian. He has never heard another Negro story about fairies. The spirit world of the Negro is usually one to be feared, full of goblins and ghosts.
'rest: arrest, arrested.
riffle: ripple.
riz: rose, past tense of rise.
roasen-year: roasting ear.
rookus, rucas: a noisy row, an angry disturbance.

rudder: would rather, prefer.
ruther: would rather, prefer.
sachayin': cavorting.
sarchin': searching.
science: proudly.
Scip: Pronounced "Sip." The original Scip was a minister, but something of a skeptic and a fatalist. (Scip Shiver was a Gullah preacher and long-term worker on Adams's farm, ed.)
'scribe: describe.
scusin': except (possibly from "excuse"), accusing.
scuse: except, accuse.
seinin': catching fish with a seine, a large net (ed.).
settin' up: a wake. When a Negro dies, his friends sit all night with the body.
set in de chair: sit in the electric chair, be electrocuted.
shet: shut, rid.
sho' or *shore*: sure, surely.
shout: a religious dance in which the feet are not crossed.
sickin': egging.
'sides: besides.
size up: estimate or judge.
skace: scarce.
sont: sent.
sperrit: spirit.
'spicious: suspicious.
spile: spoil.
spilin' for a fight: looking for a fight.
sqush: squash, squelch.
stirbance (sometimes *sturbance*): disturbance.
'stress, 'stressful: distress, distressful.
strew: scatter unpleasant gossip about.
'stroy, 'struction: destroy, destruction.
'suade: persuade.
sump'n, suppen: something.
swimp: shrimp.
swinge: singe.
Tad: Tad is a prince of storytellers, but his brother Napoleon was an emperor. No old or rehashed stories for Napoleon. He used to keep the darkies spellbound for hours at a time,

reeling out by the camp fire tale after tale, always new and original. But Napoleon's stories died with him, for nobody thought to record them.

'tain or *tay*: a contraction of "it ain't" meaning it is not. It is difficult to spell this word as the Negro pronounces it. There is a faint sound of "n" which is scarcely perceptible.

tangleroo: probably the kangaroo.

tater: A sweet potato or yam. This never means a white or Irish potato.

tay: (See *'tain*).

tech: touch.

teet': teeth.

'tention, 'tension: attention.

ter: to.

terrance: terror.

tes': test.

theu: through.

th'oat: throat.

th'ow: throw.

thoo: through.

t'ief: thief.

to'hind: behind.

toide: tide (in mimicry of the Gullah).

tonement: tournament.

tored: tore, torn.

tored out: rushed away, ran frantically away.

totes: carries.

tother: the other.

tried his self: did his best, put out extra effort.

trust no mistake: to be cautious (ed.).

trusty: a convict allowed more or less freedom of movement on his agreement not to escape. Often pronounced "trustee."

trute: truth.

turkle: turtle.

turn (*a turn er dem*): a considerable number, a pile, a bunch. An armful of wood is spoken of as "a turn of wood."

turn-over: a public disturbance, a noisy brawl.

tushes: tusks.

'twis': betwixt.

'um: them, those.
Un': Uncle.
ur: of.
varmints: opossums, raccoons, wildcats, etc.
'vide: divide.
vigus: fierce, powerful.
vomick: vomit.
wan': want was not.
war: was, were.
wase up: waste up.
we: us, also in regular sense.
weedlin': wheedling.
weeked: wicked.
wey: where.
Wha's de time?: A common salutation. Often answered by "Sorter slow" or "Time ain' so much." (Sometimes *Wuh's de time?*)
whing: wing.
wid: with.
worrums: worms.
wrop: wrapped.
wuh (often *wha'*): what, who.
wuh fuh: what, why. A common phrase usually equivalent merely to *wuh*.
wuh make or *what make*: why (ed.).
wuss, wusser: worse, bad. *Wusser* is not necessarily a comparative, but may be; *wuss* may be comparative.
yaller belly: a variety of "coota" or freshwater turtle with a yellow belly.
year: year, ear.
yourownt: yours.
zackly: exactly.
zamine: examine.
zern: discern or see.

APPENDIXES

THE CAROLINA WILDERNESS

The Poor Whites of South Carolina Depicted in a Group of Pointed Dialogues

The people of these sketches are mostly of English origin. They are the so-called crackers, the name cracker coming from the use of long whips which they were constantly cracking when they visited the towns with their wagons and carts.

Settling in the Sand Hill belt with a soil unfertile, life for generations has been difficult. They are mostly poor, undernourished, undeveloped, and illiterate. Many undoubtedly have strains of Indian and Negro blood, and many are of as pure English blood as can be found in America. Mostly cruel, with a resentment toward society, they hate alike the more successful white man and the more unfortunate Negro, whom they intend to keep in his place. However, there are exceptions, as there have come from these people some worth-while men who have made their way against all odds, and even among the most untutored, one will find here and there a chieftain of strength and ability.

Puttin' on Airs

Boze: These town folks sho puts on lots er airs; thinks deyself too good to eat like other folks.

Pede: What you got in you' mind?

Boze: I been over here to a barbecue one of 'em give. Had a whole lot er city people walkin' round dress up thinkin' they better than anybody else. They had ole man Bumby cookin' for 'em. He's the best barbecue cook in dese sandhills. Dey sont for him an' look to me like it was as fine a 'cue as I ever seen, but them people was walkin' all round there lookin' at it an' dey ask ole man Bumby all kind er questions bout how he cook it an' dis, dat, and de other. It made me mad listenin' to 'em cause I help ole man Bumby wid it.

Pede: I ain' see why you get mad cause dey come down an' talk to ole man Bumby. Don't look to me like it was no harm for 'em to ask him a few questions.

Hate: Well, you never know what them damn people' object is.

Boze: Look like they jes want to find out all ole man Bumby know den they go back an' teach it to a nigger. Next thing you know they'll be sendin' for de nigger an' ole man Bumby won't be needed for de next 'cue.

Pede: Don't you reckon some of these niggers kin cook a 'cue good as ole man Bumby without havin' to larn from him?

Boze: Ef they can, a white man ought'n to own it.

Pede: Boze, it look like you an' Hate so spiteful till you mighty nigh ain't got no use for your own self.

Boze: Now, you better hush. You 'bout to start wid some more er them fool ideas of yourn. Ef you keep on wid dat kind er talk, everybody in this precinct will be s'picious of you. Look to me like you gettin' to think you better than your equals.

Pede: I does de best I can.

Hate: You makes a mighty poor out.

Boze: De way you talks makes me grieve for your poor ole dead father.

Pede: What else happen to de barbecue?

Boze: Ain't nothin' partic'lar happen except what I was talkin' bout—the airs some of these stucked-up city people has. One on 'em axe ole man Bumby ain't he meat gitten cold. Ole man Bumby tell him he put it on last night an' de fire went out at eight o'clock in de mornin' an' dey have rain an' ain't have no more wood, an' den it don't do no good to heat meat after it git cold.

Pede: It look like ole man Bumby ain't do full justice if de meat was cold an' ain't full done.

Boze: It was good enough for de people out here, an' I ain't see where city folks is any better. I tell you de kind er thing happen. I heard one er them people say:

"There's a swarm er flies over that meat, and it's cold as ice."

An' he say:

"Ain't you kin offer a suggestion?"

An' the man he was talkin' to went up to ole man Bumby an' talk round him a little bit an' asked him some question bout de fire an' he say:

"There seems to be a few flies lighting on this meat."

An' ole man Bumby look at him an' say:

"Dere is a few flies on it, but they ain't nothin' but house flies."

Dis man look at him an' say: "Yes, dat's a fact," an' smile an' walk off.

An' I tell ole man Bumby I ain't kin see what diff'ence a few flies make.

Pede: What ole man Bumby say?

Boze: He say peoples always walkin' round tryin' to find sump'n to talk about.

Hate: Puttin' on airs.

Boze: Puttin' on airs.

Pede: Puttin' on airs?

Ten Years for Nothing

Boze: It was sho a shame de sentence dey pass on Luke.

Hate: We was talkin' bout dat to-day, sendin' a white man up for ten long years for killin' a nigger.

Boze: Dere wasn't no use for 'em to put Luke in de penitentiary. It's jes what I say bout gittin' de right kind er lawyer. Ef dey had er picked a good lawyer, Luke would er been walkin' round here free as I is.

Pede: Well, it look to me onreasonable de way Luke ack. Seems to me like his wife had much right in de penitentiary as he had.

Boze: You better keep them thoughts to yourself. It's a good thing you an' me is kin.

Pede: Well, dey tell me de way it happen Luke went off an' spend de night wid another woman, an' when he come home he wife tell him dat dis nigger axed her er unfair question, an' Luke had him arrested an' he was out on bail when Luke seen him ridin' long peaceful in de buggy an' shot him to death.

Hate: Dat's de truth, but what difference does it make? It was a nigger, an it's jes one nigger less, and then it's all wrong puttin' a white man in prison jes for killin' a nigger. I jes can't see nothin' right about it. I can't see how a jury er white men got de heart to set dere an' put one er they own color in the penitentiary for killin' a damn nigger.

Pede: Well, Hate, you an' Boze an' all of you know that this nigger was a white man's nigger an' was never known to harm a thing in he life. He was kind an' full er friendship for everybody, an' he went to Luke's house to buy some liquor. You know it was a regular place for both white people an' niggers to buy liquor, an' that poor nigger jes stood around and talked to them other niggers and to Luke's wife, and after a little while went on his way home peaceably without ever a thought that anybody had anything against him; an' Luke's wife was mad at him an' jealous bout Luke goin' off after another woman, an' told Luke what dis nigger say to her jes because she want to make him stay home, an' she knowed she was tellin' a lie when she told it. She let dis poor nigger go to his death jes because she wanted to punish Luke.

Boze: I know all dat's true, but what I don't understand is what de court want to punish Luke so severely for. It don't seem reasonable.

Pede: Luke knowed dat nigger ain' done nothin' an' jes killed him cause he thought it wouldn't be nothin' to kill a nigger. It look like Luke's wife would fret bout havin' that man's blood on her hands.

Boze: I don't see nothin' to fret about, except de mistake made in de handlin' er Luke's case. Pede, you got de wrong kind er mind, an' it's mens with your mind dat creates a lot of trouble in dis world, an' if you don't change your ways er thinkin', your mind is goin' to burst out too far in de wrong way, an' before you know it de buzzards will be pickin' your bones.

Hate: I been watchin' Pede. Course he's young, but he got a mind dat will betray some of us yet, unless he makes a change.

Pede: Well, I know a nigger is a nigger an' I know he is not equal to white people, an' I believe in keepin' them in their place, but I do think that it's wrong to go out an' butcher a man dat ain't done no harm jes because he's a nigger.

Boze: Your poor old daddy would mighty near turn over in

he grave if he heard you talk dat way. Pede, git all them kind er notions out er your head, an' jes bear in mind that we got to look out for ourselves; dat we got de nigger race against us, an' we 'gainst them.

Pede: But you don't stop wid niggers. Dere is a lot er white men you 'gainst, too.

Boze: Yes, I ain't got no use for dat class er white men dat's always tryin' to hold dey selves up better than anybody else. I'm jes as good as dey is, an' I wouldn't never miss a chance to harm one of 'em.

Pede: Some of 'em must have some good in 'em.

Hate: No matter what dey got, I hates 'em.

Pede: As bad as you hates 'em you don't slaughter 'em as bad as you do niggers.

Boze: We jes got to be a little more careful, but we sticks it to 'em when we gits a chance. But goin' back to niggers, I'd burn every nigger in de world wid a smile an' give 'em a little more fire every time dey hollered. Pede, you better mend your ways.

Hate: Think it over, Pede. Better try to improve your mind.

Boze: Well, I done tarried too long already. See you all at preachin' to-morrow. So long.

A Chain-Gang Party

Boze: How's everything, Huck?

Huck: Mighty fine.

Boze: How many niggers you got on your gang?

Huck: Court jes ended an' we got a slew of 'em. Got a few white ones, too.

Boze: De white ones ain't much use to you, is dey?

Huck: If dey come from round here, dey ain't no use at all; but if they comes from off, we works on 'em de same as niggers.

Pede: Why does you make a diff'ence?

Huck: Well, most of 'em serves they time or is pardoned, an' I has to live here where most of 'em has plenty of kin an' don't never forget; but we has a frolic when dey come from off.

Boze: Dey ain't much service when you first git 'em, is dey?

Huck: Well, dey has to be broken in, but a whip lash is a language dat all of 'em understands. Most of 'em comes out of de jail fails at first, an' we promises them amusement when we gets back to camp. You know it's 'gainst de law to beat prisoners, so we hangs dat over dey head in de day time an' keeps our promise at night when dere ain't no witnesses.

Boze: You all got any good singin' niggers over dere?

Huck: Some of de finest you ever heared. You an' Pede an' Hate come over Sunday an' we'll have a supper.

Boze: We'll be there. I loves to come over to de camp for supper. Ain't nothin' like havin' them niggers sing an' wait on you, particularly after you had 'em long enough to know their place an' how to honor a white man.

Huck: By God! All dat works under me honors white men. If dey don't, dey never leaves dere to dishonor one.

Hate: Ain't you got too many new prisoners to be botherin' wid us Sunday?

Huck: No, you all come on. Sunday guh be a big whippin' day.

Pede: What you guh whip 'em for?

Huck: Guh broke 'em in. Guh cut their hindparts off 'em wid a strap so dey won't have no desire to set down.

Boze: Dat's right. Fix 'em so dey can't set down. They'll work better.

Huck: Leave it to me. I ain't never seen one yet I can't broke in. You kin hear dat brokin'-in chune ring all over de woods. I knows how to handle niggers, an' my particular pet is one er dese educated niggers. Believe me, brother, I kin mighty nigh make him forgit how to read an' write.

Boze: We'll be there. I mighty near rather see that nigger whippin' than to eat de supper.

Huck: Well, keep your mouth shut an' I'll show you some fun to-morrow evenin'.

Boze: Look for us. We'll be over right after church.

A Nigger

Boze: We been settin' round here talkin' bout niggers.

Hate: What was you sayin'?

Boze: I was jes tellin' these boys bout de trial of this here little nigger Jenkins.

Hate: You was on the jury, wasn't you?

Boze: Yas, I were on the jury. Jes got off it about a hour ago.

Hate: What did you give him? Life or de chair?

Boze: The chair. There was one of de jurors helt out for awhile, said he didn't see no call to convict dis nigger. Had some kind er talk bout he was a mere child, an' he ain't sho he was guilty; but I helt out for the chair an' we over-rid the voice of complaint an' he got de chair.

Pede: Dey tell me dat nigger ain't done nothin'. Dat little gal jerk he sling-shot out he hand an' he had a scuffle wid her tryin' to git it back. Dat made her ma and pa mad an' dey started a hue and cry bout he throwed her down an' tried to assault her. Now, dey tell me dat's de truth. No, it don't look to me like he was guilty of nothin'. I think if dey had a stripped him an' made his pa give him a good lashin' wid a wagon whip dat would have been enough.

Boze: Well, I set on the jury an' we brought in a verdict of guilty, an' looks to me like you puttin' niggers before white folks.

Hate: Dat's what I say. A man who puts a nigger before white people ought to be lynched.

Pede: Yes, but if he ain't committed no crime it don't look like he ought to have his life took. The jury was meant to give justice.

Hate: Justice ain't got nothin' to do with it, not the way you means it. This country is over-run with niggers an' we got to pertect ourselves, our families, and our children.

Pede: But how, when this little nigger ain't commit no serious crime?

Boze: Well, he's a damn nigger an' I set on de jury an' we give him the chair an' I'm proud of it. I ain't never puttin' a nigger before a white man.

Hate: You an' me have minds alike. It's my rule to teach a nigger his place.

Boze: If they don't want 'em convicted they better not let me set on the jury, cause I promised God that every chance I get I'll uphold the white race an' turn the juice on every damn nigger I ever gets a chance at.

Hate: Pede, you one of us people. I can't bear the thought of you low'ing yourself this way. It don't sound right. You know there ain't nothin' lower in this created world than a dirty nigger. They jes live here an' take the bread out of your mouth an' mine, an' it don't take nothin' for them to get beside themselves.

Pede: Dat's so, too. I reckon you has got to teach 'em they place.

Boze: I ain't blamin' Pede so much for de way he talk. He's young. There's a good many white people round here that gets to be mighty nigh grown fore dey finds out they is better than a nigger.

Hate: That's the God's truth. It's a shame how careless some people is the way they neg-lect teachin' their children. Children are growin' up everywhere that don't know nothin'. Some of 'em, after they get grown, ain't got sense enough to sell they vote, an' most of 'em ain't got sense enough to charge what it's worth.

Boze: It's Sadday. I reckon I got to go home an' have de old woman fix me a tub of hot water, so I kin wash my skin. You know to-morrow is Sunday an' we're goin' to have a big crowd turn out for the church.

Hate: I hear the new preacher knows the gospel by heart. I reckon I'll have to be goin', too, because I promised the deacon that I'd be there in time to sing in the choir.

Pede: Well, I'll see you all at the meetin'.

Boze: They set the thirtieth for that nigger's execution. So long.

There Ain't Nothin' to Killin'

Boze: Talkin' bout killin' people, there ain't nothin' to it. I don't see what a man worry his self bout a trial for. If I has enough gainst a man, I'd set on de roadside at night an' pick him off jes like I would a bird. There ain't nothin' to it. If they ketch you an' you use your head a little bit an' know what lawyer to git, you'll come clear.

Pede: It seems to me you'd have to fret some about the trial.

Hate: Well, there oughtn to be nothin' to it. If a man do you dirt, there ain't no use to wait for de courts, cause they ain't goin' to do nothin'. The best way is to trust in God an' your gun.

Pede: Well, how does a lawyer work it in the courts?

Boze: Well, there's several little things that must not be neglected. Sometime you has to have more than one lawyer, an' you got to know how to pick 'em. Then you must have a little money, an' you can almost mighty nigh git enough by rakin' an' scrapin' to clear your conscience an' satisfy the lawyer; then you know your vote counts an' your influence at votin' time.

Hate: You're right bout what you said, but there's more to it.

Boze: I ain't finished yet tellin' you how to work it. First thing, you got to pick a lawyer that stands in with the Governor and the judges. You got to pick one that ain't afraid to have the judge round to his house for dinner and supper an' ain't scared to give him all the liquor he can drink. That's one thing you got to remember. Then you got to have a lawyer that is sharp enough to know what judge to invite to a meal, an' there's plenty of them, an' after you do that, it's well to look over the whole business an' see if you can't find a lawyer that's a member of the Legislature to jine your first lawyer. That's very important. You know Legislature makes judges, an' you can always get a case put off. If the legislator has duties to perform, the judge is only too glad to accommodate him. Another thing, it is always a good thing to have a lawyer who ain't got too good er health. The right kind of judge will always put your case off. In fact, if you use good judgment, you could git your case put off, an' put off, until all the witnesses is either dead or forgot, an' if they ain't dead they memories has become feeble with old age. There ain't nothin' to a trial. The main thing is knowin' how to pick your lawyer.

Pede: How bout the jury?

Hate: Most times the jury ain't goin' to be gainst you, an' if they is, they is ways of fixin' that, too. That is, if you got a first-class lawyer.

Pede: How can you fix that when you got enemies on the jury?

Boze: You can mighty nigh always find one friend on the jury, but even without one friend there is a way of fixin' it.

The main thing, however, is to pick the right lawyer an' be friends with the courthouse rats.

Pede: What is a courthouse rat?

Boze: Ain't no use for me to go into details bout that, but all I tell you is pick the right lawyer an' stand in with the courthouse rats.

Pede: Well, I ain't exactly understand what a courthouse rat is.

Boze: Well, I'll go this far with you. A courthouse rat hates niggers an' he don't wear no stiff collar, except—but I better keep my mouth shut on that.

Pede: To go back where we left off, you was tellin' us that the main thing was to pick the right lawyer, but you never did explain what you'd do when you had enemies on the jury.

Boze: In a case like that, if you got the right kind of judge with the right kind of lawyer, you can sometimes in very bad cases git the judge to bring a directed verdict of not guilty. There ain't nothin' else for the jury to do but come in an' say: "Not guilty."

Pede: I have heard of that bein' done, an' I heard some lawyers discussin' it an' they said it was unconstitutional; that the judge had no right to come in an' take on himself the freein' of a prisoner that the jury was liable to convict.

Boze: Them ain't no lawyers, an' ain't nobody give a damn bout the Constitution. I'm jes tellin' you how to git loose when you killed a white man, an' the way as I tell you is the way to do it, an' it has been done. You know a judge ain't nothin' but a man, an' most men are lookin' out for they own advantage. There ain't nothin' to the law, an' all this rippin' an' rearin' in the courthouse, this whoopin' an' hollerin', ain't nothin' but a lot of bluff. They got to do that to satisfy a few people who believes in the Ten Commandments, or wants to make an impression that they does.

Pede: Well, I'm larnin' every day.

Hate: Son, you jes listen to you' elders an' you'll grow in wisdom. There ain't nothin' wrong wid you. You jes need a little experience.

Boze: No, there ain't nothin' to no trial ef you know how to work it.

POTEE'S GAL

A Drama of Negro Life Near the Big Congaree Swamps

ACKNOWLEDGMENTS

It gives me great pleasure to acknowledge the assistance of Mr. William Dean, Director of the Columbia Stage Society, and Instructor of Dramatic Art at the University of South Carolina, in the technical construction of this play.

E. C. L. Adams

CAST OF CHARACTERS

In the Order of Their Appearance

Jazy
Judy
Big Charleston
Jube
Silas
Tad
Potee's Gal
Snake
Fiddler
Jew's Harpist
Banjo Player
Tamer
Hannah
Sister of Silas
Cricket
Tom
Dan
Deacon
Preacher
Brother Mose
Austin
Old Sister
Kaline
Singers, Dancers, Men, Women, Relatives, Spectators, Voices, Pallbearers.

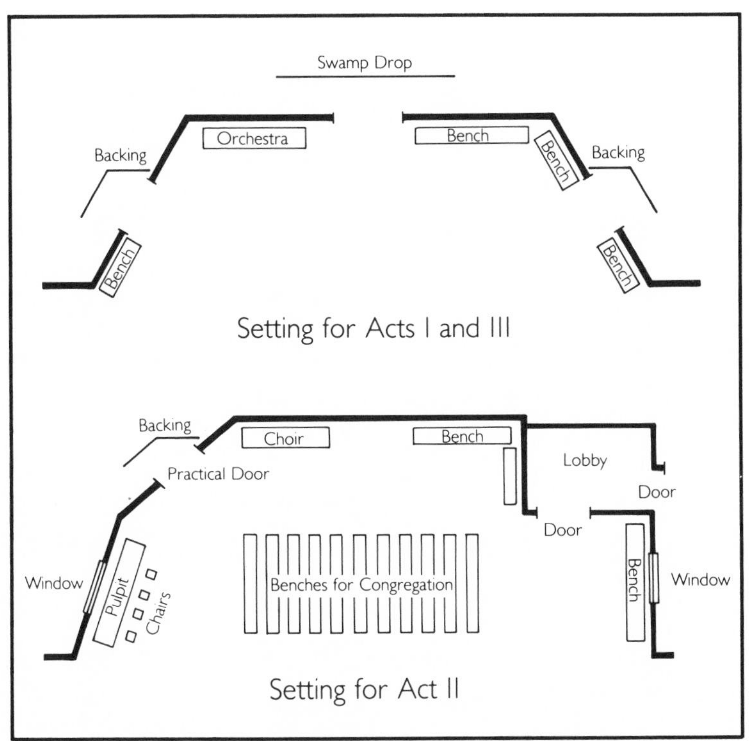

SYNOPSIS OF SCENES

Act I

A hot supper in a dance hall on a Saturday night, on a bluff near the big Congaree swamps near Columbia, South Carolina.

Act II

A small country church. Afternoon of the next day. On the borders of the Big Congaree Swamp near Columbia, South Carolina.

Act III

Same as Act I. A night in late spring three months later.
Time: The Present

The great swamps of the Congaree occupy a section in the heart of South Carolina within a few miles of the capital city, Columbia, bordering the Congaree River for a distance of about forty miles south of Columbia, South Carolina.

Potee's Gal

ACT I

(Scene: When the curtain rises it discloses a negro dance hall. It is night. Everything is in readiness for a hot supper and dance. There are benches and chairs around the wall. There is a door to the right, one to the left and a door upstage center with a window on either side. Upstage right there is a raised platform for an orchestra. Outside are heard snatches of a song, the tooting of a fife, gay laughter and talk and the beating of drums. A few people are sitting around, gradually others enter and mingle in small groups. There is general laughter and talk. In one of the groups is Jube. When the curtain rises Jazy and Judy are engaged in conversation.)

JAZY: Judy, is you guh dance wid me tonight?

JUDY: No, you're a fool. I ain't guh dance wid you.

JAZY: Wuh make?

JUDY: Well, you know how you done me de other night.

JAZY: I ain't done nothin'.

JUDY: Yes, you is. Time Coot-Duck come here, you start sidelin' off till you all got together. Make out you ain't see me atter dat.

JAZY: You wrong. I look for you every wey. You spile de whole night for me kaze I ain't kin find you. You know I ain't care nothin' 'bout Coot-Duck. You jes like all dese other wimmen—tryin' to put de blame on de mens.

JUDY: Ain't nothin'.

JAZY: I come to dis frolic tonight jes for you. Les we go an' get some hash an' rice.

JUDY: I ain't goin' no wey wid you.

JAZY: Oh, come on. Les we don't have no fuss. *(They exit together. Big Charleston, a tall, well-built, brown-skinned man wearing a blue flannel shirt open at the neck and a red bandana hung loosely around his neck, enters from the center door, looks about the crowd and suddenly sees Jube.)*

CHARLESTON: Why here's my ole pardner! *(They shake hands.)* Hello, pard! How you been? I ain't seed you since we had dat little tangle to Ten-Mile Hill. Jesus, boy! I sho is glad to see you. *(They shake hands again.)*

JUBE: Great God, Charleston! I thought you was dead. Wey you been? I ain't seed or heared er you since Father Abraham was a sucklin' babe. *(They both laugh.)* Dey tell me dat ole nigger from de trussel gang wuh been so bad been hobblin' 'round on crutches ever since. How you done it?

CHARLESTON: *(Laughing and displaying perfect white teeth.)* When he fasten me I aim to th'ow him out de window, but I missed an' th'owed him 'gainst de window sill. *(Jube laughs and Charleston chuckles.)* He is look sorter weak de last time I seed him dat night, but I ain't pay much 'tention to him, dem niggers was crowdin' me so. Dey knowed dey had a fight. We sho cleaned for 'em.

JUBE: It look like Jesus was beckonin' me dat night. Dey mighty nigh had me when I vision you standin' in de door.

CHARLESTON: Wey did you go dat night, Jube?

JUBE: I leff. I ain't been nigh dat place since. You an' me ain't work for de same white folks.

CHARLESTON: Dat's so. *(They laugh.)*

JUBE: Charleston, how you come out dat night?

CHARLESTON: Luck an' de Lord and de white folks was wid me. I went to de boss an' he cuss me out, but tell me don't fret, he'd take care of me; but he say, "Charleston, for God' sake quit brokin' niggers up an' quit messin' wid dey wimmens." He say ain't none on 'em worth a damn an' ain't worth a good man gettin' in trouble 'bout. *(There is loud laughter and talk outside. Several musicians enter, more men and women arrive. A man enters alone. It is Silas. He looks at Jube and says)*:

SILAS: Jube!

JUBE: Brother Silas!

(Jube continues his conversation with Charleston.)

JUBE: Look like we guh have a big time here tonight. Niggers comin' from everywey.

CHARLESTON: I always is like hot suppers an' dances.

JUBE: We got fine pork, rice, cornbread an' biscuit, an' dere ain't nobody dat kin cook hash better dan Tad. He got fashion Gullah Ben brung from Af'ica wid him.

CHARLESTON: You ain't say nothin' 'bout de liquor. I never was no hand at drinkin' it. I feels jes as good wid out it, but, Jube, it sho makes a frolic go.

JUBE: Charleston, is you acquainted here?

CHARLESTON: I been here in my young youth, but I ain't 'member much people.

JUBE: Dat ain't make no diff'ence. I ain't see wey dat ever kept you from havin' a good time. Dere's plenty er pretty gals comin' tonight. *(The sound of a cow's horn is heard in the distance.)* Is you hear dat horn? Dat's ole Potee blowin' for he dog, an' dat 'minds me dat Potee's Gal guh be here tonight.

CHARLESTON: Who Potee's Gal?

JUBE: I ain't know nothin' 'bout her cep she's Potee's Gal, but dere ain't nothin' never was no better lookin'. She's all spiled wid schoolin' an' edecation. She mighty nigh forget how to dance like niggers. She got a winnin' way; she diff'ent from dese other gals, an' I tellin' you now if you wants to have a good time an' ain't wants to loss a night, don't worry yourself wid her, kaze de moest she'll do is to look in your face, talk sweet an' leff you wid a smile to fret it out by you'self.

CHARLESTON: I guh get acquainted. I guh roll 'em high tonight.

JUBE: Dere's a heap er mighty pretty gals guh be here tonight.

CHARLESTON: Well, leff dat to me. I'll find one.

JUBE: Dat ain't never been no hardship on you.

CHARLESTON: Ain't nothin' no hardship if you goes at it right an' ain't waste you' time 'bout too much things. I works hard an' when I works I think 'bout my work, an' when I plays I plays hard an' thinks 'bout my wimmen. *(Both laugh.)*

JUBE: You ain't never waste too much er you' time thinkin' 'bout one ooman.

CHARLESTON: Yes, I is. I ain't thinkin' 'bout nothin' else when I'm guine wid her, but I ain't spile my time by stickin' to one ooman too long. It's jes like fishnin when you gets a fish an' makes a miration over him, you puts him on you' string an' then starts tryin' to ketch a better one. An' dat's de way it is wid me an' wimmens. Nature ain't never meant me to be satisfy wid one ooman. When I starts atter one, I wants her mighty bad, an' when I gets her I starts atter another. It's nature, it's sport an' I loves to sport.

JUBE: It's a mighty dang'ous sport. I find it ain't so hard to get wimmens, but sometimes it sho is de devil to get rid on 'em.

CHARLESTON: You know how to get rid on 'em?

JUBE: I wish to God I did. Dey done shorten my years.

CHARLESTON: Jes leff 'em like I leff Kaline. Dey get over it.

JUBE: I done tried dat. I leff 'em, but de trouble was dey wouldn't leff me.

CHARLESTON: Why, Jube, you ain't leff 'em like you meant it.

JUBE: Yes, I is; but, pardner, some er dese wimmens is fool. Dey same as a hound dog when dey gets on you' trail, dey never quit barkin' on it. Dey will angle you' mind an' wear out you' body, an' you' legs will bend like a stove-up horse. De trail ain't never too long an' God His Self couldn't dodge a ooman when she ever gets she mind set, an' she don't know wha' tired is.

CHARLESTON: Jube, you oughter try soft talk.

JUBE: Dere ain't no nuse for you to soft-talk her, kaze she know wha' on you' mind an' wha' you guh say 'fore it gets to you' tongue.

CHARLESTON: You didn't used to talk dat er way, Jube. You must er had some trouble since last time I seed you. It 'minds me of de time Mink got he wages an' gamble 'em all away. He gamble off all he clothes—all he clothes cepen he hat an' he shoes, an' dem niggers he were gamblin' wid 'fused to take anything else. *(They both laugh.)* Dey say it was a freezin' night an' dey was not guh have it say dey took everything he have an' send him home barefoot wid nothin' to kiver he self wid. An' dat night when he got home 'fore day, Dolly had every window fasten an' de doors barred an' she knowed wha' Mink been doin' an' wuh he was guh say 'fore he open he mouth, an' she wouldn't luh him come in. Dolly say he been out dis late it ain't guh hurt him to spend de rest of de night wey he been, an' de next mornin' when dey find him he had dug a hole in de side of a haystack an' crawled in, but he was mighty nigh froze to death.

JUBE: I has heared er dat nigger. But dat ain't nothin' to wha' some er dese wimmens will do to you.

(The musicians strum a little. Couples enter, chatter and laugh.)

CHARLESTON: I guine out an' see wuh I kin see.

JUBE: God be wid you, brother. Step lightly.

CHARLESTON: Jube, you too partic'lar. I'm a man, I ain't scared. I works hard, pays my honest debts and I ain't runnin' from nobody. I guh step lightly when de dance starts, but jes now I feel entitled to have my fun.

JUBE: Well, can't you have you' fun an' be careful, too?

CHARLESTON: I never was no great hand at slippin' an' dodgin'. I has my faults, but wuh I does I does in de open 'fore God an' man. I never has robbed no man, I never has run from no man an' dere ain't no reason for me to hang my head.

(The musicians commence to play. The booming of drums is heard outside. Snatches of song and laughter.)

CHARLESTON: Les we go outside.

JUBE: I guh stay here a while.

CHARLESTON: See you later, pard. *(He goes out.)*

(The strumming of the orchestra has now swelled into full melody. The crowd which has been gathering, begins to dance, and after a short while big Duffie enters and commences a solo dance in the middle of the floor. The crowd cheers him on, clapping their hands and stamping their feet to keep time. Tad stands by playing the bones. Big Duffie is dancing an African dance. The crowd laughs, enthusiasm runs high and a ring is formed around him. Jazy starts to do a dance. Judy comes forward and dances

opposite him. Potee's Gal enters during the dance which now becomes general. She is pretty, daintily dressed, has had educational advantages for a short time. She has some knowledge of aesthetic dancing. The general dancing gradually stops as she dances back and forth through the crowd, dancing up to one man and then away to another. The men applaud her, keeping time with their hands and feet, each trying to gain her favor. Then the women start dancing trying to attract the men and all look jealously at Potee's Gal. The dance becomes wild and barbaric. [Note: The men and women are dancing, individually, African Dances: Buzzard Lope, The Buck, The Shuffle, The Wing, etc.] Occasionally a man will grab a woman and whirl her around. The musicians yell words of encouragement to the crowd. The music becomes faster and wilder until Potee's Gal goes over to Silas, sits in his lap and puts her arms around his neck. Near them a boy and girl (Snake and Helen) are dancing. Part of the crowd is talking and chatting and those near the dancers group around and watch. The big drum is heard outside, some singing is heard, the drum beat is very loud and Charleston appears in the doorway. He stands smiling and looking over the crowd. He comes forward with a great deal of assurance and watches Snake's dance. Several women make up to him. He treats them all with indifference. His eye rests on Potee's Gal. Charleston signals the dance to stop by throwing a quarter, which Snake grabs and then runs out, followed by Helen. Charleston stands admiring Potee's Gal.)

CHARLESTON: Great God, sugar! I dreams 'bout you in de night. You de kind er gal I lays awake at night an' thinks about. Come on, sugar, I got honey for you' years. Les we dance. You my pickin'. Come on, chile, I ain't start to tell you de sweet things I got on my mind an' dey never will get on my tongue sweet as dey is on my mind, but I guh tell you de best way I knows how.

(Charleston takes Potee's Gal by the wrist and pulls her out of Silas's lap.)

POTEE'S GAL: I got my man. I guh stay where I is. *(Silas goes and faces Charleston.)*

CHARLESTON: Hello there, sport. You sho got taste in wimmen. *(Silas remains silent, glaring at Charleston. Charleston smiles.)* You ain't mind me talkin' wid her, is you?

SILAS: Dis is mine; go git you' own ooman; don't fool wid mient. *(He turns to Potee's Gal.)*

CHARLESTON: Don't cut me off so short, sport. Dey ain't no law 'gainst me complimentin' dis gal.

SILAS: I de law dat will stop you. Leff here.

CHARLESTON: *(Smiling)* Dat ain't de way to get rid er me. Treat me right an' I'll be fair wid you.

SILAS: I don't axe you to be fair wid me, I'm handin' you your orders.

CHARLESTON: You guine at it de wrong way. You might 'suade me, but orderin' me an' runnin' me off—dat's diff'ent.

SILAS: Dis talk ain't guh last much longer.

CHARLESTON: No, I guh end it now. You had you' chance to act decent, but now I guh gee you a chance to show how much man you is. Has you got me, brother? *(Charleston reaches forward and takes hold of Potee's Gal)* Come on, sugar, les we talk wid us feets.

POTEE'S GAL: I got my man. I guh stay where I is.

CHARLESTON: Come on. I ain't care nothin' 'bout dese niggers *(He draws her toward the center)* I guh love you, I guh make you love me an' follow me 'round, an' ain't nobody guh stop me. *(Potee's Gal resists vigorously.)*

SILAS: Don't fool wid my ooman. Leff her. *(Charleston pays no attention to him. Silas pulls Potee's Gal to one side)* You low hound, I means to kill you. I guh cut you' damn head off. *(He rushes at Charleston with an open knife in his hand. A struggle ensues. Women scream and crowd to the wall as the fight progresses. The knife falls to the floor. Charleston strangles Silas across his knee, and throws him heavily to the floor. A number of men jump on big Charleston. The women run out screeching and screaming. There is a tremendous commotion and Silas lies still through it all. Charleston grabs an ax handle from one of the men he is fighting and attacks his assailants and eventually drives them all from the hall. When the commotion ends, the stage is clear except for the Musicians, Potee's Gal, Charleston and Silas, the latter lying dead on the floor, Charleston bleeding from several cuts and bruises. Potee's Gal kneels beside Silas, shakes him and says:)*

POTEE'S GAL: Silas! Silas! *(She puts her arms around his neck and begins weeping. She rises in a terrible fury and faces Charleston.)* Silas is dead. Oh, my God! You killed him! You killed him!

CHARLESTON: *(Wiping his head with a large handkerchief)* I ain't pick no row wid him. I has to perteck myself when he stuck me wid a knife. Honey, I done it for you.

POTEE'S GAL: I didn't ask you to do nothin'. Why didn't you stay away from us? What you got to do wid Silas? Ain't nobody called you. Ain't nobody interfered with you. Ain't nobody want you, and you just bu'st in and agivate Silas. Before Jesus, I'm guh tear you down before I'm done. I'm goin' to send you travelin' the same road you sent Silas. What do I want with a low-down hound like you?

CHARLESTON: I want you; I'm waitin' for you; I'm guh have you. 'Tain't no nuse for you to be contrary wid me, I ain't start atter a ooman an' turn back. Dere ain't no need for you to think you diff'ent from de rest. Any er dese wimmen would crawl on dey knees at my biddin'. All dese wimmen b'longs to Charleston ef he wants 'em.

POTEE'S GAL: All cep me. I don't belong to you an' never will. Dese wimmen you been with is not my kind of wimmen. Dere's a heap you got to learn. You say you never start after a woman an' turn back, but this woman is guh put you on a back track with curves in it as crooked as the trail of a snake. I'm done with you. Leave me.

CHARLESTON: It don't matter wuh you say, if you please or angry, it sound to me as sweet as de chune of a mockin' bird or as soft as de fall of a jewdrop—an' when I seed you dancin' tonight, you were as pretty as a humming bird flying from flower to flower. Darlin', Charleston loves you an' is dyin' for you. Sugar, you b'longs to me. *(He grabs hold of her and kisses her.)*

POTEE'S GAL: *(Resisting him)* You low hound, turn me loose. Turn me loose. *(He holds her tighter. She struggles fiercely)* You killed Silas and before Jesus I ain't never goin' to stop till I wring a knife off in you. I'm goin' to send you travelin' the same road you sent Silas. *(Charleston throws her across the room to where Silas is lying and walks toward the center door.)*

CHARLESTON: Jes 'member wha' I say: I'm a man, I ain't scared, I ain't got but one time to die, an' I is prepared. I hasn't started yet, look for me. You mought be Potee's Gal now, but I guh tame you an' make you Charleston's gal. *(Charleston exits.)*

POTEE'S GAL: *(She looks at Silas, crawls to him, bends down and caresses his head and face)* Silas, are you dead? O God! Silas, speak to me. Silas, Silas! *(She shakes him)* O Jesus! Silas! Silas, I ain't tell you, but I love you. O Silas! I love you. Jesus, O Jesus! Help me. *(She sobs for a while then rises slowly and stands with a vacant look. Gradually she raises her head and a weird, sinister expression steals over her face. She draws herself up to her full height and clenches her fists)* Silas, I'm goin' after Charleston. I'll drag him in the dust. I'll get him and tear his heart out. O God! O Jesus! *(She exits frantically through the center door.)*

FIDDLER: *(As he approaches the body of Silas slowly)* Do Jesus! I knowed sump'n was guine wrong.

JEW'S HARPIST: *(Joining the Fiddler)* It look like we all guh git tangle up.

BANJO PLAYER: *(Joining the group)* Don't look like niggers kin have a good time lessen dey goes to fightin' an' killin' up one anudder.

FIDDLER: I ain't call dis here fightin' no good time.

BANJO PLAYER: I ain't see no 'casion for it.

FIDDLER: Big Charleston ain't have no 'casion to snatch Potee's Gal out er dat nigger's lap.

JEW'S HARPIST: Silas oughten to stucked him wid dat knife.

FIDDLER: Big Charleston is a dang'ous nigger, but he ain't no mean nigger; he's jes kind er rough. Les we don't know too much 'bout it. *(He goes and picks up his fiddle.)*

JEW'S HARPIST: I ain't know nothin' 'bout it.

BANJO PLAYER: It's niggers' business to hide wha' dey kin. It's white folks' business to find out wha' dey kin.

(They all prepare to leave. Tamer and Hannah enter.)

TAMER: *(Excitedly)* O Lord, O Lord, my Jesus! I knowed sump'n was guh happen when I seed dat little heifer come in here switchin' she self 'round, lookin' up into de faces of dese men tryin' to entice 'em wid she little fast self.

HANNAH: Mens ain't got no sense when it comes to wimmens. Dey'll kill dey self an' one anudder. Dey all on 'em act like fools when dat little gal er Potee's come 'round here. Same as th'owin' a pullet in a passel er roosters. All de roosters goes to crowin' an' struttin' an' sidelin' 'round de pullet. Dat's mens. Ain't no ooman never seen nothin' in a hussy like Potee's Gal. All men is a passel er fools. Dey ain't got no sense. A little bit er talcum powder, a red frock an' a lot er ribbons an' legs an' twistin' an' switchin' an' lookin' up in dey face invitin' like will set any on 'em crazy.

TAMER: You're right, my sister. Take a man an' a rooster an' a studhorse—dey all on 'em de same. De rooster will crow an' strut an' fight; de studhorse will squeal an' kick an' bite, an' de man will laugh an' lie an' fight, an' will do everything de rooster an' de studhorse do an' more, too.

HANNAH: Dat's de God's truth, but I loves 'em to do all dey does. Ef dey ain't do wha' dey does, dey ain't no mens an' dey ain't no count. Dey all on 'em is fool. Dey ain't got no sense, but I loves 'em dat er way, an' I sho hates to see a man like Big Charleston get all stucked up an' get his self in trouble for dat little fast gal. *(They go out together.)*

SISTER OF SILAS: *(Enters the dance hall followed by Tom and Cricket. She is screaming and weeping)* O my God! Do Jesus! *(She emits a piercing shriek)* Big Charleston done kill Silas. *(She kneels near the body)* O my Lord! O Jesus, my God! Is you take Silas? Is you take Silas? Is you take my beloved brother? *(She sways)* Is you take him, Lord, wid out geein' him a chance to say good-bye; wid out geein' him a chance to see he pa an' he ma? O Lord, dear God! *(She sways more violently)* O Jesus! My brother, my poor dead brother, my beloved brother. Wuh is I guh do? Have mercy, O, my Jesus, have mercy. Wuh make you take Silas? *(She moans a while)* Look, Lord, an' see wha' you tooken, an' look, Lord, look an' see wha' you leff. Look at all dis here trash.

CRICKET: Is you hear wha' dat ooman say? I know we ain't nothin' too much, but I don't like no ooman callin' God's 'tention to we shortcomin's.

TOM: I wouldn't pay too much 'tention to wha' she say. She ain't mean no harm. She a ooman an' she ain't got no sense, an' she want everybody to hear wha' she say to God, an' want we to look at her an' she ain't know wha' to say.

CRICKET: Well, she done call God's 'tention to we.

TOM: *(Going to the door)* Cricket, I reckon we best be guine 'fore de rural police come. Dey liable to put any on us in de chair—it ain't make no diff'ence who done it.

CRICKET: I ain't guh take nothin' to do wid it. Les we be guine. Huh?

TOM: Huh. *(Cricket turns and goes out with Tom on his heels, leaving the Sister of Silas alone with the body. She moans heavily as the curtain descends slowly).*

End of Act I

ACT II

(Scene: A small country church at Rock Hill on the borders of the big Congaree Swamp near Columbia, South Carolina, the next day. The building is made of rough lumber. There are windows in the back flats. The windows are crude attempts at Gothic, with cheap stained glass—yellow and red at the top and white below. The congregation sits on rough benches (in one church a number of old street car seats were used.) There are two aisles running across the stage from left to right, one up stage and one down stage, the

down stage aisle discontinuing at the foot lights. At the left up stage there is a large door leading into a small vestibule which in turn leads outside. At the right end of the church there is a raised platform about eighteen inches high which does service as a pulpit. In the center of the platform is a crude wooden stand covered with a cloth on which a Bible is placed. On the platform there are several chairs. These may be cheap upholstered chairs or cheap dining room chairs. In the flat on the right behind the pulpit is a window draped domestic fashion with white curtains. On the platform is an eighteen-inch table enameled white with a cheap vase filled with artificial flowers. There is a door in the flat above the pulpit. Above the door there is a large poster on which is printed the Ten Commandments. The heading is in red print, the remainder in black. From the ceiling long wrought iron hooks support two or three oil lamps. At the rise of the curtain Tom and Dan are discovered each sitting on the end of a bench.)

TOM: *(Running his hand over his forehead and drawing an audible breath)* Dis was a terrible thing de way Big Charleston act.

DAN: It sho was, but Big Charleston dis kind er nigger: when he starts fightin' he ain't got no idea 'bout nothin' but takin' care er Charleston, an', brother, he sho know how to do dat. He ain't think about wha' guh happen tomorrow, he thinkin' 'bout right now.

TOM: Ef Big Charleston ain't clean-for dem niggers, it would er been he funeral 'stead er Silas'.

DAN: An' Silas ain't been nobody' plaything. Ef Charleston ain't kilt him, he would er cut Charleston's heart strings loose. *(Potee's Gal enters and stands in the doorway listening.)*

TOM: I ain't see it end yet wid Charleston in jail.

POTEE'S GAL: He belongs in jail. Let him rot there.

TOM: He say he done it for you. Silas is dead an' Charleston is in de hands of de white folks. Dey might put him in de chair.

POTEE'S GAL: He done it for his self. Let 'em put him in the chair.

DAN: Sister, you shouldn't bear hard feelin's. Charleston's got qualities. He kill Silas kaze he want you. He ain't took no agvantage. He ain't only been fightin' Silas, but he been fightin' a drove on 'em. He ain't turn he back, he ain't run away, and he ain't leff dat dance hall till he fight he self clear, an' den he tooken he time. Dere was no voice raise agin him. All niggers who could crawl out done so, them dat ain't done it ain't been able to. He ain't never turn he back on nothin' dat look like fightin', an 'fore he leff he helt you in he arms an' tell you he done it for you.

POTEE'S GAL: I'd be doin' God's work to kill him—that carrion crow. What business has he got interferin' with me an' Silas?

TOM: Don't say dat, my sister. You ain't know wuh in store for you.

POTEE'S GAL: He said he's goin' to tame me. He's goin' to make a pet out of me. He's goin' to have me follow him around like a dog. He's goin' to make me Charleston's gal. He told me that.

TOM: But, my sister, he done it kaze he love you an' he's liable to set in de chair.

DAN: Things like dat has been done before. Charleston is a dang'ous man, but he got some winnin' ways. He tongue is soft an' he smile is sweet when he talkin' to a ooman. All de wimmens weaken for him.

POTEE'S GAL: The only talk Charleston could have that would sound sweet to me would be a groan when he twists up in the chair. He killed Silas. I'd like to see the sweat drippin' from his fore-head.

DAN: Don't say dat, sister. You mought change you' mind. Dere's a heap er wimmen dat would broke dey neck for Charleston.

TOM: If dey is put him in de chair, he will take it as he share—like a man.

DAN: De law is white; he ain't guh come to no harm from de law. Big white folks is for him an' he ain't tooken no advantage wid Silas. He were a tiger pen up.

JUBE: I hear wuh you all say. I has a mind dat Charleston will be here today.

POTEE'S GAL: How's he goin' to be here? Ain't he in jail?

JUBE: He sho been in jail, but I has a mind he guh be here jes de same.

DAN: I ain't never seen a man kill another man an' den go to he funeral.

TOM: Wuh he comin' here for?

JUBE: Dis is de house er God. Why ain't he kin come here?

TOM: I ain't think he come here on none er God's work, but you know who here, ain't you?

DAN: Potee's Gal.

TOM: You has spoken, but she won't bother wid Charleston. She heart in de casket wid Silas.

POTEE'S GAL: I ain't never want to see him. Wha' he got to do wid me?

JUBE: I never has knowed Charleston to start sump'n lessen he finish it. My sister, Charleston's comin' for you.

POTEE'S GAL: Before it's all over, he'll be guine for me.

DAN: Peace, my sister. Hush! Dis is de house er God. It's de place for weepin' an' moanin', for prayers an' for tears, for sorrow an' for hope. Dis is de house er God. Hush, hush, my sister!

(A crowd gathers in the doorway, some talking. There is general shuffling at the door. People enter and sit down, others rise and change their seats, some go to the doorway. The leader of the choir rises, then all the members of the choir rise and commence to sing the spiritual:)

"You Jes as Well Love Everybody"

You jes as well love everybody,
You got to die.
You jes as well love everybody,
You got to die.
From Monday, Tuesday, Wednesday, Thursday,
Friday, Sadday an' all day Sunday,
You jes as well love everybody.
You got to die.

You jes as well live in union,
You got to die.
You jes as well live in union,
You got to die.
From Monday, Tuesday, Wednesday, Thursday,
Friday, Sadday an' all day Sunday,
You jes as well live in union,
You got to die.

You jes as well love your sister,
You got to die.
You jes as well love your sister,
You got to die.
From Monday, Tuesday, Wednesday, Thursday,
Friday, Sadday an' all day Sunday,
You jes as well love your sister,
You got to die.

(During the singing of the spiritual, the deacon enters and is followed by six pallbearers with the casket. The Family comes next walking in pairs, dressed in black. At the appearance of the mourners, Potee's Gal shrieks.)

POTEE'S GAL: Silas, Silas! Lord, put Charleston in de chair. O Jesus! Silas, Silas! *(She moans.)*

('Relatives and friends and members of the congregation continue to enter. By now the church is almost full. Potee's Gal shrieks and moans, showing uncontrolled grief. The preacher enters from the rear of the church and steps into the pulpit. Everybody rises. He raises his hands and they all sit. By this time the spiritual is ended.)

PREACHER: *(Reading a passage from the Bible)*

Fret not thyself because of evildoers, neither be thou envious against the workers of iniquity. For they shall soon be cut down as the grass, and wither as the green herb.
For evildoers shall be cut off; but those that wait upon the Lord, they shall inherit the earth.

For yet a little while, and the wicked shall not be; yea, thou shalt diligently consider his place, and it shall not be. I have seen the wicked in great power, and spreading himself like a green bay tree. Yet he passed away, and lo! he was not. I sought him, but he could not be found. My brother and sisters, I am going to ask Brother Mose to lead us in prayer.

(While Brother Mose is praying, some members of the congregation look around indifferently, others bow their heads, some bow well forward. The women are fanning themselves. Some wipe their faces with their handkerchiefs. There is crooning throughout the congregation. At the end of the prayer, there is a general shuffle throughout the congregation as they make themselves comfortable on the benches.)

BROTHER MOSE: *(As he drops on one knee in front of the congregation:)* Most high God, our Heavenly Father, look down on your children. Have mercy, Lord, have mercy! De wages of sin is death. Have mercy, Lord, our Heavenly Father, and teach us to keep in de straight and narrow path, for all other path is beset wid briar an' rattlesnake an' moccasin. Have mercy, Lord, have mercy, Heavenly Father. Keep us feets from de road of de snakes an' de scorpion, so dat we will be prepared to enter our Heavenly home free of scars, free of wrong-doin' an' fitten for Your Heavenly presence.

Voices from Amen Corner:

Have mercy, Lord, have mercy. Look down, Lord, wid a pityin' eye on us here below.

Voice of a Brother:

Oh yes, tell us brother.

BROTHER MOSE: Lord, reach down wid You' all-powerful hand an' liff us to de Heavenly mansion. Have mercy, God. Have mercy, our Heavenly Father.

Voice of a Brother:
Have mercy, our Heavenly Father.

BROTHER MOSE: Yes, God, we puts our main 'pendence in You. Guide an' pertect us, Lord. We is in de dark.

Voices of Several Brothers:
In de dark. In de dark.

BROTHER MOSE: We ain't nowhere wid out You. Our Heavenly Father, liff us from de darkness, liff us from de night, liff us to de light, to You' mansion in de sky. Have mercy, have mercy!

Voice of a Brother:
To de light. To de light.

BROTHER MOSE: Have mercy. Have mercy. Amen.

(Brother Mose wipes the perspiration from his face and head. He steps back and sits down. The preacher steps into the pulpit and says:)

PREACHER: I am now going to call on my congregation to sing. *(They respond with:)*

"I'm on My Way to Caneyan Land"

I'm on my way to Caneyan Land,
I'm on my way to Caneyan Land,
I'm on my way to Caneyan Land,
I'm on my way, thank God, I'm on my way.

If you don't go, don't hinder me,
If you don't go, don't hinder me,
If you don't go, don't hinder me,
I'm on my way, thank God, I'm on my way.

I'm on my way to Caneyan Land,
I'm on my way to Caneyan Land,
I'm on my way to Caneyan Land,
I'm on my way, thank God, I'm on my way.

My father's gone to Caneyan Land,
My father's gone to Caneyan Land,
My father's gone to Caneyan Land,
I'm on my way, thank God, I'm on my way.

I'm on my way to Caneyan Land,
I'm on my way to Caneyan Land,
I'm on my way to Caneyan Land,
I'm on my way, thank God, I'm on my way.

Our brother's gone to Caneyan Land,
Our brother's gone to Caneyan Land,
Our brother's gone to Caneyan Land,
I'm on my way, thank God, I'm on my way.

I'm on my way to Caneyan Land,
I'm on my way to Caneyan Land,
I'm on my way to Caneyan Land,
I'm on my way, thank God, I'm on my way.

(At the end of the spiritual the members of the choir sit down, leaving the Preacher ready for the sermon)

PREACHER: My brothers and sisters, death takes on the shadows of night for the body of Brother Silas. It takes on for those who knew him the colors of darkness, but such is the will of God and such the workings of His mind. He never—

SISTER OF SILAS: *(Rising from a seat beside the coffin, interrupting the Preacher who stops until she finishes. She is in front of the pulpit. She commences shouting and whirling about with her arms held high saying:)* Listen, listen! Silas tell me he had to go. He has left me here below. *(She moans loudly)* He has left he pa an' he ma. *(She becomes quite emotional)* He were a good man. Ain't never do nothin' to hurt nobody. He tell me he want to go. Lord, why is You listen to him? Why is You take him? He work hard. He raise hog an' chicken. He in de field at sunup an' ain't come out till sundown. Jesus, O Jesus! *(She gives a violent scream)* He ain't never get jestice in dis life, an' dis preacher ain't geein' it to him now. *(She whirls around toward the aisle)* Lord, Lord, have mercy! Don't forget my lovin' brother. *(She goes on whirling and shouting)* Have mercy, my Lord, my Jesus!

(A man rises from the congregation, puts his arm around her and takes her from the church, trying to pacify her as they go out. She is moaning and screaming:)

SISTER OF SILAS: Silas, Silas! Oh, oh, Silas!

(A woman passes her baby to the woman next to her to hold for a few minutes, and a child rises and walks down the aisle away from the pulpit and joins several other children of her acquaintance. When quiet is restored, the Preacher continues:)

PREACHER: My brothers and sisters, as I was saying, death takes on the shadows of night for the body of Brother Silas. It takes on for those who knew him the colors of darkness, but such is the will of God and such the working of His mind. He never intended for us to fully understand. If He showed us everything, we would think we knew as much as He does. God has put death amongst us to impress us with the importance of living the right sort of life.

Voice of a Brother:
De right sort of life.

(There is moaning and crooning throughout the congregation. Potee's Gal rises. She is very emotional and shrieks:)

POTEE'S GAL: Lord, why have You taken Silas? Alone, alone. *(She gives a piercing scream)* My God, I'm alone! Why have You taken Silas? Silas! Oh my God, my God! O Silas!

(A woman sitting above Potee's Gal and one behind her force her to sit down.)

PREACHER: God has let death drop upon us like a dark and angry cloud.

Voices in the Congregation:
Angry cloud. Angry cloud.
Shrill Voice of Old Woman:
Dark, dark and angry cloud.

PREACHER: Lightning flashes and thunder rolls.

Voices in the Congregation:
Thunder rolls. Thunder rolls.

PREACHER: And lightning flashes, flashes and strikes. It may be you or me, for thunder is the voice of God and lightning is the flashing of His eye and the thunder bolt He hurls from His heights on high. He does not miss you, my brother or my sister. His aim is always true, and your mortal body is destroyed. Such is the will of God and the cloud that has dulled the world and your senses rolls away, and the soul of the dead is either lifted into the world of eternal light, or cast into the everlasting shadows of unending night amidst the flames and groans of the sinful and the wicked—cast down, down, down into the night.

(There are moans and wails from all parts of the congregation.)

PREACHER: Brother Silas is dead,
He rests from his labor,
And he sleeps,

Shrill Voice of Sister:
He sleeps, oh, he sleeps.

PREACHER: Where the tall pines grow
On the banks of a river.

Another Voice:
On de banks of a river.
Several Voices:
On de banks of a river.

PREACHER: His trouble is done,
He has left this world
On the wings of glory.

Voice:
On de wings of glory!

PREACHER: Out of life's storm,

Another Voice:
On de wings of glory!

PREACHER: Out of life's darkness,

Several Voices:
On de wings of glory!

PREACHER: He sails in the light
Of the lamb.
Away from his troubles,
Away from the night,

Congregation:
In the light, in the light of the lamb!

PREACHER: He's gone to the kingdom above,
In the raiment of angels,

Voice of Sister:
In the raiment, in the raiment of angels!

PREACHER: To the region above;
And he sleeps,

Voices Chanting throughout the Congregation:

He sleeps, oh, he sleeps,
On de banks of a river.

PREACHER: Where the tall pines grow,
On the banks of a river.

Congregation:
Wid de starry crowned angels,
On de banks of a river.

PREACHER: And the flowers are blooming
In the blood of the lamb.

Shrill Voice of Sister: (Taken up by congregation chanting and swaying:)
De blood of de lamb!
In de blood of de lamb!

PREACHER: And the birds are singing,
Where the wind blows soft
As the breath of an angel;
And he sleeps,
Where the tall pines grow
On the banks of a river.

Voice:
An' he sleeps!
Another Voice:
Wey de tall pines grow.

PREACHER: And his spirit is guarded

Several Voices:
On de banks of a river.

PREACHER: By a flamin'-faced angel,

Sister:
Yes, Jesus, a flamin'-faced angel,
On de banks of a river.

PREACHER: Standing on mountains of rest
And he sleeps where the tall pines grow,
On the banks of a river,
Where the wind blows soft
As the breath of an angel,
He sleeps where the tall pines grow.
He sleeps, oh, he sleeps.

Congregation:
He sleeps, oh, he sleeps.

PREACHER: May God in His mercy and loving kindness look down with pity on Brother Silas and rest his soul in peace.

(During the sermon the congregation sways, beat their hands against their thighs or their knees and move their feet, keeping time with the rhythm of the Preacher's sermon.)

PREACHER: The congregation will sing.
(They respond with:)

"Set Down Servant"

I know you tired, set down,
I know you tired, set down,
I know you tired, set down,
Set down and rest a little while.

Refrain:
Oh, set down, servant, set down,
Oh, set down, servant, set down,
Oh, set down, servant, set down,
Set down and rest a little while.

I know you been runnin', set down,
I know you been runnin', set down,
I know you been runnin', set down,
Set down and rest a little while.

Refrain:
Oh, set down, servant, set down,
Oh, set down, servant, set down,
Oh, set down, servant, set down,
Set down and rest a little while.

Know you been cryin', set down,
Know you been cryin', set down,
Know you been cryin', set down,
Set down and rest a little while.

Refrain:
Oh, set down, servant, set down,
Oh, set down, servant, set down,
Oh, set down, servant, set down,
Set down and rest a little while.

Talked wid de death angel, set down,
Talked wid de death angel, set down,
Talked wid de death angel, set down,
Set down and rest a little while.

Refrain:
Oh, set down, servant, set down,
Oh, set down, servant, set down,
Oh, set down, servant, set down,
Set down and rest a little while.

You know your time comin', set down,
You know your time comin', set down,
You know your time comin', set down,
Set down and rest a little while.

Refrain:
Oh, set down, servant, set down,
Oh, set down, servant, set down,
Oh, set down, servant, set down,
Set down and rest a little while.

(The spiritual concluded, the Preacher calls upon some of the friends of Silas to say a few words.)

PREACHER: Now, my brothers and sisters, we have with us some of the close friends of Brother Silas, and I am sure that we would all like to hear from some of them. I will call on Brother Tom to say a few words in behalf of our dead brother.

TOM: *(Rises and goes to a place in front of and below the pulpit)* My brothers and sisters, Brother Silas was my dear neighbor. I has knowed him from de time he was born and I knowed his fore-parents. Brother Silas was a hard-workin' man, an' he 'tend to he own business, an' he was a kind an' friendly man. When anybody cross him, he always stand up for he self, but he was too quick to fight an' wouldn't take nothin' off er nobody. Ef you insult him, he were too quick, an', my brothers an' sisters, dat de casion er he bein' in de casket right here in front er we. De good Book tells we dat "A soft answer turneth away wrath." Dat were de main fault of our brother. He ain't know nothin' 'bout a soft answer, an' his days been shorten in de land. Dere's a heap I could say 'bout Brother Silas, dere's a heap er good dat you all ain't know 'bout *(Looks at his watch)*, but I must stop so dat you kin hear from some er he other friends. *(He resumes his seat.)*

PREACHER: My brothers and sisters, Brother Tom has told you a few things about the deceased. I would like to ask Brother Daniel to say a few words.

DAN: Brothers and sisters, I so full er grief over de death of our beloved brother an' a friend of my youth, dat every word about him is said wid a achin' heart as he lays here in he casket at rest. It brings to my mind all things dat happen betwix' us. To show wha' kind a man Brother Silas were, ef I ain't have a thing an' Brother Silas got it, he would 'ny he self to help me out. I own up dat he were much too hasty, but, my brothers an' sisters, in de years dat I knowed him dere never was a cross word twix him an' me. We ain't never have nothin' but true friendship an' lovin' kindness. He would give away everything he got, an' do it wid a smile. Him an' me was guine to see a gal, an' Brother Silas find out she like him better dan she do me, an' he jes say to me: "Dan, dere ain't nothin' kin come between me an' you, much less a ooman, to casion we to fall out, so I guh gee her to you an' I ain't care wha' purpose you make of her." Dat's de sort of man was Brother Silas. My time is short, so I will end. May God bless de memory of our dead brother.

PREACHER: Now, my brothers and sisters, you have heard what the intimate friends of Brother Silas had to say. I feel that you are all satisfied that he rests in the arms of his Maker. All of you who would like to take a last look at the body of Brother Silas, rise and come this way, then go back to your seats. *(The choir leader commences to sing:* "If You See My Master Huntin' Somebody" *which is taken up by the rest of the choir and the congregation.)*

"If You See My Master Huntin' Somebody"

If you see my Master
Huntin' somebody,
Jes tell Him I said:
Send me, send me.

If he want somebody
To carry His gospel,
Jes tell Him I said:
Send me, send me.

Don't send my mother
Nor neither my brother,
Jes tell Him I said:
Send me, send me.

Don't send no liar
Nor neither no pretender,
Jes tell Him I said:
Send me, send me.

(The spirituals continue until the end of the act. The congregation passes into the aisle and walks past the casket.

They cross in front of the casket and pass on down the opposite aisle. The relatives and a few friends remain around the casket moaning loudly, shouting and screaming. The pallbearers pick up the casket and start to leave the church. The moaning increases in intensity and volume. There are piercing shrieks and screams. The choir leader begins singing another spiritual which is taken up by the rest of the congregation:)

"I'm Goin' to Live So My God Can Use Me at Any Time"

I'm goin' to live so my
God can use me
At any time,
At any time.
I'm goin' to live so my
God can use me
At any time,
At any time.

I'm goin' to pray so my
God can use me
At any time,
At any time.
I'm goin' to pray so my
God can use me
At any time,
At any time.

I'm goin' to talk so my
God can use me
At any time,
At any time.
I'm goin' to talk so my
God can use me
At any time,
At any time.

I'm goin' to shout so my
God can use me
At any time,
At any time.
I'm goin' to shout so my
God can use me
At any time,
At any time.

(The singing of the spiritual gets louder, the congregation, shouting as they pass out. Note: Shouting in this instance means a religious dance in which there is swinging and swaying and in which the feet are not to be crossed. Shouting, does not mean 'shout' in the ordinary sense. Frequently they jump up and down whirling around and around with their arms extended above their heads. As the body of Silas passes Potee's Gal, she throws herself across the casket shrieking at the top of her voice:)

POTEE'S GAL: Let me die! Jesus, let me die. I want to lie in de same grave wid Silas. Bury me wid Silas, O Jesus! O Jesus! O Lord! I'm goin' to send Charleston de same road he sent Silas. O Lord, let me sleep in de same grave wid Silas. Silas, O Silas!

(Suddenly a man rises from the rear of the church. He goes toward the casket and as he gets closer we recognize Big Charleston. He lifts Potee's Gal away from the casket and the procession goes on its way singing and shouting, while Big Charleston holds her close to him and tries to comfort her.)

CHARLESTON: Hush, baby. Don't you cry. Dry you' eyes. Charleston guh take care of you. Sugar, quit you' fretin', Jes put you' 'pendence in Charleston, honey. Hush, baby. Dat's all right. *(The procession has passed, leaving Charleston and Potee's Gal alone in the church. He sits on the end of a bench with Potee's Gal in his lap. They sway gently from side to side)* It's all right, honey, honey. *(The spiritual dies*

away in the distance and the curtain descends slowly.)
Honey!

End of Act II

ACT III

Scene: Same as Act I, a night three months later. It is late spring. Outside of the dance hall a hot supper is taking place, accompanied by loud laughter, occasional booming of a drum and playing of a mouth organ. Voices are heard singing:

"I Was Ridin' on a Hump-Back Mule"

Ole marster bought a pretty yellow gal,
He bought her from de south;
Her hair was wropped so very tight
She couldn't shut her mouth.

Refrain:
I was ridin' on a hump-back mule,
I was ridin' on a hump-back mule,
De only song dat I could sing
Was ridin' on a hump-back mule.

Took her to de blacksmith shop
To have her mouth drewed small,
She backed her years drewed a great big breath,
Swallowed blacksmith shop and all.
Refrain

Head look like a coffee pot,
Nose look like de spout,
Mouth look like a fireplace

Wid de ashes taken out.
Refrain

(There are several groups talking inside the hall. Some people are sitting, some sleeping; one girl is openly flirting with a boy. The musicians are on the platform. They are talking quietly. When the song outside comes to an end, Dan speaks:)

DAN: Is you hear dat song, "I was Ridin' on a Hump-back Mule?" I was jes thinkin' 'bout de tale Cricket tell we 'bout de time he been on Flat Lake fishnin by his self, an' he say he hear de cries er all kind er night birds, an' alligator bellowin' till dey shake de earth, an' bull frogs wid voice so deep dey sound like dey come out er de bottom of a well. Cricket say de night been so silent dat when all dem sound bus out on de night air, it got to be a strain on him. He say it were bad enough wey he been—look like it wusser ef he leff, so he tried to pacify he self by singin' dat song, an' when he finish sump'n pass he years like a breath er air an' set on a log right 'side er him, an' when he look he seed it were a ole owl. 'Fore he could move, dat owl whirl 'round an' look at Cricket an' say: "I like dat piece you was singin'. Gee us another verse." Cricket say he blood run cold from de root er he teet' to de back er he eyeball an' down to he toenail.

TOM: Great God! Dat's when I would er leff dat swamp.

DAN: From wha' Cricket say, dat's zackly wha' he done.

JUBE: An' I don't reckon he loss no time.

DAN: Cricket say he don't know how he git out, but he sho er one thing: dat he come out in a straight line. He say he ain't look back but one time, an' it seem to him like every rattlesnake an' moccasin in dat swamp was runnin' a race wid de varmints tryin' to see which on 'em could get to him first. He say he see several things in front on him, but dey ain't nothin' look wuss dan wha' behind him. He say he always had a desire for whings, but he ain't need 'em dat night.

TOM: It's good thing people comin' to dis frolic tonight don't have to pass through dem swamps.

DAN: Dey tell me dey's a wagon-load on 'em comin' from Pine Bluff an' niggers from 'round de burnt mill sent word dey was all on 'em comin'.

TOM: Dere's a heap er danger on de road. All on it ain't in de swamp.

DAN: You has spoken, Tom. Dey got Israel tonight.

TOM: How come?

DAN: De officers hem him up wid a load er liquor. Dey mistooken him for a stranger an' dey shoot him through de leg, an' when dey find out who it was, it were too late.

TOM: Israel worked for dem big stiller, an' he had free passage.

DAN: De stiller cussed dem officers out an' tell 'em ef dey ain't 'tend to dey business right, he guh clean 'em out an' put mens in dey place wuh got some sense.

TOM: Dey sho is some good lookin' wimmen comin' tonight from Pine Bluff an' de burnt mill. Les hope dey won't have no trouble. Dese good lookin' wimmen will help to make de party go.

(Tad enters and stands in the doorway holding a cleaver and a big spoon. He makes a clatter with them. Everybody pays attention to him and Tad says:)

TAD: If you all hongry, you better come on. I got hash an' rice for you. 'Member, now, I ain't want you all to do wha' ole man Robin done at de settin'-up when ole man Paul die.

JAZY: Wha' he do, Tad?

TAD: Wait a minute, luh me tell you how it was. Ole man Paul had went off in a trance an' ain't been dead. Ole man Robin was preachin' his funeral an' when he start to preach he say:

"O Lord, bring Paul back. We want to see him again. Lord, we need Paul back here. We lost one er our best neighbors. Dey any way to bring Paul back, for God' sake bring him, for we sho want to see Paul again." While he was preachin' he had both eyes shet tight hollerin' in a loud voice:
"Lord, I want to see Paul again."

When he looked around, everybody in de house

were gone out. He was dere by his self. He seen de sheet on Paul risin' up an' Paul gettin' up on de coolin'-board. He hollered wid a loud voice:

"Stand back, Paul. Don't you budge. Don't you budge."

Straight through de loft an' de gable end er de house he went. He didn't have time to find de door. He bust de gable end er de house out wid he head an' went through landin' on his head an' next on his feet. He went home an' crawled under de bed, an' his wife an' chillun were persuadin' him for a long time to come out to find out wuh happen. He said:

"Ole man Paul die, but he come back again. Dey say dat a man don't rise till de resurrection, but I raise Paul in one night."

I don't want you all to do like ole man Robin. You don't have to go through de gable, de door is big enough. *(Tad goes out yelling)* Dis way for hash an' pork. Come an' get you' rice.

(At the same time the crowd whistles and talks as they move off after Tad. The clanging of a plow hoe is heard. Tom starts out, but Dan with a twinkle in his eye detains him. Tom and Dan lag behind and go to a corner when all are off. Tom takes a pint of corn from his hip pocket. They drink. Charleston enters with Potee's Gal.)

CHARLESTON: Tad an' dem out to de barbecue pit. Ain't nobody here but you an' me.

POTEE'S GAL: I ain't worryin' 'bout nobody else long as I got you, darlin'.

CHARLESTON: It ain't make no diff'ence to me ef ain't nobody come. I got de prettiest gal on de Congaree from Columbia to Wateree.

POTEE'S GAL: And you are never goin' to change dat tune?

CHARLESTON: *(Putting his arm around her)* Ain't never. Dat's guh be my onliest chune.

POTEE'S GAL: Les see if you kin do dat waltz I was teachin' you. *(They dance with a very slow motion looking into each others eyes.)*

CHARLESTON: Gal, I more rudder be here wid you dan in heaven.

POTEE'S GAL: I feel so good when I'm wid you, it look like sump'n guh happen.

CHARLESTON: Don't talk dat er way. Ain't no nuse to start crossin' a creek 'fore you get to it. Ain't I here wid you?

POTEE'S GAL: Charleston, I don't b'lieve you'll ever leff me. You couldn't look dat er way out er you' eyes if you had another mind.

CHARLESTON: De first time I seed you, I knowed you'd be Charleston's gal. *(The drum is beating, the crowd cheering)*

POTEE'S GAL: Les we see what all dat is.

(The beating of the plow hoe is heard accompanied by shouts, cheers and yells. Potee's Gal and Charleston exit in the direction of the barbecue. Tom starts out in the direction of the noise and Dan says:)

DAN: Wait a minute. *(He takes a quart bottle from his pocket, looks around)* I got more music in dis little vial dan all dat music out dere. Les we have another little nip. *(Dan takes a long drink.)*

TOM: Dat ain't no nip. Dat's a google you swallow.

(The noise of the crowd is heard outside. Fearing discovery, Dan hides the bottle. Jube enters.)

JUBE: Dere sho been a turn-over down to de ole street 'bout a ooman—every kind er mix-up. Niggers fightin' every which er way.

TOM: Wha' de matter ail 'em?

JUBE: Ole Sister start sump'n.

DAN: Dat's wha' Ole Sister good for—carryin' news an' puttin' pizen out.

JUBE: She done put pizen out up de street, an' den she pass on to put pizen out somewey else.

DAN: *(With a touch of sarcasm in his voice)* You ain't think all dat 'bout Ole Sister, is you? Ain't I see her in church an' meetin' look like she always prayin' an' beggin' God to forgive poor sinners? *(They all laugh.)*

TOM: She tongue forked jes like a snake's. One half on it drips prayers, an' tother half turns loose ruination. Ole Sister's business is other folks' business.

JUBE: Ole man Daniel tell we dat way back in slavery time dere been a nigger, dey call him Gab'el. He say Gab'el been a kind man. He perteck everything in trouble—mens an' wimmens—but other times he ain't take nothin' to do wid nobody. Ole man Daniel say Gab'el been courtin' a pretty gal, an' one day one er dem ole sister spiled her name an' run to she friend an' tell tales to everybody. She jes strewed dat little innocent gal's name till one day she swallow a handful er bottle glass, an' Ole Sister had her time moanin' at de settin'-up an' at de funeral walkin' 'round lookin' pious as a buzzard hoppin' 'round a carcass.

TOM: Hell must be full er Ole Sisters. Dey got generations on 'em pen up together for de punishment of poor sinners.

JUBE: It must be wuss dan bad.

DAN: Les we be leffen. *(They start off and all pause at the door.)* Who dat comin' yonder? Dat's Ole Sister now. Do Jesus! Les we be leffen.

JUBE: Les we make Austin sing dat song er he ownt. Get up dere, Austin, an' sing dat song er you' ownt. Come on, les we have it.

(Austin stands on the Musician's platform and commences to sing "The Liar." When he gets to the first refrain, Old Sister enters and stands looking on suspiciously.)

"The Liar"

Jes let me tell you how a liar will do:
He's always comin' wid something new,
He'll steal your heart with a false pretense,
Makin' out like he's your bosom friend;
Yes, an' when he find out you believe what he says,
Then dat liar's goin' to have his way;
He'll bring you news about women and men,
And make you fall out with your dearest friend.

Refrain:
If you don't want to get in trouble,
If you don't want to get in trouble,
If you don't want to get in trouble,
You better leff dat liar alone.

When the liar takes a notion to 'fend and prove,
He lays around his neighbors till he gets the news;
And nearly every day when you look out,
You see dat liar comin' to your house;
He'll tell you such a lie, it will surprise your mind,
And he'll mix a little truth to make it shine;
Yes, and when he gets his business fixed jes right,
Then dat liar goin' to cause a fight.
Refrain

And when everything is in perfect peace,
Here comes dat liar wid his deceits;
He make pretend he loves you so well
Dat everything he hear he must come and tell;
Let me tell you, my sister, if you jes knew
What a certain somebody tells me about you.
He studies up a lie and he tells it so smooth,
Until you think undoubtedly dat it must be de truth;
And he'll urge you for to trace de tale,
And if you don't mind you'll be put in jail.
Refrain

A hypocrit and a liar both keeps up a fuss,
They both are very bad, but a liar is de wuss;
Dey come to your house in a powerful rush,
He say he can't stay long for I must go to my work,
I jes come to tell you what somebody say,
Then he'll take a seat and there stay all day.
He'll tell you some things that will cause you to pout,
Then at last he will borrow you out;
He knows that he owes you and if you ask him for pay,
He'll fall out wid you and stay away.

("The Liar" is greeted with enthusiastic applause and cheering and whistling. Old Sister comes down stage:)

OLD SISTER: My brothers and sisters, may God's blessings and mercy and loving kindness rest on you all. I don't come to dese kind er place wid out a prayer on my lip. Dancin' is sinful an' it is only in my earnestness to do God's work dat I is here wid my hand helt out to help de sinner, for my heart like my lips is bustin' wid prayer, an' my eye is well up wid tear. I axe God, our Heavenly Father, dis night to luh repentance and forgiveness dog de footsteps er sin.

SEVERAL VOICES: Amen! Sister is talkin'. In de name er de Lord. Amen!

OLD SISTER: De mercy of God rest on you' heads. *(She passes out. Tom starts to sing, the rest of the group taking up the song:)*

"Old Sister Don't Like We Nohow"

Well, Ole Sister don't like we nohow,
Well, Ole Sister don't like we nohow,
No! no! no! no! no! no!
No . . . oh! no . . . oh!
Well, Ole Sister don't like we nohow,
Well, Ole Sister don't like we nohow,
No! no! no! no! no! no!
No . . . oh! no . . . oh!

(They all burst into laughter.)

DAN: *(Imitating Old Sister)* You shouldn't talk dat er way, my sister. I don't come to dese kind er place wid out a prayer on my lip. I ain't come to dance an' hot supper cep wid de hope er doin' service for God.

(This is received with loud laughter and loud chattering. Kaline enters.)

KALINE: Dey sho havin' some party tonight.

TOM: Honey, you looks good enough to eat.

KALINE: I wants to look dat er way.

DAN: You looks like a rose.

KALINE: Does I? *(Rolling her eyes and smiling seductively.)*

TOM: You looks like a apple.

KALINE: If I looks like a rose, ain't none er you guh pick me; an' if I looks like a apple, ain't none er you guh bite me.

TOM: I was merely expressin' my desire. You ain't kin help dat no more dan I kin.

KALINE: You is welcome to you' desire. Dat's all I kin gee you. I hope dat satisfy you.

DAN: If you ain't change you' mind, satisfy ain't got nothin' to do wid dis compersation.

(Charleston enters.)

KALINE: Charleston!

CHARLESTON: Kaline!

KALINE: Is my eyes right? Is dis you sho nuff?

CHARLESTON: Dis is me. Wey you come from?

KALINE: Charleston, wha' kind er way dat you done me? You leff me an' make out you went to hunt a job, an' I ain't seen you since.

CHARLESTON: I leff you an' went to hunt a job. I meant to come back.

KALINE: Leff me wid you' chile to nurse an' raise.

CHARLESTON: My chile? Wha' chile!

KALINE: Ain't you know you leff me wid a baby?

CHARLESTON: Honey, I ain't know you have a baby. I ain't know nothin' 'bout it.

KALINE: You leff me to bear my burden alone, an' you ain't done nothin' to help me—nothin' to help you' chile.

CHARLESTON: I aim to come back, but I ain't know nothin' 'bout no baby.

KALINE: I am here, Charleston. God must er sent me here. I ain't know I guh see you tonight. You must go back wid me.

CHARLESTON: Wha' do my baby look like?

KALINE: He's guh be a man, Charleston, an' he look jes like you. Dey calls him Little Charleston.

CHARLESTON: Stay here. I brought a ooman wid me tonight. I'll take her home, an' I'm comin' back for you.

KALINE: Charleston, dis ain't guh be like when you went to hunt a job? Is you comin' back?

CHARLESTON: God knows I'm coming back for you.

KALINE: You fool me one time, an' you leff me wid a chile—you' chile.

CHARLESTON: Honey, I owns I done you wrong. I ain't meant to, but I'm comin' back to you. I sho would like to see dat little nigger.

KALINE: It's you' chile—you' chile an' mine, but in my heart I knowed I was guh see you again. I knowed I wasn't guh loss you. Charleston, my life ain't been but one thing—thoughts er you an' us baby. He's a man, Charleston, a little man. He looks jes like you. *(She puts her head on his shoulder)* You he daddy.

CHARLESTON: Me? Me? I ain't never thought to have a chile. I ain't never thought to be a daddy. I done wid sport, I done wid fightin', I done wid wimmen. I ain't thinkin' 'bout nothin' but you. Yes, honey, I'm guine wid you. I wants to see my chile. *(He puts his arm around Kaline and gently draws her to him)* Forgive me. I ain't meant to leave you an' stay 'way, an' I ain't never thought er no chile. Honey, I wouldn't er harm a hair er you' head. Me an' you an' Little Charleston.

(Potee's Gal enters.)

POTEE'S GAL: Charleston, wha' de matter ail you? Wuh make you leff me dis er way?

CHARLESTON: Oh, I jes been walkin' 'round. Dan an' Tom call me.

POTEE'S GAL: Charleston, you lyin' to me. Who dis ooman I see you talkin' wid?

CHARLESTON: Come on, les we go home. I'm done tired er dis frolic.

KALINE: You ain't guine till you have some more talk wid me, is you?

POTEE'S GAL: Wuh you got to do wid it? If I wants to take Charleston home, I'm guh take him.

KALINE: I ain't see wey you got no claim on him.

POTEE'S GAL: I like to know wuh make I ain't got no claim on him. Charleston's recognize as my man. I hope him in he trial. I took him out de chair when he kill Silas, an' ain't nobody got nothin' to do wid him but me. He promise me an' God he ain't guh never leff me. I like to know wha' you got to do wid him.

KALINE: I ain't got nothin' to do wid dat. Charleston was my man 'fore you knowed him. He got a chile by me.

POTEE'S GAL: You might try to put dat chile on Charleston. I ain't reckon you know who dat chile' daddy.

KALINE: It ain't make no diff'ence wha' you think. I'm guh take Charleston wid me. Come on, Charleston, an' leff dis little hussy. *(She takes his arm as if to go. Potee's Gal pulls him back and flies at Kaline in a terrible fury. Charleston goes to Kaline to see if she is all right, when Potee's Gal flies at Charleston and stabs him in the back. He groans and sinks to his knees, and as he falls he grabs Potee's Gal and breaks her neck on his knee and sinks to the floor, and Potee's Gal falls across him. Kaline is stunned and stands staring at both of them for a moment then she takes the body of Potee's Gal and pulls it away from Charleston. Kaline kneels beside Charleston's body. She kneels moaning and swaying as the curtain descends slowly.)*